SNOWBALL

MAÑANA, MAÑANA

'Ever dreamt of a new life in the sun? This is the story of one couple who tried it... with hilariously unexpected results... a warm-hearted mixture of disaster and hilarity'
Daily Mail

'A wealth of funny stories about a large circle of local eccentrics'
Sunday Times

'Kerr has an ability, reminiscent of D.H. Lawrence, to capture the overwhelmingly oppressive feel of physical fatigue on a hot day'
Monocle magazine

'People are already making comparisons between *A Year in Provence* and *Mañana, Mañana*. But, at the risk of committing travel writing heresy, some readers may like 'Mañana' better. It's often funnier, grittier and more textured... captures the Mallorcan landscape and character'
BookPage

'contains good insights into the challenges of living as a new arrival in a small community and also coming to terms with a new way of making one's living... a treat to read'
Anglo-Spanish Society

VIVA MALLORCA!

'*Viva Mallorca!* is a gem of a book... witty and amusing... A great book to take down to the beach with you, but be warned... you won't be able to put it down'
Celebrity Mallorca magazine

'Book of the Month... riveting reading'
Spanish magazine

'Kerr is a great storyteller and makes astute observations of the Spanish and the British... an enjoyable and at times hilarious book'
Viva España magazine

'an endearing insight into life in rural Mallorca and a characteristically humorous portrait of its colourful inhabitants'
A Place in the Sun magazine

A Basketful of Snowflakes

ONE MALLORCAN SPRING

A Basketful of Snowflakes
ONE MALLORCAN SPRING

PETER KERR

Oasis-WERP

A Basketful of Snowflakes

Published by Oasis-WERP 2012

ISBN: 978-0-9573062-3-3

First Published by Summersdale 2005

Copyright © Peter Kerr 2002

www.peter-kerr.co.uk

Book illustrated by Peter Kerr
Illustrations copyright Peter Kerr © 2005
Cover design © Glen Kerr

Cover photograph © Eduardo Miralles
for the Fomento del Turismo de Mallorca

CONTENTS

If you had suddenly been where I've been,
Under the sun among the almond flowers,
If you had dreamed and seen what I have seen,
The old grey olives and the old grey towers:
If, in bewilderment, there had come to you
Over the hills, beneath the evening star,
The tinkling of sheep bells, or the blue
Gleaming from where the happy wild flowers are:
If you'd been wafted to that fairyland,
And in delight been lost and lost again,
And walking with me, waved a friendly hand
To children smiling with the eyes of Spain,
And in full day beheld the young moon fly…
Then you had sworn the same sweet oath as I.

'Sweet Oath In Mallorca' by John Galsworthy
(1867–1933)

– ONE –

MISADVENTURES OF A PARTY ANIMAL

'Your animal is illegal, *señor.*'

'Ill*egal?* How can *this* be illegal?'

'*Hombre*, it is a public health hazard!' The customs officer was adamant, and he swept a finger under his heavy, black moustache to prove it. 'Without the proper *certificado*, it cannot be granted entry into Spain.'

I thought Jock Burns was about to burst a blood vessel. 'The proper cert*ifi*cate?'

'*Sí, señor. Un certificado oficial.*' The officer brushed his moustache in the other direction to emphasise the point. '*Es absoluta*mente *necesario!*'

Jock gave a little laugh. One of those nervous little laughs that you'd expect to be released by a homicidal maniac about to do chainsaw topiary work on a fellow human. 'But, for Pete's sake, man,' he spluttered, 'who the hell ever heard of a certified *haggis*, for crying out loud?'

It was the time of year that Mallorcans call *Las Calmas de Enero*, The Calms of January, a few winter days that invariably take on the quiet qualities of spring on that most enchanting of Mediterranean islands. But the spirit of *Las Calmas* had exited Palma Airport the moment Jock had been stopped and his suitcase opened by the official at the gate in International Arrivals.

'You should have declared possession of this, *señor*,' he'd said, gingerly peeling back the shroud of tinfoil covering Jock's jumbo-size haggis. '*Animales*, dead or alive, are not allowed entry without the necessary paperwork.' He'd then taken a closer look at the haggis, his top lip curling in undisguised disapproval. 'Pigs are especially prohibited. The risk of swine fever or foot-and-mouth disease. *Coño*! A potential disaster for the pig farmers of Mallorca!'

'A haggis is *not* a pig!' Jock snapped. 'In fact, it's not even a bloody animal!'

'It looks like a dead piglet to me.' The customs officer leaned back and inhaled a cautious, one-nostril sniff. '*Sí*, and it smells like one, too!'

I could hear Jock slowly counting to ten under his breath. '*Mira, amigo*,' he eventually purred, smiling coldly at the customs man while reaching out a hand to whip the entire covering of tinfoil from the haggis. 'Look closely, my friend,' he crooned in flawless Spanish. 'Do you see any legs, trotters, a head with an apple in its mouth, tusks, a snout, a curly tail?'

Jock paused.

The customs officer looked at the haggis as closely as he thought prudent, raised a cynical eyebrow, then shook his head – warily.

'Or,' Jock continued, his voice rising with the colour in his cheeks, 'do you perceive evidence of a pig's eye, or even a pig's arsehole, perhaps?'

Another slow, frowning shake of the official's head.

'Well then,' Jock exploded, 'it can't be a fucking pig, can it, *amigo*!'

Still being very much a rookie resident of Mallorca myself, and nowhere nearly as fluent in the Spanish language as Jock, I was forever amazed by his confident, sometimes aggressive, manner in dealing with officialdom when it stood in his way. But he had lived and worked in the country since the latter years of the dictator Franco, and he obviously knew that he could get away with saying things to members of the liberal 'establishment' of today that might have risked arrest back then. For all that, it was clear that no amount of verbal bulldozing was going to shift this customs man's resolve by a single centimetre.

'The creature will be impounded and placed in quarantine until you can provide me with the relevant paperwork,' he stated flatly.

'Would that include his passport?' Jock sarcastically enquired, though (shrewdly in my opinion) in English. Then, hearing my barely-suppressed snigger, and never one to resist playing to an appreciative gallery, he added (perhaps not so wisely) in Spanish, 'You know, official proof that he's Angus MacSporran – male – born Edinburgh, Scotland – loyal subject of Her Majesty the Queen of Britain and Grand Empress of Haggisonia?'

Expressionless, the customs man produced a large plastic bag from under his table. He held it open at arm's length. 'Place it in here,' he said. 'You have three days in which to satisfy regulations, then the beast will either be deported or destroyed. The choice will be yours, as will the cost.'

Much as he disliked it, Jock knew that there would be no point in arguing any more on this particular occasion. 'OK,' he rasped. 'Just make sure you quarantine him in a cold store, *amigo*. I'll be back – but *pronto*!'

As Jock turned to leave, I could have sworn that I glimpsed a shadow of a smile lurking mischievously under the customs officer's moustache. Could it be, I wondered, that here was a government official with a sense of humour – at least one that outdid Jock's limited powers of patience?

'Three days!' he barked after Jock, the spectral smirk mutating into a snarl. 'Three days, *señor*, or it will be *adiós* to your… 'agees!'

What had started as a pleasantly normal and potentially uneventful day for me was suddenly shaping up to be something of an 'experience'. But then, days in the company of Jock Burns invariably did.

Being January, it was the peak of the orange harvesting season and, therefore, the busiest time of the year on our little farm of Ca's Mayoral, nestling in a hidden valley in the Tramuntana Mountains of Mallorca. It was the start of the second year of a new life that my wife Ellie, our two sons and I had launched ourselves into – perhaps a tad more enthusiastically than astutely – after giving up our beef-rearing and barley-growing holding in Scotland. Our fifty-acre farm 'back home' had simply become too small to be viable in the big-is-beautiful climate that was now prevailing in agriculture locally, so, more on a whim than by good guidance, we decided to risk all by selling up and buying this little farm that we had literally stumbled upon when on holiday in Mallorca. The tiny detail that we knew absolutely nothing about oranges, or fruit farming of any kind for that matter, had been conveniently put to the back of our minds. Fate had provided us with an opportunity to farm in the most entrancing of settings on a beautiful Mediterranean island, and it was an opportunity that we were determined not to miss – for better or worse.

It hadn't taken long for us to discover that, not merely was it likely to be for the worse, but perhaps even for complete ruination. Our ignorance of this type of farming had blinded us to the fact that the orchards had been neglected for years and many of the trees were in a state of dangerously poor health. But, with the advice and assistance of our elderly Mallorcan neighbours and, in particular, with some expert 'doctoring' by local tree maestro Pepe Suau, total disaster had been averted. Now, after a year of dedicated toil, intermingled with interludes of zealous nail-biting, we could see that the trees were well on the way to full recovery and were already yielding respectable quantities of good quality fruit. *And*, we were making ends meet – just.

'Forty kilos of clementines, fifty of mandarins and a hundred of Valencias,' said Ellie as she ticked off the order for oranges from Señor Jeronimo, the local fruit merchant who bought virtually all of our crop, save for a few kilos that we sold to mothers of school chums of our younger son Charlie, who had just turned thirteen. 'He'll be along to pick them up later this morning.'

We had worked out a routine whereby, whether Señor Jeronimo collected the fruit or we delivered it to his warehouse a few kilometres along the coast in the town of Peguera, he would usually give us a note of his requirements for the next day at the same time. This meant that we could then pick the fruit in the cool of the evening, load the plastic crates onto our tiny Barbieri tractor and trailer, then cart them back to the farmhouse, all ready to be finally checked over and weighed in the morning. It was a simple system that worked well and ensured that the fruit we sold him was absolutely fresh. We only picked enough to complete each order, so no unnecessary storage was involved. This also meant, of course, that we had no fruit instantly available should an unexpected order suddenly come in. Fair enough, that didn't happen very often, but it did on this particular morning.

'That'll be another hundred-and-twenty kilos each of mandarins and Valencias,' said Ellie, who had gone inside to answer the phone while our elder son Sandy and I stacked the last of the crates for Jeronimo in the shade of an old carob tree by the gate to the lane.

I wiped the sweat from my eyes. 'Jeronimo's business is certainly booming today,' I puffed.

'They're not for him,' said Ellie. 'They're for French Andy.'

French Andy, or Andreu, to give him his proper name, was a contact we'd inadvertently made through the school, which our Charlie and Andreu's two young children attended. It was one of those chance meetings that had turned out to be fortunate, not just because Andreu and his wife Josephine were exceptionally pleasant young people who had soon become friends of ours, but also because he was a director of his family's fruit import-export business. This was an extremely impressive enterprise, with branches in France, Africa, England, mainland Spain, and now also in Mallorca, the place of his father's birth. We'd always believed that, realistically, the relatively small amounts of fruit that we could produce at Ca's Mayoral would be of little interest to a firm dealing in such vast quantities as his. However, kind and sensitive a chap as he was, Andreu realised that we needed every cent of income that we could lay our hands on just to get ourselves established, and so, whenever a suitable occasion arose, he would give us an order for whatever he felt we'd be able to supply.

'Wants them at his warehouse out at the airport by two o'clock this afternoon,' said Ellie. 'He's trying to make up a shortfall on a shipment going over to Marseilles. Says he could do with as many ripe lemons as we can rustle up as well.'

Though only just after eight in the morning, it was already shaping up to be a typical *Calmas de Enero* day, with the temperature in the valley already matching what would be regarded as very acceptable in Scotland at the height of summer. It was going to be a warm one, and the prospect of doing an extra stint of fruit-picking in the full heat of day wouldn't normally have appealed. But we were talking about a sizeable order here – and French Andy always paid in cash.

'OK,' I grinned at Ellie and Sandy, 'let's get those baskets, ladders and secateurs organised. We've got work to do! Yeah, and very pleasant work it'll be at that!'

Neither Ellie nor Sandy looked totally convinced.

'So, ehm, there'll be a bit of overtime money in this for the hired help, I take it?' said Sandy, more by way of a statement of fact than a query.

At nineteen, our son Sandy was at that age when the difference between getting pocket money from his parents and real wages from his employer meant a lot. The wages we'd managed to pay him at Ca's Mayoral to date had amounted to no more than pocket money – and sometimes not even that. Though reluctantly, Sandy had already expressed doubts about committing his future to life on this little farm. Ellie and I knew that, deep down, he craved the sort of modern, mechanised, more extensive type of farming he was used to in Britain. But he had supported our coming to Mallorca as a family, and knowing as he did that we had a struggle on our hands to turn this run-down little spread around, he had decided, without any pressure from us, to stick with it and help us all he could until the summer at least. Then he would make a final decision about staying or returning 'home'.

We were getting precious little more for a kilo of oranges in Mallorca than we would have paid for a single orange in the UK, so the money to pay Sandy a decent wage simply wasn't there – yet. But today's order from French Andy had come as a pleasant surprise, the sun was shining, the birds were singing, the valley was bathed in that magically calm atmosphere of January, and the surrounding mountains looked even more serene than ever. I felt light-hearted, and strangely big-hearted too – if not more than a little guilty about having kept Sandy on such a short financial rope for so long.

'So, do I get that overtime loot or not?' he pressed, his wry smile indicating that he was only half kidding.

'You bet,' I grinned, slapping his back. 'In fact, even better than a bit of overtime money, I'll give you half of what French Andy pays for the whole consignment today. How about that?'

Sandy squinted at me as if I'd just sprouted horns. 'You're pulling my leg,' he said.

I shook my head. 'No, it's only fair. You deserve a wee bonus occasionally. You've worked hard for it.'

'Half, you said? You'll give me *half* the boodle for the fruit?'

'Certainly will.'

'Well,' Sandy smiled, 'like you said, let's get those baskets, ladders and secateurs organised!'

'And, uhm, what about the other half of the workforce?' The tone of Ellie's voice was the very epitome of commercial no-nonsense.

'Come again, dear?' I replied, feigning puzzlement, but knowing full well what was coming.

'The other half of your workforce. Me! I think I deserve a bonus as well.' She turned to Sandy. 'Agreed?'

Sandy gave a knowing wink and nodded his head.

'And an equal one, at that,' added Ellie, with a sweet smile in my direction. 'So, dearest,' she said, giving *me* a pat on the back, 'I'll have the other half of the French Andy boodle… *if* you don't mind.'

The phone inside the house rang before I could answer her.

'I'll get that,' Ellie told me, ' – ehm, while you're thinking about my *offer*, OK?'

Sandy and I got on with loading the required amount of empty crates onto the tractor and trailer.

That was Jock Burns,' Ellie announced when she returned. 'Phoning from Edinburgh. He's on the next flight to Palma. Tells me he's bringing a haggis. A really big one. Wants you to pick him up at the airport this afternoon.'

'Well, that should work out just fine,' I breezed. 'I'll be at the airport delivering the oranges to French Andy's warehouse in any case. No problem.'

'Correction. *One* problem. You'll never get there in time if only two of you are going to pick the fruit. And you can't let Jock down – not after all he's done for you.'

Ellie liked playing these little games. She handled all our finances anyway, did all the banking, paid all the bills. Interestingly, although she hadn't bothered to learn much spoken Spanish before we came to Mallorca, she *had* made a point of perfecting the art of writing cheques in her adopted language, complicated numbers and all. In fact, she was the only person who knew exactly what our monetary situation was from day to day, week to week, month to month. So, for all I knew, she may well have been about to divert half of today's windfall income to her personal purse in any case. She, like Sandy, needed and deserved her own spending money, after all, and I had absolutely no problem with that. Knowing Ellie, though, it was more likely that she'd end up putting anything she gleaned from today's takings into the general housekeeping pot as usual.

'But what about *my* bonus?' I said, playing her along. 'I reckon we should divvy Andreu's money up three ways.'

'Bosses don't qualify for bonuses,' Ellie came back. 'Not in this firm, at any rate!'

I could have argued about who the real boss in this particular outfit was, but we had work to do, so the game was over, for the moment at least. That said, I did harbour a sneaky little hunch that I might just win it yet, given half a chance.

'OK, you win, Ellie,' I sighed. 'You get the other half of the French Andy boodle. Now, come on – let's pick those damned oranges while we still have time!'

Jock didn't waste any time in starting his campaign to have his haggis released from custody. He was a Scotsman on a mission.

'Drive me straight to the British Consul's office in Palma, son,' he instructed me before we'd even left the airport. 'It's in the Plaça Major, smack in the middle o' the city, but there's an underground car park nearby, so *no problema*.'

Coincidentally, I knew that car park intimately, having had a rather painful run-in with a carload of nuns in its subterranean bowels shortly after arriving on the island. On that occasion, I'd been rewarded with a suspiciously unmerciful flat tyre, a bruised shin and a whack on the head for having swept selfishly into the only available parking place ahead of the nunmobile. I was relieved to note that there were no motorised holy sisters in evidence when I drove in this time.

'I hope this isn't a daft question, Jock,' I said as we scurried up the flights of stone steps leading from the Carrer

Riera to the Plaça Major, 'but how can the British Consulate help you to import a haggis illegally into Spain?'

'Wheels within wheels, son,' he replied. 'Make sure ye're a member o' the right clubs and societies, then make the most o' yer connections. That's how to survive on this island, by the way.' He gestured towards one of the open-air bars that proliferate in the Plaça. 'You sit there while I go and see Her Majesty's man in Mallorca. Oh, and order me up a beer, eh. I'll only be a minute.'

Palma's main square is, I suppose, fairly typical of the popular image of Spanish big-city *plazas* – a large, paved quadrangle (in this case, a rectangle), enclosed by handsome, arcaded buildings. Although it was still technically winter, many of the south- and west-facing upper-floor windows had their slatted shutters closed against the sunlight, lending a sleepy effect to the mellow, pastel-painted façades, and disguising the fact that business was being carried on as usual in the warren of offices within. I'd been in the Plaça Major a couple of times during the summer, when its central expanse had been full of market stalls, selling everything from leather belts to handmade jewellery and all manner of handicrafts, souvenirs and nick-nacks aimed at the hundreds of rubber-necked tourists drifting around. There had even been a few street artists, 'human statues' and buskers doing their respective things and adding something of a bohemian buzz to the place then. But today, the Plaça was comparatively empty. As ever, of course, there were a few sharp-suited businessmen stepping briskly to or fro with their distinctive little leather 'handbags' tucked under their arms. There was also a scattering of holidaymakers, either casually looking in the windows of the shops that squat beneath the arched flanks of the square, or sitting outside the almost-deserted cafés sipping drinks. But, essentially, the Plaça was in as near a state of hibernation as it was ever likely to be. I liked it.

I took a seat outside the bar Jock had indicated and ordered two beers from the tired-looking waiter who instantly appeared at my side. Paradoxically, it was probably the slackness of trade that was making the poor fellow weary. Spanish waiters are justifiably renowned for their professionalism, and they do seem to thrive on being busy – although I often wonder what their feet, if they could talk, would say to them at the end of a long, hot day of serving tables during the peak tourist season. 'Do us a favour and get a desk job,' most likely. But then, I mused, it would be amazing what the accumulation of a few months' generous tips would do to silence the barking of even the most aching of 'dogs'.

'*Un poquito flojo hoy* – a little quiet today?' I remarked when he returned the beers. I gave him a sympathetic smile.

He reciprocated with a heavy sigh. '*Pues sí, señor,*' he monotoned, exuding enough pathos to fuel a wake, '*es un poquito flojo.*' It was, he agreed, a little quiet. With that, he ambled forlornly back to his lonely vigil by the café entrance to sigh once more and patiently await the arrival of his longed-for summer hordes.

He'd have been in his mid-thirties, I guessed, and, although obviously every inch the super-efficient *camarero*, who wouldn't have looked out of place serving tables in the dining room of a swanky five-star hotel, he did have something of the 'farm boy' about him. It was difficult to pinpoint what gave that impression. Maybe it was his slightly loping gait, perhaps his large hands, or it could just have been the wistful way he stared up at a little flock of overwintering martins that were skimming the rooftops for flies and surveying the deep eaves of the buildings for imminent nest-building sites. He was, I fancied, one of many of his generation in Spain, who had forsaken the hard life of the small family farm to work in supposedly easier, better-paid, tourism-related jobs, just as the sons of most of our Mallorcan neighbours in the valley had done.

I thought about our own two boys and what the future would hold for them now that I had committed the family to a way of life that was dying out, even for the native Mallorcan country folk themselves. We already knew that Sandy was having doubts about his own long-term involvement at Ca's Mayoral, and I worried about young Charlie too, but for entirely different reasons. Essentially, he was still the same good-natured, fun-loving kid who'd been brought up to work along with us in all weathers on our farm back in Scotland. That mud-on-his-boots, both-feet-on-the-ground element to his upbringing would never leave him, I hoped. Yet there were distractions for a lad of his age living on a holiday island like Mallorca. Invaluable though his outlook-broadening experience at the international school was proving, his newfound friendship with the offspring of some exceptionally rich parents and his obvious attraction to their ostentatious lifestyles was a source of concern for us. Whatever the future held for Charlie, it was becoming less and less likely that it would involve picking oranges for a living, no matter how viable a fruit-farming business we *might* eventually manage to develop. And such viability was still very much conjectural in any case.

While I wouldn't say that I'd spent *all* of our first year at Ca's Mayoral in a secret state of panic, there had been those nail-biting moments when setbacks made me wonder if I'd brought the family all this way on a fool's errand. But maintaining an outward appearance of confidence had been my maxim, though whether that hoodwinked either Ellie or the boys is doubtful to say the least. To their credit, though, they never revealed even the slightest hint that they suspected I might occasionally have been wavering in my resolve. Every functioning family needs a worryguts, when all's said and done, and I'm sure the three of them were quite happy to let me wear that mantle in our household.

However, they had recently managed to convince me that a more relaxed attitude towards the future would be beneficial to us all. Having spent all of those first twelve months working, almost manically at times, at improving the health of the trees and generally doing everything possible to restore the fortunes of the farm of Ca's Mayoral, the time had come, they'd reasoned, to actually start *enjoying* the place a bit more. Sprucing up the previously less than spick-and-span state of the interior of the house had become, therefore, the main priority, followed closely by a few schemes to establish 'recreational amenities', which would, Ellie claimed, add much more to the value of the property than the cost of creating them. And I had to concede that the theory was sound. If the long-term profitability of Ca's Mayoral didn't materialise in the way we hoped (and we were already realising that the farm probably *was* on the small side), then it would be sensible to make the most of developing the appeal of *every* aspect of the property, just in case we were ultimately obliged to raise the finances to expand – somehow.

Two of those recreational amenities, an illuminated barbecue area within a little pine grove in the lee of the high wall by the lane, and a games-room conversion of the big *almacén* store/workshop that occupied much of the ground floor of the house, were already nearing completion. A prerequisite of these projects had been that we undertook as much of the work as possible ourselves, without unnecessary resort to paying tradesmen. Frugality wasn't just an option in that respect; it was absolutely mandatory. When you're obliged to calculate your solvency in oranges on a little *finca* like Ca's Mayoral, it's surprising how resourceful you suddenly become in the DIY stakes!

But the next item on the list of leisure-activity developments was one that, no matter how vital our need to watch the pennies, we'd have to rely on the experts to tackle. The construction of a swimming pool isn't something for amateurs to have a bash at. Many were the times I'd privately regretted having suggested the need for a pool to Ellie after one particularly hot and sweaty day working in the fields during the furnace-like heat of summer. But she had seized upon my moment of weakness like a ferret going in for the kill against a hypnotised rabbit. Since that day, my increasing mastery of the Spanish art of *mañana*ness had allowed me to buy time, but not to sweep aside completely what was liable to be an extremely expensive undertaking. Every time I'd tried, Ellie had merely plucked some more bristles from my *mañana* broom, until now the time had come when I was sweeping with a chunk of bald wood on the end of a stick. Gomez, the pool-builder, would be coming with a contract based on his verbally-accepted estimate in the morning.

The sound of Jock's voice only just saved what was left of my fingernails from a terminal nibbling session.

'Sorted!' he shouted as he strode over to join me. 'Angus MacSporran is free!' He raised his shoulders and grinned. 'Or he will be in an hour or so.' He then gave me one of his conspiratorial winks of near-Masonic intensity. 'Like I say, son, make yer contacts and then make the most o' them. That's how ye get things done on this island.'

How Jock had managed to sweet-talk the British Consulate into liberating an incarcerated haggis, when it was common knowledge that even holiday-making Brits who'd had all their money stolen couldn't even bum a fiver off them, I didn't know, and I didn't bother to ask. As Jock's wife Meg once said, Jock had more strings to his bow than all the Merry Men in Sherwood Forest put together. Springing the stuffed innards of an animal from jail was just one more to add to the collection, which already included a career as a teacher in the international school that Charlie attended, a nightly job as a keyboard player and singer in a popular tourist hotel in the resort of Palma Nova, and a gift for making contacts that had earned him the reputation of being able to move, shake and 'fix' just about anything for anyone.

He downed his beer without bothering to take a seat. 'Wow!' he burped, rubbing his prodigious midriff. 'I'd murder for a few Franks. Haven't had any decent nosh since the all-day breakfast at Edinburgh Airport – apart from the pigswill on the plane, that is, and there wasn't nearly enough o' that.'

Jock's a big chap, and he has an appetite to match. He also has a penchant for rhyming slang, and I already knew enough of his street-poet vocabulary to recognise 'Franks' as being an abbreviated form of 'Frank Zappas', or *tapas*, those classic Spanish titbits that Jock regarded as compulsory top-up fuel between main meals.

I was feeling a bit peckish myself. 'OK,' I said, 'let's get the waiter to tell us what they've got on offer here.'

Jock wagged a cautionary finger at me. 'No way, boy. Strictly for the tourists, this place. Rip-off. Nah, just follow me. I've got a wee bit o' business to do along the street, so we'll have a pit stop en route.' He winked again. 'I know just the place.'

For all his generously-proportioned physique, Jock could get off his mark when he had a mind to, and he clearly wasn't in the mood for dawdling today. He was off down the flights of steps from the square as nimbly as if he were dancing barefoot on hot coals. I tagged along as gamely as I could in his slipstream.

'Leave the car where it is,' he called to me over his shoulder, turning left at the foot of the steps and plunging into the stream of pedestrians flowing this way and that along the pavement. 'We'll never get parked again where we're going.'

We were in the Plaça Weyler, a busy thoroughfare that links two of Palma's most spectacular tree-lined avenues, the Passeig dels Born (popularly known simply as 'the Born') and the Passeig de la Rambla ('the Rambla'). I'd driven along here a few times, but the need to concentrate on avoiding a collision in the wacky races that the circulation of traffic in central Palma tends to resemble had always prevented me from noticing, far less appreciating, any of the surrounding buildings. And there are a few really interesting ones in this part of the city, as witness a group of Japanese tourists, cameras and video recorders at the high port, gazing awe-struck at the flamboyant *modernista* architecture of the old Gran Hotel, the forerunner of and inspiration for several such intricately-sculpted frontages in the area. A clever fusion of Gothic-derived elaboration and classic Spanish understatement, the *modernista* style owes more to the past than even to the 'present' of the early twentieth century when it first emerged. Just opposite the Gran Hotel (now an art gallery), is a building which, although less aesthetically noteworthy than its celebrated *modernista* neighbours, can nonetheless boast having its picture featured in more tourist guides to Palma than perhaps any other structure in the city – save for the imposing bulk of the famous Sa Seu Cathedral itself. I'm referring to the little Forn des Teatre bakery whose green, red and gold 'art deco' shopfront is also reproduced on circular cardboard boxes containing *ensaimadas*, the island's iconic, lighter-than-air, spiral pastries, that are lovingly carried as edible souvenirs onto dozens of charter flights out of Palma Airport every day in summer. Right next door is the always-busy Bar Central, and it was in there that I thought Jock would wheel for his craved Frank Zappas. But I was wrong.

'Too many tourists,' he shouted back at me, as if reading my thoughts. 'Come on, son,' he urged, increasing his stride. 'Keep up, eh. Time's money.'

I glanced at my watch. Four o'clock. By now, I'd normally have been picking oranges back at Ca's Mayoral. But any twinges of conscience that I might have felt for having left Ellie and Sandy to fill tomorrow's order for Señor Jeronimo without me were quickly dispelled by recalling what Ellie had said to me following Jock's phone call from Edinburgh earlier in the day: 'You can't let Jock down – not after all he's done for you.' And she was right.

They say that everyone needs a guardian angel, and although even Jock himself would admit that it would take an aeronautical engineer of extraordinary talent to design a pair of wings capable of flapping *him* all the way up to a vantage point above the clouds, he *had* proved himself to be an invaluable source of help and advice since the day we'd decided to settle in Mallorca. Coming originally from the same town as ourselves in Scotland, Jock probably felt a bit protective towards us anyway. Home-town bonds can be very strong, particularly when people are far away from their common roots. But the good deeds and favours Jock had done for us went well beyond that. Without the benefit of his guidance, for instance, the rigmarole involved in obtaining permission from the Spanish government to buy Ca's Mayoral might well have put us off embarking on our Mallorcan adventure in the first place. Before Spain's entry into the European Union, the restrictions imposed on foreigners buying more than a fairly modest amount of *rustica* land in the Balearic Islands were both rigid and vigorously adhered to. Since the total ground area of the *finca* of Ca's Mayoral happened to exceed the prescribed limit, the legal jiggery-pokery involved in surmounting an apparently insurmountable problem would not have been possible, it's fair to say, without the skilful intervention of Jock's connections. He'd also negotiated advantageous terms for Charlie's enrolment at the school where he taught, he'd found us the best deals available for buying everything from cutlery to cars, and he'd always been there for us in times of difficulty – even setting up the police investigation into a housebreaking that we'd been the victims of shortly after arriving on the island. Yes, Jock had done a great deal for us, so missing one evening's orange-picking to help him attend to a 'wee bit o' business' today was the least I could do to reciprocate in even the least commensurate of ways.

We ploughed on in tandem along the Carrer Unió, soon emerging at the top of 'the Born' at the pavement peninsula that accommodates the outdoor tables and chairs of the Bar Bosch, arguably the most popular of all such see-and-be-seen cafés in central Palma.

'Too many tourists?' I shouted ahead to Jock. His nod confirmed that I'd correctly anticipated his reaction to the crush of customers sitting looking at the world, wheeled and pedestrian, passing round and through the square now dedicated to Rei Joan Carles, the name in the *mallorquín* language of Spain's King Juan Carlos I. The coffers of the Bar Bosch wouldn't benefit from a pit stop by Jock today. We waited at the kerb by the traffic lights.

I could tell by the swagger that had been developing in his step that Jock was becoming increasingly chipper as the feeling of self-satisfaction at having pulled off another victory against bureaucracy kicked in. As I mentioned earlier, Jock was never shy to grab a chance to show off to an appreciative audience, and, although habitually a couple of paces behind, I knew I'd be the gallery he'd once more be playing to on this occasion. Having seen this mood-change often enough before to guess what his state of heightening bonhomie would result in, I braced myself for embarrassment.

'*Toujours la politesse!*' he exclaimed through a beaming smile to an elderly couple crossing the square towards us when the lights went to green. Their startled expressions revealed that they neither knew who Jock was nor understood what he'd said. Offering inappropriate greetings in fractured, phrase-book French to total strangers in the street gave Jock a real kick when in this frame of mind. I was relieved that, this time at least, nothing more offensive than 'Good manners at all times' had been his chosen salutation – nonsensical though it was in the given situation. There would be more to come, however.

We strode on into the Avinguda de Jaume III, a long, straight street with a distinctly smart air about it, arcaded on both sides, and recognised as both the mecca for serious shoppers in Palma and one of the city's most prestigious business addresses. The perfect arena for Jock in full exhibitionist mode.

'*Les collants de ma tante!*' ('My auntie's tights!'), he smiled repeatedly to a procession of senior citizens, accompanied by their tour guide, shuffling down the busy pavement in the opposite direction. He alternated this with a polite, '*Quelle est cette odeur?*' ('What's that smell?'), doffing an imaginary hat as he spoke.

I was intrigued to note that a few of the recipients of Jock's absurd greetings attempted to return them verbatim, although patently clueless as to what the words actually meant. Ironically, '*Toujours la politesse*' was clearly their motto, even if it wasn't Jock's while this particular devil was perched mischievously on his shoulder.

A gaggle of mini-skirted, teenage girls was his next target, and it was for them that he'd saved his pièce de résistance. They were exiting the Gelatería Ca'n Miquel, happily guzzling a selection of made-in-house ice creams that enjoy the reputation of being the best in town, if not on the entire island.

Marching purposefully past, Jock hailed the young ladies with a cordial, '*Sur le pont d'Avignon*!', responding to their coy titters with an even more affable and romantic-sounding, '*Avez-vous des cancres*?' (Have you got crabs?').

'What the bleedin' 'ell was that git on abaht?' I overheard the leader of the pack enquire of her companions in a broad Cockney twang as Jock advanced out of earshot.

'Search me, Samamfa,' one of her chums shrugged. 'All that Spanish lingo's fuckin' Greek to me. Know what I mean?'

So, not for the first time, Jock had got away with making his spoof-Gallic salutations without even a mild rebuke in return, never mind a poke in the eye. Whether it was all down to pure luck or to an uncanny gift for differentiating between nationalities simply by their appearance, I don't know, but whatever the basis for his bizarre (and risky) behaviour, Jock got a buzz out of it – and it showed. When he turned to wait for me at the top of the street, he had a grin on his face like a slice of melon, his cheeks were flushed, unbridled glee was glistening in his eyes, and his shoulders were shaking to the rhythm of a symphony of wheezy sniggers. The schoolteacher had morphed into the schoolboy – temporarily, I hoped.

He led me into a small shopping arcade, which, although a tributary of the busy main street, could easily be by-passed by the uninitiated without noticing it was there. It was the archetypal location for one of Jock's many favourite, known only to the locally *au fait*, watering holes in Palma.

'The Frank Zappas in here are the berries,' he said, combining rhyming slang with a Scottish colloquialism denoting excellence.

He shepherded me into the Bar Ca'n Miquelet, a somewhat gaunt-looking corridor of a place that had precious little in its appearance that would have attracted me had I been passing by on my own. But that's the secret of many of the best little eateries in Spain. The quality of their food is paramount, and if their décor happens to be on the plain side of plush, then the good news is that this is usually reflected in the prices. Ca'n Miquelet was no exception.

'Ye'll never get better Carnegies than these, son,' Jock enthused as he stabbed his fork into one of a generous serving of Carnegie Halls – meatballs, or *albóndigas*, as they're called in Spanish. He swept his free hand in a dramatic arc and added, 'Aye, and not a bloody tourist in sight.'

It wasn't really that Jock disliked tourists. In fact, one of his main sources of income, his evening job as a hotel musician/entertainer, required that he got on well with them. And, being a naturally gregarious sort of chap, he did genuinely enjoy their company, and had even established lasting friendships with many of the hotel's holiday-making regulars over the years. But he also liked to get away from all of that sometimes. He loved mixing with the locals and speaking to them in their language – not just the 'standard' Castilian of mainland Spain, but also the *mallorquín* dialect of Catalan, its use once suppressed by Franco, but now actively and proudly promoted as the traditional vernacular of the island. Jock grabbed every chance he could to exercise his considerable command of both tongues, and frequenting little *tapas* bars like this was guaranteed to provide just such opportunities. But he had other things on his mind on this occasion. Jock was on a mission, and as soon as he'd scoffed enough Frank Zappas to replenish his depleted energy tanks, we were off again.

'Just need to pay a quick visit to the *Majorca Daily Bulletin*,' he told me as he got back into his stride out in the street. 'Just need to place a wee ad or two.'

The 'Daily B', as it's affectionately known in Mallorca, is something of an institution among English-speaking residents of and visitors to the island. And it's not just a newspaper that keeps its readers up to date with what's going on in the world. It's also an in-print gossip shop in which all manner of harmless Mallorcan tittle-tattle is bandied about, it's a source of useful information about island life, customs and cuisine, and it provides a truly effective noticeboard for just about anything that anyone would want to sell, buy, hire or rent. Whether you're a dog-owner looking for someone to clip your pooch's toenails, an out-of-work sword-swallower hungry for engagements, or a multi-millionaire seeking a buyer for your mansion, the small-ads pages of the good-old 'Daily B' are where to tout your stuff.

Jock had planned this expedition well. The 'Daily B' offices are located just round the corner from the Bar Ca'n Miquelet, in the Passeig de Mallorca, a wide avenue skirting the banks of the Torrente La Riera, Palma's so-called 'river', which only really appears following one of the monsoon-like downpours that occur infrequently throughout the year. Jock's approach to the girl at the advertising desk revealed yet another of his various personae – this one the smooth-talking entrepreneur. I wasn't surprised to note that, the moment he adopted this guise, he effortlessly shifted his accent from his native Scots to a laid-back mid-Atlantic drawl. It's a way of talking he automatically slipped into if he felt his audience might be impressed more by a worldly-wise sophisticate than by a street-wise wheeler-dealer. Very often, however, the dividing line between the two turned out to be narrow in the extreme, although I'm sure Jock didn't see it that way.

Casually leaning an elbow on the counter, he pulled a lopsided smirk, then said to the girl, 'Hey, honey, you're lookin' real good. Wow, amazin' likeness!' He glanced at me. 'I mean, Pedro – did ya ever see a ringer for Jennifer Lopez like this before?'

Taken aback, I shook my head – hesitantly. 'Ehm, well… no.'

Unimpressed, the girl stared at him – stonily. 'Can I help you, sir?'

Undaunted, Jock proceeded with his spiel – confidently. 'It's like this, sweet lips,' he smouldered in a George Clooney baritone, 'I have this, uhm, ethnic extravaganza I'm producin' here on the island in a coupla weeks, and I, uh – I need a deal for your best advertisin' rates.' He winked conspiratorially. 'If ya catch my drift, gorgeous.'

'Would these be full-page or half-page display ads you require, sir? To run daily, bi-daily, or weekly? Full colour, I presume?'

Jock shifted uneasily on his feet. 'Uhm-ah, no. What I had in mind, darlin', was more kinda – .' He looked furtively over his shoulder, leaned towards the girl and muttered out of the corner of his mouth, 'What I had in mind was a coupla three-line entries in the personals. One next week, one the week after.'

'So,' the girl said, straight-faced, 'we're talking about a fairly *minor* extravaganza here, are we, sir?'

I smiled inwardly. Jock had met his match here.

'There could be a complimentary ticket in it for ya, baby,' he said, a suggestion of desperation creeping into his approach, '– *if* we close the right deal for the price of the ads, that is.'

With a bored look and without ceremony, the girl pushed a form over the counter to him. 'The small ad rates are printed at the top there, sir – in *cents* per word! No discounts, except for long runs. If you still want to put a notice in the paper, print the details in the space provided, then give me the form back.' She then moved swiftly along the counter to attend to another customer, leaving Jock mumbling curses to himself.

'There could be a double helpin' of haggis in it for ya as well, beautiful!' he called after her in a last-ditch attempt at soliciting a bargain price. Ironically, the cost of his two little ads was likely to amount to less than the value of a dollop of specially-flown-in haggis anyway. But, being a Scotsman through and through, Jock was compelled to try his best for that cut-price deal, even if it meant he'd end up being out of pocket by clinching it.

His entreaty fell on deaf ears. In a moody silence, he ultimately placed the ad with the girl, paid up the full whack in cash, turned on his heel and headed for the door. 'Incidentally, miss,' he barked at her before making good his exit, 'that Jennifer Lopez lookalike thing I mentioned? Yeah, well, I was referrin' exclusively, of course, to the size of yer ass!'

The age of chivalry had taken yet another step backwards, as Jock strode purposefully forwards and (prudently) out into the street.

Jock's annual Burns Suppers had already earned a reputation among expats and natives alike as being one of the highlights of the Mallorcan social calendar – though firmly ensconced at the unpretentious end of it. Their popularity had grown on the success of that very precept having been adopted from the outset. Over the years that Jock had organised these events, the practice of paying formal tribute to the memory of Scotland's national bard, Robert 'Rabbie' Burns, was never allowed to weigh down the essentially happy-go-lucky atmosphere of the occasion. It was a fun formula that 'rantin', rovin' Rabbie' himself would have approved of, I'm sure.

From tentative beginnings before an audience of little more than a dozen émigré Burns afficionados in the little dining hall of the school where he worked, Jock had seen his Mallorcan Burns Nights steadily grow in popularity and size until, this year, he had decided to push the boat right out by elevating proceedings to the 'extravaganza' status that he'd boasted about to the girl at the *Majorca Daily Bulletin*. And if that had been a slight exaggeration on Jock's part, then he could be forgiven. Extravaganza or not, this year's event would certainly be the most adventurous and, consequently, the most expensive he'd ever put on.

Even the cost of taking a few days off work to fly back to Scotland – ostensibly to visit his ageing parents, but equally, I suspected, in order to personally select and transport the first pageant-proportioned haggis ever to grace his Burns Suppers' table – would have given Jock severe palpitations of the wallet. To add to his financial anxieties, he had also arranged to fly out, again for the first time ever, a five-piece Scottish Dance Band, a piper, a well-known Scottish singer and two Highland dancers. Attempting to wring a piddling discount from the ads girl at the 'Daily B' would have been only one of many such outlay-saving ploys that Jock would already have tried to pull off, of that I was sure.

During the return drive out to the airport, he explained his annoyance at having had his haggis 'arrested' by the

Spanish customs earlier. The forthcoming Mallorcan Burns Night wasn't going to be the first one at which haggis had been served. Indeed, the obligatory Burns Supper fare of haggis, mashed tatties and 'neeps' (Swede turnips) had been served up every year since that first experimental celebration of the bard's birthday in the school dining hall. But it had always been the tinned variety of haggis that had been on offer, a couple of cans at a time having been brought over from Scotland throughout the preceding twelve months by a succession of Jock's obliging friends and family members when visiting the island on holiday. Not that there was anything wrong with tinned haggis, Jock was quick to stress. On the contrary, its quality was regarded as being up there with the best. And it goes without saying that, when presented with an individual portion on a plate, not even the most knowledgeable of haggis buffs could tell whether his helping had been spooned from a tin or a skin.

No, it was just that, to pay ritual homage to a haggis in the time-honoured Burns Night way, a 'proper' one, the bigger the better, and essentially sporting an outer covering of a sheep's stomach, had to be paraded from kitchen to presentation table with all the pomp and pageantry that Rabbie's 'great chieftain o' the puddin' race' deserved. And this was the first time, after all those years of working towards it, that Jock had managed to arrange a bash big enough to warrant the appearance of a worthy example. That nit-picking customs man couldn't have touched a more sensitive nerve, therefore, than he had when threatening to have Jock's precious show haggis 'deported or destroyed' – and at Jock's expense too!

What's more, Jock pointed out to me as we entered the customs area at the airport, no bugger had ever objected to a tinned haggis being brought into Spain, so why deny entry to a real one?

I told myself that officialdom probably had a perfectly plausible reason for that – namely that one variety of haggis 'meat' was enclosed in a hermetically-sealed container, whereas the other wasn't. On the other hand, maybe it was just that Jock's obliging friends and relations had been fortunate enough never to have had their luggage searched. Whatever, it certainly wasn't a point I'd have risked taking up with the Spanish customs. And I was relieved to discover that Jock was of the same mind – though clearly set on having the last word on what he saw as the unnecessary hassle he'd been subjected to today.

'My 'agees, if you please?' he said in Spanish to the same customs officer, flashing him the briefest of humourless smiles. 'I believe that the papers – the *certificados oficiales* – that will enable you to issue a permit for my *animal* to run wild in Spain have been faxed to you, *sí*?'

'Ah, yes indeed, Mr Burns,' the officer replied in perfect English. He nodded his head and smiled genially back. Though perhaps not quite in the Antonio Banderas league of drop-dead, Latin good-lookers, when he was in this amicable state of mind, the officer's face did have a touch of that distinctive Spanish handsomeness about it. Swarthily dignified and patently self-confident would be how I'd describe it. The smouldering toreador look. His parted lips exposed a ribbon of gleaming white teeth to contrast with the black pelmet of his moustache, whilst also accentuating the golden glow of his lightly-tanned skin.

'Looks like a bloody liquorice allsort,' Jock mumbled to me from behind a cupped hand.

'One moment, please, Mr Burns,' the officer went on, apparently not having caught Jock's caustic quip. He produced some forms from a desk drawer, flicked through them, extracted the relevant ones, then presented them to Jock. 'You will find everything to allow the legal immigration of your little friend there,' he stated. 'And, uh, you will be relieved to learn, sir, that no passport will be required for him.' He'd said this in all seriousness – or so he'd have had Jock believe. But, watching him closely, I was pretty sure that the same mischievous smile that I thought I'd detected after his earlier detention of the haggis was tugging gently at a corner of his mouth again. 'Now, Mr Burns,' he said, 'I will arrange for the release of Master MacSporran from his cell.'

Jock glowered, but said nothing.

The customs man spoke the required command into an intercom, and a few moments later Jock and his precious haggis were reunited.

Jock still said nothing.

'I must apologise for associating your sausage with a pig when I first saw it,' the customs man smiled as he handed Jock a form to sign.

'It's not a fuckin' sausage,' Jock grunted under his breath, while testily scribbling his moniker on the paper. I could sense that he was trying desperately to dredge up all the self-restraint he could. He was having the mickey gently but pointedly taken, and he knew it.

'It looks like a sausage to me,' the customs man stated offhandedly, but without animosity. 'Yes, and I see from the paperwork here that the haggis is actually made from certain obscure parts of a sheep,' he then remarked. He smiled cordially again. 'Awful, I think you call it in English, no?'

For the second time that day, I thought Jock was about to explode. '*Offal!*' he snapped. '*Offal* is what it's called!'

The officer inclined his head in a that's-what-I-said sort of way.

'Offal!' Jock reiterated. 'That's O-F-F-A-L, right?'

The officer inclined his head to the other side, this time in a what-the-hell's-that? sort of way.

'Offal!' Jock snarled again, the schoolteacher in him coming out as he eyeballed the customs man with an imperious glare. 'That's off-*al*, not fucking aw-*ful*! Offal – the edible entrails of an animal, according to the dictionary. In the case of a haggis, that specifically means the pluck of a sheep, OK?'

'Pluck?' The customs man inclined his head both ways, this time accompanying the movements with a puzzled frown. 'What is a… pluck?'

After taking a deep, temper-controlling breath, Jock proceeded to painstakingly explain that, together with a spicy blend of oatmeal and suet, the essential ingredients of a haggis were the finely-chopped components of the sheep's pluck, namely the heart, liver and lungs. Offal, in other words – all stuffed into the 'bag', which was actually the sheep's stomach.

The customs man turned up his nose. 'And you *eat* this?'

Jock didn't reply, but stood squinting apprehensively at the officer, waiting for his delivery of the inevitable *coup de grâce*.

'Well, sir,' the official said with a slightly derisive chuckle, 'that certainly sounds awful to me. And I do mean awful, as in A-W-F-U-L. Right?'

I had to physically restrain Jock as he made to lunge over the desk, ranting about how the officer had a bloody cheek to take the piss out of a haggis when, in all probability, one of his own favourite dishes would be *Frit Mallorquí*, an island speciality made from the roughly chopped *asadura de cordero*, the heart, liver and lungs of a bloody sheep! In other words, the pluck – just the same as in a haggis, except that the Mallorcan sheep's 'bits' were mixed with potatoes, onions and peppers instead of oatmeal.

'And not stuffed back into the donor's guts again,' the customs man appended by way of a final dig as I bundled

Jock out of the door. '*Adiós, señores*,' he shouted after us, laughing freely now. '*Feliz fiesta escocesa, eh*! Have a happy Scottish party! Ah, *sí*, and that goes for your little *animal*, too!'

Jock gave him a one-fingered salute in response, to which the officer jovially replied, 'And God save your gracious Queen of Haggisonia!'

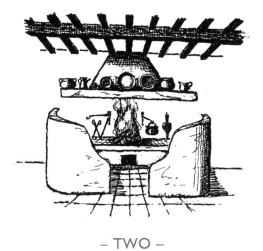

– TWO –

MONEY DOESN'T GROW ON TREES

When I finally got back to Ca's Mayoral that evening, Ellie and the boys were waiting for me in the kitchen.

Ellie was filing her fingernails, an essential maintenance task after a day working in the orchards. 'We picked all the oranges to fill Jeronimo's order for tomorrow,' she told me, looking up briefly from the job in hand.

'Yeah, I noticed all the full crates stacked in the *porche* as I came in. You did really well, both of you. Thanks a million.'

'We did really well, the *three* of us,' Charlie piped up. 'I mucked in with the picking when I got home from school.'

I could have sworn that I felt French Andy's wad of notes twitch nervously in my hip pocket at this piece of news.

'So that'll be a slice of the fruit-pickin' dough for me as well, huh?' Charlie ventured hopefully.

I gave my hip pocket a calming pat. 'Try not to speak in that phoney mid-Atlantic accent, Charlie,' I yawned. 'I've heard enough of that from Jock today.'

'He can't help it,' Ellie said. 'All the kids at his school talk that way. You know that well enough, so stop trying to change the subject.'

'I take it, Dad, that you did get the boodle from French Andy?' Sandy probed.

I took the roll from my pocket. 'Yes, yes, don't panic. It's all here.'

Charlie rubbed his hands.

This gesture didn't go unnoticed by his elder brother. 'Don't kid yourself, Charlie. There aren't three halves to an orange, and the same goes for the French Andy money. Half to me, and half to Mum. That's the deal.'

'Don't gimme that,' Charlie came back. 'I did my bit, so I'm due my cut. That *should* be the deal!' He looked at me for back-up.

'Listen, sprog,' Sandy cut in before I could respond to Charlie's plea, 'there are more than twenty full crates out there, and it'd be stretching even your over-fertile imagination to claim that you picked enough oranges to fill more than *one* of them.'

'Bullshit, big brother! If I picked less oranges than you, it's only cos you'd started before I got home from school. I still deserve a fair slice of the dough!'

'Not out of my share, you don't! Who do you think does the work around here on all those weekends you're away poncing about on luxury yachts and things with your millionaire chums? Nah, get lost, Charlie. Dad says the French Andy money's a bonus, and half of it's mine!'

These little feuds between the boys were becoming more frequent. Maybe it was just sibling rivalry. Brothers will be brothers, after all. Yet I could see Sandy's point, in as much as working on the farm was his *job* and his means of earning a wage, meagre though it was. Charlie, meanwhile, was still a schoolboy and, therefore, still the financial responsibility of his parents, whether he helped with the farm work or not. That he did help wasn't a big deal, however. It was a prerequisite of being a member of a family like ours – hands-on small farmers, whose very existence depended on every member of the family pulling his or her weight. Although Sandy had also been expected to do his bit when he was Charlie's age, whether he'd actually done more work to help out in his spare time than Charlie was doing now was debatable. But the difference between Sandy's social life with his schoolmates in Scotland then and the one that Charlie was enjoying in Mallorca now was always likely to distort the truth of the matter, whatever it was. Had Sandy, when only thirteen, spent less time playing football and all the other 'normal' things that kids do for fun at weekends in Scotland than Charlie was now spending 'poncing about on luxury yachts and things'? Probably not. But Charlie did have a more 'glamorous' leisure-time life than Sandy had previously had, and that, compounded by the difference in their ages, was probably the real source of this brotherly bickering. Though not intending to afford the matter more importance than it deserved, Ellie and I *were* becoming increasingly aware of it.

'We'll see if we can slip a wee bonus into your pocket money this weekend, Charlie,' said Ellie, ever the timely pourer of oil on potentially troubled waters. 'A little extra something for the extra work you did today.'

'That's just typical!' Sandy grumped. 'Money for nothing for Charlie. I mean, he already gets his jeans and T-shirts and fancy trainers bought for him. Yeah, and all with highfalutin designer names at that, just so's he can swank about alongside his rich-kid schoolmates. And now he's gonna get extra pocket money, just for picking one measly crate of oranges. Bloody typical!'

While there was some truth in what he'd said about the fashion fads that kids subscribed to in international schools like the one Charlie was now a pupil at, we'd never succumbed to the demands of any such peer pressure that Charlie might have been subjected to. On the contrary – Ellie's female addiction to shopping, particularly for clothes, was tempered by her having a canny eye for a bargain. So, Charlie's school rig-outs since coming to Mallorca had comprised items which, whilst perhaps carrying in-vogue 'name' labels, never stretched the limits of Ellie's carefully calculated and devoutly adhered-to budgets. Consequently, Charlie's casual and trendy school clothes were unlikely to have cost us any more, relatively speaking, than Sandy's more mundane school wear had done at the same stage of *his* scholastic life.

For all that, I could still appreciate how Sandy felt. He was at an age when money, his *own* money, was becoming increasingly important to him as his natural instinct towards independence developed. At the same time, it was only natural that Charlie would aspire to enjoying the material things that some of his new friends, the children of extremely well-off parents, probably took for granted. He'd be super-keen to grab every penny of extra pocket money he could get his hands on. Suddenly, the harsh financial realities of our new life were threatening to strain our family bonds at the seams. I could now see that there was going to be much more to making a success of this Mallorcan venture than just turning a profit from growing oranges.

For the moment, though, my main regret was ever having allowed my sudden attack of big-heartedness to spur me into being so free with French Andy's fruit money in the first place. But it was too late to go back on my word now.

I counted out equal shares into Ellie's and Sandy's waiting hands.

'And, as your mother said, ' I advised Charlie, whose optimistically outstretched palm remained empty at the conclusion of the boodle-split, 'we'll see if we can lob you a bit extra for your pocket money next time. But,' I quicky added, 'don't think that I'll make a habit of it. You've got to do your share of chores here like the rest of us – and nobody's on piecework!'

On the face of it, that may have seemed rather harsh on a kid of Charlie's age, but what I'd told him was a fact of life, nevertheless. If he'd been developing an expectation of exacting more money from us every time his farm-work input happened to exceed the norm (and he was never called on to do any more than was absolutely necessary, and certainly never as much as would encroach on the time he *should* have spent studying), then it was an unrealistic attitude that had to be nipped in the bud. He was never going to be the spoilt son of wealthy parents, and if it meant being a bit blunt in stressing the point when the occasion arose, then so be it. Meanwhile, given the down-to-earth upbringing he'd had, we could only hope that the common-sense side of his nature would prevail, no matter what temptations he might be exposed to by mixing with the 'high life' set of Mallorca.

I looked at him enquiringly for a sign of feedback to the rebuttal I'd just given him.

He hunched his shoulders into a stoical shrug and said, 'Cool. That's cool with me, *padre*.' Then, stuffing his empty hands into the pockets of his Calvin Klein jeans, he smiled and added, 'Yeah, no sweat. I'm wise to where you're coming from. Money doesn't grow on trees, right?'

I couldn't resist a fleeting smile of relief at Charlie's surprisingly perceptive reaction. 'Not on this little farm,' I replied. 'Not enough to chuck about willy-nilly, at any rate.'

'A penny saved is a penny earned, right?' said Charlie, quoting another of my favourite sayings.

I nodded sagely. 'Never more so than when you're trying to build a new business – and a new life – like we're doing here.'

Charlie ambled forward and awarded me a we're-all-in-this-together pat on the arm. 'Like I say, *padre*, it's all cool by me.' He gave me the thumbs-up and added philosophically, 'Hey, relax – missing out on a slice of the French Andy dough is *not* a problem for me, OK?'

Sandy, who, until this moment, had been leafing through his share of the money, and had been tempted by pangs of conscience, I suspected, to peel off a note or two for his younger brother, suddenly glared pop-eyed at him and gasped, 'You crawling little creep! How insincere can you get? I mean, that performance deserves a bloody Oscar!'

With that, while Charlie allowed himself a smug little smirk, Sandy folded his wad and stuck it in his pocket – intact.

Ellie, I noticed, had already committed her half of the money to the security of her purse. She shot me an expectant smile. 'Well, it's Friday night and we've all worked really hard this week. Don't you think you should be treating us to some way of enjoying the fruits of our labours, so to speak? You know – getting ourselves into that more *relaxed* attitude to life here that you agreed to?'

I knew what Ellie was angling for – eating out, her favourite pastime, apart from rummaging through dress shops. The boys knew what she was getting at as well.

Charlie wagged a finger at her in the manner of Jock Burns in schoolteacher mode. 'Ah, but,' he cautioned, 'you forget, *madre*, that *padre* is stony broke – now that he's given all his French Andy stash away.' He fired a cutting glance at Sandy, who merely puckered his lips and rolled his eyes disinterestedly ceilingwards.

'Don't you believe it,' Ellie laughed. 'Your father's flogged more oranges to Jeronimo in the past seven days than in any fortnight since we came here.' She gave me a playful nudge. 'So, come on, Scrooge, let a few moths out of your wallet. Your hired helpers deserve to live a little *once* in a while!'

I'd noticed, on coming into the kitchen earlier, that the table hadn't been set. It normally would have been by that time, so Ellie obviously hadn't prepared a meal for tonight anyway. However, it had indeed been a week of harder-than-usual work for her in the orange groves, so no-one could deny that she deserved a break from cooking. Not that she ever needed much of an excuse to take one of those. But that aside, the latest flurry of friction between the boys would only have served to increase her determination to gather us together for some family bonding round the dinner table. Though not, if she could help it, round our own!

'Well,' I said with a sigh of mock resignation, 'if we're going to go to the wall, we may as well enjoy ourselves on the way. Let's eat out.'

Sa masía means 'the farmhouse' in *mallorquín*, and the Restaurante Sa Masía is, or rather was, just that, athough its honey-stone walls resound these days to the babble of convivial conversation instead of the bleating of the sheep and goats that grazed its little pine-screened fields in centuries past. It's in the style of a typical Mallorcan *senyoríu*, or country 'mansion', in that the frontage of the main house conceals an inner courtyard, a *clastre*, formed by a rectangular enclosure of more modest stone buildings. These were intended for housing, not only the farm's animals, but also the families of those employed by the *senyór*, the owner of the estate, to tend his livestock, work his land and harvest his crops.

The Restaurante Sa Masía sits back from and above the main Andratx-to-Palma road, near the peaceful (as its name suggests) Costa de la Calma urbanisation and about a third of the way between Andratx and the city. Although we passed by it every day when doing the seventeen-mile drive to take Charlie to and from school at Sant Agustí on the western outskirts of the capital, we had only eaten there once before. That had been at the invitation of two visiting friends, as a token of their gratitude for having been our house guests at Ca's Mayoral during their two-week summer holiday. As they'd insisted that they'd be picking up the tab, we hadn't been too concerned about noting the menu prices when ordering, but the general ambience of the place had suggested that the cost of eating there would be on the expensive side of average for Mallorca. As it turned out, the quality of the food added weight to the assumption.

More modest in scale than many Mallorcan *senyoríus*, partcularly those bulky, fortified examples high in the Tramuntanas that were built both to afford shelter from the harsh winter weather of the mountains and to provide protection from marauding bandits in olden times, the façade of the Restaurante Sa Masía has an unmistakably welcoming appearance to it. Its single-storey frontage is homely-looking, as opposed to loftily-grand, yet built in the classic *hacienda* style that instantly reminds you that you're in Spain.

In homage to the farm's workaday past, a wooden cart sits parked in front. But, instead of sacks of almonds or sheaves of oats, all it's burdened with now are tubs of geraniums, their scarlet flowers tumbling in glorious profusion over wooden-spoked wheels and two empty shafts, between which a drowsy donkey, in this very spot, might once have been stealing a welcome rest from its labours. To one side of the building, a play area for the younger children of the restaurant's clients has been constructed in a little corral where pigs used to root in the dirt. Well, exasperated parents might remark, at least there's been no significant change there!

Typically, you enter Sa Masía through a central archway that leads to the inner courtyard, which is where we'd dined alfresco with our friends on that balmy summer evening. And totally beguiling wouldn't be too extravagant a description of the setting. Candlelit tables were set discreetly apart throughout the cobbled *clastre*, splashes of warm light from hanging lanterns casting the mellow stone of the surrounding farmstead into gentle relief. Here and there along the walls, billows of bougainvillea clambered past snugly-shuttered windows, scaling the eaves of the buildings to smother their aged roof tiles in glorious lava flows of mauve and pink. Then, as the shadows of dusk crept into every corner of the courtyard, star after star appeared in the darkening sky above, and the soft strumming of a Spanish guitar melded with the tinkling flow of water from the *fuente*, the 'fountain of life', around which this little *senyoríu*, like all others, had of necessity been built.

It was, of course, a scene and an atmosphere that had been carefully stage-managed to captivate the summer visitor to Mallorca. It bore little relationship to the spartan conditions that would have prevailed for the families who'd lived within these four walls in the days when Sa Masía had been a working farm. And the attire of the waiters, while calculated, no doubt, to add a note of authenticity to everything, could just as easily have succeeded in accentuating the theatricality of it all. They were dressed in traditional Mallorcan costumes of baggy, striped *pantalones*, girded at the waist with broad sashes and gathered below the knee above white stockings. Crimson waistcoats were worn open over full-sleeved shirts, also pristine white. It was hardly the practical garb of farm hands. But the waiters sported their outfits with apparent pride, and, lulled by the nocturnal chirruping of crickets in the surrounding pines, it would have taken the most unromantic of souls not to have been seduced by the summer-night magic of Sa Masía – no matter how deftly contrived.

But this was now Mallorca in winter, and a chill had descended on the island with the setting of the sun, the drop in temperature all the more marked after the unseasonable warmth of the *Calmas de Enero* day. As we approached, we could see that the inner courtyard was in darkness, save for the pale glint of moonlight on the cobblestones. Gone were the candlelit tables of summer and the cheerful chatter of suntanned diners, the only sound now the hushed sigh of a night breeze whispering through the pines. A welcoming light spilled out through a half-glazed door inside the archway.

Ellie led the way. 'Looks like they're open for business,' she said. 'Phew! For one horrible moment I thought we were out of luck.'

'Don't worry, I'd have treated you all to fish suppers at the English chippie in Palma Nova instead,' I told her, dropping the hint that I was already going all of a financial flutter at the prospect of what this culinary excursion to the Restaurante Sa Masía might cost.

'Don't be such a cheapskate!' she scolded. 'We're surely worth more than some takeaway hake-and-chips in a paper bag.'

I chose not to argue the point. I could see from the eager grins on the boys' faces that I'd have been in a minority of one in any case. But, while I followed Ellie inside, the smells wafting out of the kitchen instantly put a smile on my face as well. There's something wonderfully unique about the smell of Spanish country cooking. I've tried to define it, but it's just too complex to analyse accurately. It has a lot to do with the tang of woodsmoke, combined with the rich fragrance of hot olive oil, and a whiff of grilling meat or seafood so potent that you can almost taste it. Ultimately, though, you have to leave it to your nose to convey the message that words can't adequately express. My nostrils were already telling my taste buds best-selling stories as I thanked the costumed waiter who opened the door for us.

'*Guten abend, meine dame und herren,*' he smiled with a polite little bow. Overhearing us talking as we came in, he'd obviously mistaken our east-of-Scotland accents for German, a not-infrequent occurrence in a part of the island extremely popular with German folk, resident and holiday-making alike.

Not wanting to risk embarrassing the waiter, I elected not to correct him, but to reply in my best Spanish instead. After a good year of practice, I was quietly confident that my pronunciation of at least the most often-used phrases in my repertoire was now indistinguishable from that of a native Spaniard.

'*Buenos tardes, señor,*' I smiled back, then asked for a table for four. '*Una mesa para quatro, por favor.*'

'Ah,' he beamed, 'English, eh?' He beckoned us to follow him.

Suitably deflated, I decided it would be simpler not to pursue the subject of nationalities further – particularly one that might be regarded by the waiter as being of the hair-splitting variety anyway. Automatically calling all Brits

'English' tends to be a fairly common inaccuracy abroad, and there are times when it doesn't do any harm to remind the mistaken party that Britain comprises more than just one country. But I wasn't of a mind to risk boring the baggy *pantalones* off a well-meaning Mallorcan waiter with a brief history of the United Kingdom. There were more rewarding things in prospect.

'Please,' he said, while showing us to a table near an inglenook, in which a welcoming log fire had been lit, 'sit you here, *señores*. It makes a little cold out tonight, no?' As a mark of respect for my brave attempt at speaking Spanish-sounding Spanish (or maybe just to humour me), he then handed out multi-lingual menus, conspicuously opened for each of us in turn at the Spanish-language section.

'What's *Rodets de Vedella Empinyonats*, Dad?' Charlie asked as soon as the waiter had left. 'Hey, I hope *rodets* isn't a misspelling of rodents. I've been suckered into eating that Mallorcan rat stew before!' Charlie was referring to a dish from the town of Sa Pobla in the north of the island, where an old recipe is based on the meat of large rat-like creatures that live in the nearby lagoons and salt marshes of La Albufera. I'd once fooled him into ordering it in a restaurant by telling him the meat was chicken.

'You're the one who's learning Spanish at school every day,' I pointed out, 'so you should be telling *me* what it means. Let's face it, your education's costing me enough!' I jerked my head towards the inglenook's open fire, which Charlie happened to have his back to. 'Some size of a log that,' I casually remarked.

While he looked round to admire the blazing chunk of olivewood, I swiftly thumbed through the menu until I found the page with a little Union Flag in the top corner.

'But just to improve your vocabulary, Charlie,' I said offhandedly, 'I can tell you for nothing that the dish you asked about is actually small barrels of veal, with a stuffing of minced meat laced with pine nuts. *Empinyonats*, as you'll observe, contains the letters P-I-N-Y and O. That spells *pinyó*, which, of course, is the local word for a pine kernel.'

Charlie turned back round, his face wreathed in a self-congratulatory grin. 'Yeah, I'd already sussed all that from the English-lingo bit of the menu, *padre*. I just wondered if you had, too, that's all.'

I cleared my throat. 'Nobody likes a smart-arsed kid, Charlie.' I grunted, then, head down, concentrated on studying of the bill of fare.

Ellie and Sandy concealed their smirks behind raised menus, craftily flicking the pages back and forth between the Spanish and English sections. Like them, I was well enough accustomed by now to the names of the most popular Mallorcan dishes when straightforwardly itemised on the menus of the humbler bars and *tascas* that we were in the habit of frequenting. But here, the more 'creative' combinations of the same basic ingredients had been given names to match – and, to make things even trickier, some were in *mallorquín*. So, having already been caught with my linguistic trousers down, I followed Ellie's and the boys' suit without further comment. I flicked.

The waiter returned with little pre-prandial dishes of olives and slivers of raw carrots and mild green peppers, together with a basket of crusty bread and a dip of garlicky *all-i-oli* mayonnaise.

It's the Spanish way not to drink wine without eating something, and I'd long since subscribed to the view that it follows that the reverse should also be the case. Why eat, even 'picks' of olives and things, without drinking some wine? I asked the waiter for a *jarra* of the house *vino tinto*, and he was back in a jiffy with an earthenware jug of what turned out to be a typically muscular country wine. Its colour was as dark as bull's blood, its taste resolutely on the macho side of delicate, its strength clearly to be treated with respect. I did as Spaniards do with such robust table wines, and topped up my glass with a generous splash of *agua con gas* (sparkling mineral water). I was careful not to totally emasculate the wine, however, and its lulling glow was soon spreading through my veins. Feeling more mellow with each sip, I sat back and contemplated our surroundings.

In keeping with their courtyard counterparts, many of the original features of Sa Masía's interior had been retained, and their rustic charm shown off to maximum effect. The inglenook, so characteristic of old Mallorcan country houses, wasn't just a large, recessed fireplace, but rather a room within a room, big enough to accommodate an entire family within the enfolding shelter of its high-backed benches. As well as being the focal point of the farmhouse kitchen, such an inglenook, in the days before central heating, would have been a cosy winter haven in an otherwise cold and draughty house, especially when the icy Tramuntana gales blasted down from the north. The cooking would have been done over its open hearth, and within its reassuring confines the resultant meals would have been eaten. The inglenook was, in effect, the living heart of the household. I've also heard it described as a family sanctuary, in which, at the end of a day of toil in the fields, the post-supper silence would be broken only by the ticking of the clock and the crackling of the fire – and, no doubt, the occasional snore.

Characteristically, the bell-shaped chimney breast was painted white, offsetting the smoke-darkened wood of the mantleshelf, on which an array of terracotta jugs, *greixonera* cooking dishes and copper utensils were lined up as they would have been when still in daily use. But now, their only purpose was to state a theme that was repeated on other shelves throughout the room. These, together with randomly-hung clusters of painted plates, provided an aptly simple adornment to the otherwise plain, whitewashed walls.

It seemed that the main restaurant, appearing spacious enough to cater for fifty or more diners, had been created by knocking a few smaller rooms into one. And the result was totally in keeping with the intended *mallorquina rustica* image. Even the practical idea of the inglenook's cushioned stone benches had been borrowed to provide seating at tables in little intimate corners that the demolition of the internal walls had created. The overall effect was one of snug, homely comfort in an atmosphere that, like the summer courtyard, gave a fair, though understandably modified, taste of a bygone age. It was a concept that chef Amadeu had skilfully carried over to the cuisine.

His 'special of the day', our waiter told us, was sea bream, or *dorada* – always a delicious fish, he acknowledged, but all the more so when baked in a jacket of rock salt, a precise skill of which Amadeu was a recognised expert. I readily opted for that, while Sandy ordered *Faisán a la Frambuesa* (pheasant with a raspberry sauce), which, he commented, though perhaps a little Freudianally, sounded more Scottish than Mallorcan to him. Charlie went for the *Rodets de Vedella Empinyonats*, having become even more attracted to them after noting that their meat stuffing was laced with, not just pine nuts, but truffles as well. To the best of my knowledge, he'd never tasted a truffle in his life, but he'd obviously learned somewhere along the way that they were expensive. Ellie, meanwhile, had selected the less extravagant-sounding *Conill amb Ceba* (rabbit with onions).

Sandy shook his head. 'Honestly, Mum, one of those days you're gonna sprout long ears.'

'Or maybe even buck teeth,' Charlie chipped in. 'Yeah, we'll have to start calling you Bugs!'

Ellie was rather predictable in her choice of food when eating out. But, in fairness, it wasn't *always* rabbit. Equally often it was squid – but not *Calamares a la Romana*, those golden, fried-in-batter squid rings that even the most unadventurous of eaters find attractive when in Spain. No, when Ellie ordered squid, and it *was* fairly frequently, it had to be in its entire, undisguised, as-the-fisherman-caught-it state. Not a dish for the squeamish of eye, and one that I'd been surprised to see Ellie taking to so enthusiastically, particularly as she baulked at comparatively innocuous-looking Mallorcan delicacies like snails. But she genuinely liked nothing better than a whole squid, simply grilled on a wood-fired *plancha*, and served with plenty of lemon wedges. But there was no squid on the menu tonight.

'Just as well,' I said. 'Growing rabbit ears is one thing, but I worry about what you might sprout if you go on eating so many squid.'

Ellie replied with a dismissive sniff and a devil-may-care toss of her head. 'You needn't worry. You'll notice that I *always* cut the testicles off and bin them.'

The boys and I were accustomed enough to Ellie's innocent, but often priceless, slips of the tongue to allow that fairly mild one to pass without comment. We knew what she meant. I only hoped she did as well!

She'd certainly known what she was about when she ordered that deceptively humble-sounding rabbit dish. Amadeu had taken one of the most common and unpretentious of Mallorcan country recipies and turned it into a *tour de force*, endowing it with a taste and texture that Ellie claimed was as near perfection as she'd ever experienced. And she knew her rabbits. Served in a *greixonera* earthenware bowl, chunky cuts of meat were luxuriating with silky ribbons of onion in a gravy enriched with ground almonds, herbs and white wine. The flesh was so tender, Ellie assured us, that it fell away from the bone as easily as Charlie could be distracted from his homework. No higher praise could be lavished on Amadeu's culinary expertise.

I couldn't have been more generous in my endorsement of the *Dorada a la Sal* either. The bream arrived looking a bit like a fish-shaped mummy in its body-hugging sarcophagus of toasted salt. However, once that oven-hardened crust was broken, what was revealed was white fish cooked to succulent perfection, and so delicious that, if he'd known about it, Tutankhamen himself would probably have ordered one to be entombed with him for his delectation in the afterlife.

The boys, not surprisingly, didn't bother to wax so lyrical about their chosen dishes. They didn't need to. The silence that prevailed during their devouring of them spoke volumes. It also turned their burped, end-of-meal pronouncements of 'Good, eh?' and 'Not too bad!' into superfluous understatements of hyperbole.

My compliments to the chef, via the waiter, resulted in the customary placing on our table of a bottle of Mallorcan *hierbas* liqueur, to be enjoyed, compliments of the management, over coffees. The fact that I was the only one drinking it meant that, in order not to appear ungrateful and risk offence, I was obliged to force myself into downing all four glasses of the delectable, anise-flavoured, green potion on my own. I ignored Ellie's muttered jibe about the sacrifices I made my family at times, and savoured each tangy-sweet drop.

The strident sound of stringed instruments being energetically plucked and strummed stirred me from the half-tipsy reverie I was drifting into. Then a harmony of male voices as robust as the house wine drew my eyes towards the door, where a quintet of young men in period costumes were entering the restaurant, singing Mallorcan folksongs while accompanying themselves on guitars and lutes. They were students, the waiter told us – from the university in Palma – probably studying law – going the rounds of restaurants at weekends – busking for a bit of extra money – to buy books – or wine!

They moved from table to table, like a troupe of wandering minstrels in a medieval court, making hearty music and bowing to every diner who tossed a few coins into the hat of the sole non-instrumentalist member of the group, who was strategically stationed in the middle of their colourful little procession. Even if, to the terminally cynical, their impromptu appearance had contributed to that subtly-contrived atmosphere I mentioned before, I felt, in my current mellow mood, that it had actually added a touch of authenticity to the olden-days Mallorcan ambience I'd become increasingly pleased to wallow in. The effects of the house *vino tinto*, the *hierbas* and the olivewood warmth of the inglenook were weaving a soothing spell, and I was happy to submit to it.

The arrival of the waiter with the bill delivered a sobering slap, however. Or, rather, I thought it would.

'You know,' I said, checking the total with a benevolent eye, 'if I'd known this place was such good value for money, I'd've picked something a lot more expensive-looking from the menu when our chums were paying last summer.'

'No doubt,' Ellie concurred, 'but you're on the bell tonight, Rockefeller, so get your money out.'

And, in saying that, she'd unwittingly fed me the perfect cue I'd hoped for when letting her believe she'd won her little extortion game that allowed her to bag half the French Andy money.

I patted my pockets. 'Oh no!' I groaned, my face falling. 'Would you believe it? I've forgotten my wallet!'

Ellie arched her eyebrows. 'Believe me, if it's true that a fool and his money are easily parted, then you're up there in the Einstein league.' Leaving me to unravel that tangled compliment for a moment, she reached for her handbag. 'Ah well,' she said with an exaggerated note of stoicism, 'it all comes out of the same pot at the end of the day, I suppose.'

But before she could open her purse, the most surprising thing happened. Sandy leaned over the table and grabbed her wrist. 'Wait a minute, Mum,' he said, 'this one's on me.' With that, he produced his own half share of the French Andy windfall and placed it on top of the bill on the little silver tray. 'That should cover it, I think.'

Ellie and I started to object, explaining that we'd only been kidding each other, playing out that little joke from earlier, having a silly leg-pull. There was no way, we insisted, that we could let him blow all of his bonus money on what had been, first and foremost, a *family* treat.

But Sandy would have none of it. No, he insisted, he, like everyone else in the family, had to make a financial contribution to this new *relaxed* attitude to life that we'd agreed to adopt. He glanced ruefully at the heap of notes he'd just parted with, then said under his breath, 'It's not as if I've got anything else to spend it on, anyway.'

'That's right,' Charlie breezed, 'it's not as if he's got a cute little *señorita* to take nightclubbing in the bright lights of downtown Andratx or something.' His self-congratulatory giggle and look of anticipated approval met with an awkward silence from Ellie and me, and a glare from Sandy that would have stopped a fighting bull in its tracks.

It certainly wiped the grin off Charlie's face. While it was obvious that his wisecrack had been blurted out without thinking, and was merely a bit of non-malicious showing off, it had clearly touched a sensitive point as far as Sandy was concerned. At that moment, however, we could only assume that Sandy had taken exception to Charlie's remark because, inevitably, he'd found it impossible to forge relationships with young people of his own age in a rural location where none existed any more. He'd solve that problem in his own time and in his own way, of that we were sure. And Ellie, for one, had made no secret of her hope that finding the right *señorita* would tilt the balance of his decision-making in favour of committing his future to a life in Mallorca. But that was something that would either arise and resolve itself or not in the fullness of time. For now, though, my only feeling was one of relief when Charlie stepped swiftly into the conversational hiatus with an offer of unexpected generosity…

'Tell you what,' he announced, 'seeing as how Sandy's picking up the tab for the meal, the least I can do is lob in ten per cent for the tip.'

While three jaws dropped in formation, he held up a reassuring hand and said, 'OK, OK, I know I didn't get anything for helping pick the oranges for French Andy, but I still want to make a contribution towards this new *relaxed* way of life we're into. Fair's fair, right?'

Three disbelieving heads nodded in unison.

'But I didn't think you had any money,' I eventually ventured.

'Hey, absolutely spot on, *padre*! Totally skint, in fact. Yeah, and that's why I wondered if you might consider giving me the tip money on tick… uhm, until the next pocket money pay-out, that is.'

'Charlie,' I said, my pay-out hand dipping grudgingly into my pocket, 'for you, money really does grow on trees!'

And soon might the miracle come good for the rest of us, too, I silently prayed.

Ellie, meanwhile, smiled maternally.

Sandy mimed a puke.

– THREE –

HORSES FOR COURSES

Pablo Gomez the builder was a self-made man. He was also a very likeable man, stockily built, in his mid-fifties, and cheery of disposition. Unfortunately, however, he didn't share Ellie's affection for mimosa trees (at least not her one), and that was the start of his problems. He had arrived, bang on time, at eight o'clock on that appointed morning. Amazing, I mused, how punctual builders can be when they want you to sign a contract or a cheque. But Pablo came highly recommended for reliability in all aspects of his profession, and from no less an authority than Jock Burns' wife Meg.

As a hairdresser, Meg didn't profess to know much about bricks and mortar, of course. But her salon on the outskirts of Palma was a renowned hotbed of information on every aspect of Mallorcan life, so her advice on the merits of one builder as opposed to another was about as guaranteed to be correct as you could hope to get from anyone. Pablo Gomez's company, she assured us, might not be the cheapest around, but Pablo was honest, employed only the best tradesmen, and kept a personal eye on every job he undertook. 'Oh aye,' Meg had insisted, 'he'll be the very man to build yer swimmin' pool for ye, flowers.'

Certainly, if Pablo's background was anything to go by, he was a man who had never accepted anything but the best as far as workmanship was concerned, and to prove it, he'd built up a thriving business empire from literally nothing. As a young man, he'd arrived penniless in Mallorca from one of the poorer provinces of southern Spain, settling, like many others from that part of the mainland, in the south-western corner of the island. But, unlike most of his fellow 'immigrants', Pablo hadn't been content to be just another labourer working on the sites of the new hotels and apartment blocks that were pushing up like concrete mushrooms along the coast. He wanted a piece of the profits pie for himself. So, recognising the potential that existed in tourism-related construction work, he set up in business on his own in the then nascent resort of Peguera.

With no capital behind him, and with a wife and young family to support, the only way Pablo could succeed in his venture was to work all the hours that God provided, every day, every week, every year, doing any building job, no matter how menial, that came his way. Now, almost thirty years later, the fruits of Pablo's endeavours (and risk-taking) were there for all to see, and he wore the trappings of his deserved success with a commendable degree of modesty. His big Mercedes car was only *second*-top of the range, for instance, and his much-extended old farmhouse down on the outskirts of fashionable Port d'Andratx had an indoor swimming pool that was rumoured to be of *less* than

Olympic proportions – though only just. Having come up the hard way, Pablo always erred on the safe side of ostentation. But, on a more serious note, he had neither forgotten his humble roots nor had he lost his habit of getting personally involved in every project his company took on. This applied to our proposed swimming pool, and it mattered little to Pablo that it was an undertaking that paled into insignificance compared to most of the contracts he was involved in these days. 'Many a mickle makes a muckle' was a dictum, albeit supposedly Scottish, that had served Pablo well in his life. His more poetic Spanish version of the same was, 'Every little counts, said the mouse, when he pissed into the sea.'

I liked Pablo's line in philosophical thinking. Ellie, though, was more concerned with his attitude towards mimosa trees – at least her one. The problem was that the little tree, which was a golden eruption of fluffy popcorn flowers in winter and spring, stood right in the middle of the yard through which Pablo's digger would have to be driven to get to where the pool was to be situated. Pablo was apologetic but adamant. The tree would have to go.

The word 'no' means the same in both English and Spanish, so Ellie didn't have to expend too much breath, or overstretch her vocabulary, in stating her case.

Pablo looked gravely at the tree, shaking his head and fingering his moustache. '*Es un problema grande,*' he muttered. He thought for a minute, then turned and walked back to the gate, took a tape measure from his pocket and extended it across the opening. There was more bad news, he called over to us. The gateway was too narrow for the digger to pass through, so part of the wall would have to be demolished as well.

Now it was my turn to put my foot down. That wall was a thousand years old or more, I pointed out – possibly even dating as far back as the Arab occupation of the island. It was said to have carried water from the mountains to the old mill along the lane, a building also steeped in history, but which had now been turned into a weekend *casita* by Tomàs and Francisca Ferrer, the Mallorcan couple who'd sold us Ca's Mayoral. I had no hesitation in telling Pablo that, although I was only an *extranjero* from a land far away, my conscience wouldn't allow me to further sully the heritage of the island by destroying even half a metre of that wall.

Once I'd made that high-principled statement, however, I couldn't help feeling a bit guilty about its underlying duplicity. In truth, I was slyly hoping that protecting the integrity of the wall would provide a credible reason for the swimming pool project being shelved right there and then. Any such twinges of remorse quickly faded, though, as I visualised so many red-threatened figures remaining joyously black on our bank statements. It was a feeling of relief consolidated by the sight of Ellie standing four-square and resolute in front of her beloved mimosa tree, her arms folded, a look of near-Amazonian determination on her face. No way would Pablo Gomez be allowed to harm one precious panicle of that tree. Yes, the chances of the swimming pool ever being built now were looking hearteningly slimmer by the moment.

But my feeling of elation was to be short-lived.

'I have the *solución*,' Pablo beamed, visions of multiplied black figures on *his* bank statements clearly restored. 'We will simply use a smaller digger!' *Los señores* need worry no more, he promised. Our wall and mimosa tree would remain unscathed.

Dammit! I thought. Doesn't life have a way of kicking you in the teeth hardest just when your smile is at its widest?

His particular problems over, Pablo strode jauntily over the yard and produced an envelope from his pocket. 'Here we have the contract for your signature, *mi amigo*.' He gave me a slap of encouragement on the shoulder. 'Then we can commence work, so that you and your *familia* will soon be enjoying yourselves in your new *piscina*, no?'

'Ehm, the use of a smaller digger,' I ventured, ever hopeful, ' – it will cost us less, *sí*?'

Pablo gave me a smile that showed a mix of admiration for my game attempt at saving money and pity for the inevitable futility of it. He chuckled softly. 'Ah, no, no, no, *señor*,' he said with a determined shaking of his head, 'the use of the smaller digger means that the excavation work will take longer. So…' He left the obvious unsaid.

I thought I'd double-check anyway. 'So, it'll cost me more – is that what you're saying?'

Instead of replying, Pablo gestured towards the mimosa tree and then the gateway. He pulled a one-shoulder shrug. The choice was clearly ours. Save money by losing the tree and a bit of the wall, or save them both by losing a bit of money.

'OK, so how much more for the smaller digger?' I asked. If I was to be the latest incarnation of Pablo's peeing mouse, I needed to know what level he expected me to raise the high tide mark to.

Pablo gave me another pat on the shoulder – a calming one this time. '*Hombre*,' he crooned, a gently-reprimanding note to his voice, 'I am a businessman, but a fair one.'

I held my breath in anticipation of the sting.

'Yes, I am a fair man,' Pablo reiterated, 'but I am also a practical one.' He then went on to inform me that the extra cost of using the small digger for the excavations would normally be in the region of ten per cent. However, if I paid his bill for this stage of the work on the same day that he presented it, the increase would be waived. Why, he said, he wouldn't even alter the already-agreed price in the contract. He offered me his hand. '*De acuerdo*?' Did we have a deal?

We did, I said, and promptly shook on it. Pablo was all smiles as he climbed into his Mercedes, the duly signed contract safely back in his pocket. '*Hasta mañana*,' he called through the open window. He'd be back to see the digger start work in the morning. '*Hasta luego, eh!*'

I felt my wallet trembling again. Now that there was no escaping the economic realities of it, the swimming pool idea appealed even less than before. I sensed another nail-biting session coming on. 'I hope we're doing the right thing,' I said to Ellie, while I weakly waved goodbye to Pablo's smiling face in his rear-view mirror.

'Of course we are,' she replied with a self-satisfied nod. 'You'd never have forgiven yourself if you'd let him chop down my mimosa tree.'

I shook my head in despair. 'The trouble with you, Ellie,' I muttered, 'is that you've got absolutely no sense of proportion.'

'Yes I have!' she chirped, then turned and walked, almost skipped, back towards the house. 'It'll be eight metres by four, and I can't wait to jump in at the deep end.'

'I think I already have,' I mumbled to myself. 'And I can't even bloody well swim!'

Good as his word, Pablo was back first thing the following morning. When I walked out of the back door, he was standing beside one of his firm's pick-up trucks in the yard, smoking a huge cigar and talking to a tiny man of about his own age. The little fellow was wearing grubby, blue overalls and a blank expression. He was also wearing a flat cap that looked a couple of sizes too small for his head, which, in turn, made his head look a couple of sizes too big for his body.

'Ah, *mi amigo!*' Pablo grinned when he saw me. '*Buenos días, eh!*' He shook my hand, then introduced his companion as Luis, who also answered to the nickname of Groucho – so called, Pablo explained, because of his ready wit and irrepressible sense of humour.

Pablo chuckled a little after saying that, and I knew why. Groucho looked as if he'd had a sense-of-humour transplant, and he'd been the donor. Although the sun was shining brightly in a perfectly clear sky, Groucho gave the impression that his own little cloud was stationed permanently just above his head. Its shadow was invisible but infectious.

'*Mucho gusto,*' he frowned, taking my hand in an iron grip, his fingers feeling as if they were sheathed in thick sandpaper.

I returned his salutation, checked my own fingers for fractures and grazes, then asked Pablo when the digger would be arriving.

He chuckled again.

I asked again.

Pablo then gave a nod and a wink to Groucho, who shuffled over to the truck and came back toting an *espuerta*, one of those two-handled, rubber basins that Spanish builders use for everything from carrying materials in to shielding their faces from the sun when lying down for a snooze at siesta time. Cradled in the *espuerta* was a mattock-like hoe, with a concave, triangular blade set at right-angles to its short wooden shaft. I recognised it as an *aixada*, a simple, all-purpose tool, used as much by farmers to carve furrows in the soil as by building-site labourers to mix cement, or – significantly, as it would turn out – to dig with. Pablo gave *me* a nod and a wink next, then inclined his head towards Groucho, drawing my attention to those two items he was carrying.

Pablo grinned proudly.

Groucho scowled dejectedly.

I gaped aghast, first at Groucho, then at Pablo. 'He – Groucho – *Groucho* is the small digger? But – but I was expecting you to bring a mechanical one! You know – a tractor thing, with hydraulic arms and a bulldozer blade and scoops and everything!'

Pablo took a leisurely puff of his cigar, then shrugged one of his most nonchalant shrugs. '*Hombre!*' he smirked, gesturing in the direction of the gateway and the mimosa tree, exactly as he'd done the previous day. 'Horses for courses, eh!'

Suddenly, I wished I'd insisted on having a clause in the contract stipulating a completion date for the pool, and including the imposition of a hefty penalty for Pablo if he failed to meet it. But I hadn't. What I did have were visions of Groucho taking several years to dig an eight-by-four-metre grave, in which, long before it was finished, my bank manager would be compelled to bury me.

Something I hadn't bargained for, however, was the prodigious strength and energy that lurked within that puny-looking body of Groucho's. Diminutive though he was, Groucho soon showed that, singlehandedly, he could do the work of a whole gang of burly, six-foot navvies. And I never once saw him using his rubber *espuerta* to cover his face when having a siesta. That's because he never took a post-lunch nap. He didn't even have any lunch to speak of. All he ate, after asking our permission, were some oranges picked from the trees during the few short breaks he took from his labours. Ellie was concerned for his survival, but her invitation to join us for lunch in the kitchen had been politely declined. If you ate a decent breakfast, Groucho told her, you didn't need much more to keep you going until evening. *Madre mía*, eating too much during working hours, he claimed, only slowed you down.

Groucho's breakfasts must have been packed with a colossal amount of protein, if the volume of earth he dug and shifted during the day was anything to go by. Yet his down-at-heel appearance and hangdog expression suggested that he wasn't accustomed to treating himself to big, juicy, energy-packed steaks all that often – if ever. Yes, I got the impression that Pablo's little digger would have occupied a permanent place at the bottom end of the Gomez company's pay scale.

Groucho's somewhat timid request to me at the end of his first day tended to confirm this.

Would the *señora* of the house be requiring all her snails tonight? he enquired. My puzzled look prompted him to point northwards. The clouds building up over Ses Penyes Mountain, he explained, indicated that rain was on its way. He had noticed, he continued, that there were signs of much snail activity on the tall stalks of the wild fennel that grew here and there round the boundary walls of our fields. The rain would bring the snails out during the night, of that he was certain, so if *la señora* would allow him to collect some – just one small bucketful, and not enough to reduce her own snail-gathering tally by any noticeable degree – he would be most grateful. He dipped his head apologetically and mumbled that he hoped the *señor* would forgive his impertinence.

When I gave his back a little pat and told him that *la señora* didn't like snails and that he could help himself to as many bucketsful as he wanted, he first looked at me in a way that suggested he thought Ellie could be a candidate for admission to a happy farm, then his face creased into a delighted grin. The skin of his cheeks instantly took on a comfortably distressed look, like the leather of an old sofa when sat upon, clearly implying that the task of smiling was something that Groucho's facial muscles didn't have to cope with very often.

It made me feel guilty about having a luxury like a swimming pool built, and I was stung into realising just how relative were the worries I harboured regarding its likely strain on our finances. For here was a man for whom being given the opportunity to harvest a few freebie snails had been the highlight of the day – perhaps of the week, or even the month. And he was in the process of creating *my* luxury for me with his bare hands.

Instantly, I regretted having given him that little pat on the back. It had been a well-intentioned gesture, made spontaneously, but I cringed inwardly when I realised that it might have been regarded as patronising by Groucho. He may have seen me as the condescending foreigner, so well-off that he could afford to treat with contempt such a valuable source of nourishment as the snails that nature, and the luck of life's draw, had gifted him. That could well have been Groucho's opinion of me at that moment, and I couldn't have blamed him if it was. For all I knew, the snails that Ellie could afford to turn her nose up at were probably an important source of the energy that Groucho's back-breaking work demanded and on which his livelihood depended.

Also, despite his apparent lack of worldly means, he was a proud man. I'd already been made aware of that when offering to help him out by carting away his excavated earth with our tractor and trailer. I was very kind, he'd said, but he was sure there were many more important things for my machinery to be doing on the farm. He would continue to work away, as always, with the equipment that Pablo provided. He'd even refused my offer of the use of a wheelbarrow. '*Gracias, señor,*' he'd said, 'but when Pablo Gomez thinks I need a wheelbarrow, he will bring me one. He has many in his yard.'

Groucho's pride manifested itself in his work, and he took pride in the execution of that work without assistance from anyone. The gaping, rectangular hole in the ground that one day would be our swimming pool was going to be dug *aixada*-ful after *aixada*-ful and the spoil removed *espuerta*-ful after *espuerta*-ful by Groucho, alone and unaided. To my astonishment, this wiry little man seemed genuinely unfazed by the prospect. Clearly, he'd been there and done it all before, even if he wasn't wearing the proverbial T-shirt.

Groucho was already at work when I went outside at seven o'clock the following morning. He'd arrived long before sunrise, he told me, the hours of darkness being the best in which to find snails. Also, he stressed, he had taken the precaution of pushing his old moped along the last couple of hundred metres of the lane so as not to risk the noise of its rattly, old engine waking us up. And, he said with that lugubrious smile returning to his face, the hoped-for rains had materialised during the night, so his snail-gathering had been a great success. His smile quickly faded into a look of slight bewilderment. Was I *sure*, he checked, that my wife would not like some? After all, he had found many more snails than he'd expected to, and he didn't want to be greedy.

Being careful not to appear in any way condescending this time, I made what I hoped was a plausible-sounding excuse for Ellie's abnormal taste in food. I told him that she had a rare allergy to mollusks – even to their cooking vapours. I then swiftly changed the subject by asking him if he'd like a brandy to fortify himself after his earlier than usual start this morning. I knew very well that many Spanish men like to kick-start their day with a stiff shot of their favourite tipple, either straight or splashed into a strong coffee. It was an accepted custom of the country, but I feared that Groucho's fervent dedication to his labours might have excluded him from being a participant. He may well have believed that early-morning alcohol, like too much food during the day, would only slow him down. The instant grin that wrinkled his leathery skin suggested otherwise, however.

'*Sí, señor,*' he gushed, an unfamiliar note of good cheer raising the pitch of his voice by a good octave. *Sí*, a little *copita de coñac* would be most acceptable, *gracias* – uhm, if the *señor* was having one himself, *naturalmente*.

Now, here was an unforeseen dilemma. As much as I approved of, even admired, the local habit of taking a nip first thing in the day to jolt one's still-drowsy metabolism into life, it was, nevertheless, a practice that my northern European constitution was ill-equipped to handle. So far, my only attempt to enter into the spirit of the thing had come about because of a chance meeting with a well-known Andratx wag called Jordi Beltran a few months earlier. I'd popped into one of the town bars at about nine o'clock one morning, intending to do nothing more venturesome than have a coffee while waiting for a chatting congregation of unhurried farmers to vacate the counter space in a nearby hardware store.

Jordi, being a typical Mallorcan, was no drunkard, but he could fairly be described as an imbibing imp, a cheerful little fellow who never let work on his tiny *finca* interfere too much with his social drinking. This he undertook in a wide selection of bars in the area. Jordi's gregarious nature compelled him to strike up a conversation with anyone who looked likely to collaborate, and if his target happened to be a Brit on whom he could practice his proud command of English-language swear words, then so much the better. That's roughly how I'd got to know Jordi myself, and we'd since become firm friends, with Jordi also proving to be a valuable source of local knowledge in all matters agricultural. And it was on just such a subject that he was laying forth to some other local worthies when I walked into the Bar Cubano that morning.

'Hey, damn, forking baster, man!' he grinned on catching sight of me. He immediately cut short his lecture and homed in on me. 'Drink? OK, Jordi be buying! No bloody bugger worries, mate, oh yes!'

Jordi's English, I should mention in passing, had been learned during many years of working in a factory in the Midlands of England. Most of that time he'd roomed with an Asian family, and more recently he'd befriended an itinerant Australian who was holing up in Mallorca between spells of roughnecking in the Middle East oilfields. The complexity of Jordi's accent and the quality of his vocabulary reflected this rare mix of ethnic influences.

I got my intended coffee all right that morning. Several coffees, in fact. But each of them, on Jordi's insistence, had been converted by the barman into a *rebentat* by being spiked with whisky. The spirit added to the coffee to make a *rebentat* can be brandy, rum, a liqueur, or whatever the partaker fancies. Spanish *coñac* is the Spaniard's favourite, but Jordi assumed that, as I was a Scotsman, whisky would be my chosen poison. Whether it actually was or not was of no consequence, because even a moderate intake of *any* spirit at that early hour would have had the same effect on me. All I wanted to do afterwards was sleep. And, as Ellie was swift to remind me when I eventually got home from the Bar Cubano, my having a kip in the morning would most certainly not be conducive to the expeditious completion of all the improvement work that still had to be done on our run-down little *finca*.

No, my northern constitution just wasn't equipped to react positively to taking swigs of strong booze that early in the day. So, how was I to respond to Groucho? I neither wanted to spoil his pleasure in having a nip, nor appear to him like an abstemious foreign wimp. However, the devious devil of diplomacy whispered a persuasive fib in my ear...

'*Discúlpeme*, Groucho,' I said. 'Forgive me if I don't join you in a *copita*. But I've, ehm – well, I've already had a couple this morning. Whiskies in my porridge at breakfast, that is. It's the Scottish way, you know.'

Groucho accepted that excuse with a little smile of approval. No doubt my liver did as well.

And so commenced a daily routine that had the effect of encouraging Pablo Gomez's 'small digger' to work with even more than his previous high level of enthusiasm, albeit still of the melancholy variety. Ironically, this redoubled appetite for the job was also to lead to his penny-watching employer getting some of his own back. But more of that later.

The regular morning shots of brandy seemed to add extra vim to Groucho's already admirable stamina as well. After little more than a week of hacking away with his trusty little *aixada* hoe, all of the topsoil in the pool area had been removed, and the underlying layer of heavy clay was already being pared steadily down. To me, this was a remarkable enough achievement in itself, but when I looked at the neat surrounding embankment that Groucho was concurrently forming with each individually-heaved basinful of dirt, his physical performance started to assume truly Herculean proportions.

Pablo Gomez turned up every day to check on his employee's work, a formality which Groucho acknowledged with no more than a brief glance in his direction and, occasionally, a grunted '*Hola!*'. Pablo's questions, though brief in themselves, were answered with even briefer grunts of '*Sí!*' or '*No!*'. Groucho never stopped working for a second. If I hadn't known better, I'd probably have taken all this as a sign that Groucho resented his boss's niggling attentions and, in all likelihood, disliked the man anyway. Given the vast gap that existed between their respective lots in life, no-one would have been too surprised at that. Envy and enmity are first cousins, after all. Yet, as it happened, the reality of the situation was very different.

During the fleeting conversational moments that Groucho granted himself while sipping his morning *coñacs*, I learned that, like all of Pablo's workers, Groucho had nothing but respect for him and the success he had achieved. Many of the longer-serving of these men had come originally from the same underprivileged area of southern Spain as Pablo; some, like Groucho himself, even from the same village. They'd all moved to Mallorca for the same reason – to better themselves by taking advantage of the huge demand for workers being generated by the burgeoning tourist industry. Having had no opportunity to do anything but sporadic manual work where they came from, it usually followed that they become labourers on the island's countless building sites.

All of them, including Pablo Gomez, had been in the same boat, yet he was one of only a few who had succeeded in dragging himself up by his bootlaces to become a successful businessman in his own right. Many of the others, like Groucho, had moved no further up the employment and social pecking order since the day they'd arrived in Mallorca all those years ago. And Pablo had had no more chances laid at his feet than they'd had. The difference was that Pablo had siezed whatever opportunity he saw, no matter how small, and he'd worked hard to make his own luck. His way of sharing that luck had been to ensure that none of his old colleagues ever wanted for a job, if he could possibly provide one. And, Groucho freely admitted, if that meant such arduous tasks as excavating the hole for a swimming pool by hand, the job was there for the individual to accept or reject. For Groucho, the choice was easy to make. In his view, Pablo Gomez was a good and generous man, though never *over* generous. And why should he be? He wouldn't be in a position to offer employment to anyone if he was. And that, in Groucho's considered opinion, was the crux of the matter. Pablo paid the money. Groucho dug the dirt.

I may well have been witnessing an example of labour relations that would soon become as obsolete as the use of a donkey on Mallorcan farms. But, for the present, it was a system that worked, and to the obvious satisfaction of both parties. Also, it provided me with an opportunity to see first-hand that the popularly-held belief that the Spanish are a lethargic, work-shy people is the mother of all fallacies. What's more, although the daytime temperatures rose as the hole in the ground deepened, Groucho quarried on regardless. No matter how warm the noonday sun, he didn't even bother to take off his little flat cap, far less his shirt. Like all of his *compañeros* from the south of Spain, the blood of his Moorish ancestors still flowed through his veins as cool as the waters of a Saharan oasis.

Eventually, when the hole in the ground had become too deep and the surrounding wall of earth too high to make it possible for Groucho to dispose of his basinsful of spoil by merely chucking them upwards, one of Pablo Gomez's many wheelbarrows was duly delivered on site, complete with a few wooden battens to serve as ramps. The Gomez/

Groucho 'small digger' excavation system was running as smoothly as clockwork.

Naturally, none of this feverish activity went unnoticed, or uninspected, by our neighbours. Pep, the studiedly-crusty old farmer from the ramshackle little *finca* over the lane, was first on the scene.

It was late on a Sunday afternoon, the one time of the week when he would have been pretty sure that the 'digger' wouldn't be working. I saw the unmistakable outline of his lean frame ambling into the yard and round the side of the house as I was driving the tractor back through the orchards with a load of crated oranges on board. Hearing me coming, he looked across and gave me a cursory nod. He was wearing his customary scuffed leather bomber jacket and baggy old trousers. As ever, his trademark red neckerchief was tied nattily to one side. Unashamedly scruffy though he was in his working garb, that neckerchief and his black beret, pulled down over his forehead with calculated precision, combined to give him a curiously suave appearance – a bit like a rakish, down-on-his-luck toff from an ancient silent movie. It was Pep's very own version of style, and he flaunted it. He lit a hand-rolled *cigarrillo* as I approached, then sauntered to the edge of the swimming pool excavations at the front of the house.

'The sky will never give you enough *agua* to fill an *aljibe* as big as that!' he scoffed. '*Coño*, this is Mallorca, not Scotland or the monsoon jungles of the Congo!'

He was alluding to the age-old practice in Mediterranean climes of diverting the precious winter rainfall from the house roof into an *aljibe*, or underground holding tank. The water so gathered would keep the household going for the predominantly dry remainder of the year, if winter rainfall and prudent subsequent usage happened to balance out.

There was already just such a reservoir beneath the west terrace at Ca's Mayoral, and big as it and the roof area of the house were, we'd found that we still had to supplement the accumulation of rainwater with a few tanker-loads of the bought variety during the latter months of summer. Pep had noticed that, he'd put two and two together, and come up with twenty-two.

'*Tío*,' he said, referring to me familiarly as 'uncle', even though he was almost old enough to be my grandfather, 'no matter how many *aljibes* you dig, and no matter how much it rains, you cannot store more water than it is possible to collect from one roof.' He gave a snort of derision. '*Cuarenta putas*, you do not have to be a scientific genius to understand that!'

When Pep used his '*cuarenta putas*' oath (meaning 'forty whores'), you knew that he was well fired-up and unlikely to brook any contradiction of his opinions. So I didn't try. Always best on these occasions, I'd discovered, to let him vent his spleen uninterrupted. That way, you hedged your bets in case he was only pulling your leg, which you never knew about until the moment he chose to spring it on you. To cut him off in mid-tirade served no purpose other than to increase the amount of wheezily-laughed satisfaction he got from putting one over on you.

I let him rant on about how we'd be better off throwing out our washing machine to conserve the water the heavens gave us for free, instead of wasting good money on the truckloads of the stuff he'd seen being pumped into our *aljibe*. Not that it was any of his business, he hastened to add, but if we wanted to make a success of farming in Mallorca, we'd better get to grips with the fact that water was a commodity worth more than all the newfangled, so-called labour-saving contraptions that wives wanted in their kitchens these days. Using a tub and a scrubbing board hadn't done women any harm in the past, and *no*body bought water then.

After mumbling that he was glad *he* didn't have a wife to squander his hard-earned pesetas, he paused to draw breath, or rather to take a deep drag on his *cigarrillo*, which contained a noxious shag made from his prized (by him) home-grown tobacco. This resulted in the usual mini fireworks display of sparks, crackles and pops, culminating in purple-faced convulsions of suppressed coughing and spluttering. Ah, *sí*, and another thing, he continued once normal breathing had been resumed, had we ever stopped to consider how much water we wasted by taking all those baths that people seemed hellbent on taking nowadays? *Madre de Dios*, he'd heard that some extravagant idiots now took a bath every week! Every *week! Coño*, it meant that, in a family of four like ours, one week's bath water would add up to enough to keep his entire flock of twenty sheep drinking for a whole year!

I thought it best not to tell Pep that all of us actually took, if not a bath, at least a shower, not just once a week, but sometimes twice a *day*. He'd probably have had a seizure on hearing such a scandalous disclosure. I was fairly certain of that, because he'd once proudly admitted to me that two baths a year was his limit – one at the end of summer, one in spring. Any 'specially-targetted' ablutions that might be required occasionally in the interim could be undertaken without squandering any more than a kettleful of hot water. *Caram*! he barked, nobody could ever accuse *him* of having smelly feet! But, just as important as the judicious use of water, he went on, patently revelling in his diatribe now, your health was safeguarded by taking only six-monthly baths, because essential body oils wouldn't be washed off your skin more often than was absolutely necessary in the interests of personal hygiene.

I chortled as I recalled that my own grandfather, himself a no-frills, both-hands-to-the-plough farmer like Pep, had been an avid advocate of exactly the same principle.

But Pep wasn't amused. 'Why do you giggle?' he rasped. He then inclined his head backwards and squinted accusingly at me from under the overhang of his beret. '*Hombre*, you doubt the truth of what I say, uh?'

He seemed suitably pacified, however, when I explained that his sanitary ideology had been shared by my grandfather.

'So, not all people in Scotland are stupid enough to waste water,' he smirked. '*Va bé.*' That was fine.

In my own defence, I told him that, at Ca's Mayoral, all of the household waste water went into the septic tank, and we regularly pumped it out to irrigate our tomatoes and other vegetables. So, the waste water wasn't in fact wasted, but efficiently recycled.

Pep chose to ignore that piece of information, which I was fairly certain he already knew about anyway. He wedged his cigarette firmly in the corner of his mouth, stuffed his hands into his trouser pockets and nodded at the hole in the ground. '*Bueno*, how do you intend to fill an *aljibe* of those vast proportions? Do you plan to build another house here as well? *Coño*,' he exclaimed through a burst of *cigarrillo* sparks, 'it will have to be the size of a king's palace for a roof big enough to catch all the rain it will take to fill that!'

Without waiting for any response, he then enquired why I was going to need so much water in any case. We had a good, reliable well that provided sufficient *agua* to irrigate the trees, and if I followed his advice about the folly of using a washing machine and taking too many baths, the winter rains collected in our existing *aljibe* would more than provide for all our domestic needs. Pep angled his head back again, one eye closed this time, the other peering at me, its mischievous glint inviting me, daring me, to contradict him.

'It's less than a metre deep at the moment,' I offered as a clue to the truth. 'It'll have to be at least twice that depth before it can hold enough water for what I've got in mind.'

He laughed a gurgling, chesty laugh, while dusting the resultant shards of burning tobacco from the lapels of his bomber jacket. 'Ay-y-y, *guapo*,' he growled, 'now I understand. A fish farm! I know about these things. *Sí,* they rear trout in them in Scotland. *Sí, sí, sí,* I heard about it on the radio once.' Still laughing, he shook his head and swatted the air. 'Pah! You are wasting your time, *tío.*'

He proceeded to tell me that they already bred trout in Mallorca – in the Gorg Blau reservoir, away up in the shadow of Puig Major, the highest mountain in the mighty Tramuntana Range. *Hombre*, the reservoir had been stocked with trout for the past thirty years. It was full of them! Where did I think the fancy Palma restaurants that fleeced the foreign *turistas* got them? But, he stated, his expression pointedly earnest now, the Gorg Blau was a great lake, which made my hole in the ground look like a pockmark on a leper's arse in comparison. Also, the lake was fed by an endless supply of free water from the snowy peaks of the surrounding mountains. How could I expect to compete with all that, especially if I had to buy water by the tanker-load?

Pep motioned towards Groucho's excavations with a sideways twitch of his head. 'Anchovies,' he said.

'Anchovies?' I queried.

'*Sí.* No matter how deep you make it, this *cisterna* will only accommodate a small shoal of puny, little fish like anchovies – and even they will make a *desastre* of your fish farm business, because they can only live in the sea.'

It was becoming increasingly obvious that, as I'd suspected all along, Pep knew perfectly well that what we were standing gazing into here was the makings of a swimming pool. The chances were that he'd already gleaned this information by ambushing Groucho in the lane and pumping him for inside information at the end of his very first day of digging. Pep's fish farm hypothesis, therefore, had only been a red herring thrown into the conversation to make me feel as embarrassed as possible about admitting the truth. And the ploy was succeeding.

Pep stood there, inscrutably weighing up my reaction to his anchovy jibe, roguishly relishing every moment of my discomfort. He eventually broke the awkward silence by telling me, poker-faced, that I could always use the *cisterna* for breeding frogs in. They were freshwater creatures, after all, and he knew a marshy hollow up on the north-facing side of Ses Penyes Mountain where I could get frog spawn by the bucketful at this time of year. All I'd have to do then would be to set up a deal to export the farmed frogs' legs to France, and, *cuarenta putas*, I'd make a fortune! Provided, he added with exaggerated indifference, I didn't mind living with a green-scummed, stagnant pond right outside my front door. On the other hand, he concluded dryly, the tuneful, nocturnal song of the pond's inhabitants would probably compensate for the accompanying stink.

Pep was in top tormenting form, and I knew when I was beaten.

'OK, we're actually making a swimming pool here,' I confessed in a low mumble, making a half-hearted attempt at sounding blasé.

'*Qué?*'

'*Una piscina* – a swimming pool.' I even surprised myself at how ashamed I sounded.

'*Perdón?*'

'Well, Ellie and the boys think it'll be a good idea. I mean, I don't actually swim myself, so, you know, I –'

'*Una piscina*? *Una… PIS-CEE-EE-EE-NA?*'

'*Sí,*' I confirmed, looking down at my feet like a schoolboy owning up to stealing apples.

Pep spat his half-smoked *cigarrillo* onto the ground. He took a sharp intake of breath, followed by a stumbling step backwards, as though he'd just been kicked in the chest by his mule.

'*Una pis*-cee-ee-ee-*na*?' Pep was whispering now, his facial expression a masterpiece of overplayed melodrama. He was staring at me as if I had just been convicted of shepherding a blind nun into a street of speeding traffic, while simultaneously stealing her tin of money collected for the inhabitants of the local orphanage. His look couldn't have made it more clear that I was now regarded as a piece of breathing dog dung.

'So,' he continued, 'you have joined the enemy. You are about to become just another of those foreign layabouts who come here and buy our little farms to use as playthings.'

I was about to attempt to assure him that nothing could be farther from the truth, but Pep wasn't finished with me yet.

'Just think how many sheep or goats you could buy with the fortune you will spend on this – this – this rich man's *extravagancia!*'

If this was a leg-pull, it was a good one. I was now feeling lower than that piece of living dog's turd after it had been trod on by another blind nun, and to even hint to Pep that I thought he might be joking would only have made matters worse. I said nothing.

Pep said plenty more, rounding off his shame-inducing diatribe with, '*Sí*, and, just think of how much more orange-growing land you could have bought for the cost of this…'

(he paused to look disdainfully down into the hole) '… this – this waste of precious water. Swimming pools? *Jesús*, *María y José*, the farmers of this once-green island will soon be ploughing a desert!'

While there was, in fact, more than a grain of truth in what he said, the irony of the situation was that I was having the pool built to *add* value to our little farm, so that, if needs be, I'd be able to raise money to help us buy more of that very orange-growing land he was referring to. There was no point in trying to convince Pep of the logic of that way of thinking, however. Truth to tell, I was now even less convinced than before of the logic of it myself.

Pep took one final disparaging glance at the excavation work, tutted woefully, wished me a good evening, then ambled off. He stopped at the far corner of the house, turned and announced, 'Even I myself can swim, *tío*. Ah *sí*, and you would be able to swim also, if, like me, you had gone sponge-diving for a living in Cuba.'

I already knew vaguely that Pep, like many from Andratx before him, had spent some time in Cuba when a young man, though somehow the images of a daring, youthful free-diver and Pep, the cantakerous old peasant farmer, didn't quite match up. But I had no reason to disbelieve him.

Maybe, I reflected, I'd eventually have to ask old Pep for swimming lessons, if I wasn't to go under, both virtually and literally.

Before sauntering off, he gave me his customary John Wayne salute of farewell, and I could have sworn that I noticed a glimmer of rascally fun sparkling from those impenetrable little eyes of his. Had he been teasing me with that same droll, Mallorcan sense of humour that the customs man had caught Jock with during the illegal haggis episode? Time, as ever, would tell. But, for the moment, Pep had me floundering about in a sea of indecision and self-doubt, while he went about his business with the relaxed confidence that only comes from being born into a generations-old way of life. No doubt, in his eyes, I was still the *loco extranjero*, the silly foreigner. And I probably always would be, no matter how hard I tried to be otherwise.

As Pablo Gomez had sagely asserted: 'Hey, *amigo mío*, horses for courses, eh!'

– FOUR –

SAINT ANTHONY'S FIRE

The Mallorcan calendar is liberally peppered with saints' days and their accompanying fiestas. Some of these are purely local celebrations of a particular town's canonised patron, whilst others are holidays (veritable 'holy days') that mark more widely-observed religious dates. Included in the latter category is the Fiesta of Saint Anthony, or, as he's known in *mallorquín*, Sant Antoni, the patron saint of animals.

On 17 January, processions of pets and farm animals are blessed by being sprinkled with holy water as they pass by their local churches in towns and villages across the island. I've heard it said that, over the years, the occasional over-enthusiastic priest has been butted in the balls by a billygoat or had his robes ripped by a Rottweiler that didn't take kindly to being sloshed with water, no matter how holy.

But the custom of anointing animals continues, whether the blessed creatures appreciate the spiritual significance of it to themselves or not.

However, it's on the night *before* Sant Antoni's Day that the real festive jollifications take place, given that they're of a predominantly secular nature. And, if any animals do decide to participate in the fun, it's at their own risk, for the Eve of Sant Antoni is bonfire night in Mallorca, and things *can* get a bit noisy.

Tradition has it that the celebratory lighting of these fires relates directly to the belief that the associated hermit-saint could cure a previously-incurable illness, which consequently became known as Saint Anthony's Fire. This is a particularly nasty ailment, described, under its medical names of 'ergotism' or 'erysipelas', as being characterised by fever, headache, vomiting, and red, raised lesions, especially on the face. The skin, apparently, feels as hot as it looks. Hence the malady's popular name. No wonder that, long before the scientific marvel of antibiotics brought this highly-contagious condition under control, Anthony the miracle-working 'fireman' was sainted.

But the legend of Sant Antoni is unlikely to be much in the thoughts of those whose main concern is simply to enjoy a good-going fiesta in his name. And that's one of the wonderful paradoxes of Spain. On such religious occasions, piety, no matter how solemnly practiced, is seldom allowed to get totally in the way of the devoted having a damned good time as well. A celebration should be just that, after all, and the Spanish are masters of the art.

The charitably-inclined of them are also very adept at eliciting a bit of *dinero* from their fellow citizens when in festive mood. In Palma, for example, a figure dressed as Sant Antoni, accompanied by two men disguised as the 'demons' who feature so prominently in Mallorcan folklore, can be encountered a few days before the feast day selling raffle tickets in a street named after another saint, Miquel. Why they don't do this in the Plaça Sant Antoni instead, I don't know. Maybe Sant Miquel's patch of the city is simply a better pitch as far as the volume of passing 'targets' goes. Anyway, the top prize in the raffle is – appropriately enough, considering the link to the patron saint of animals – a pig. In fact, Sant Antoni himself is often depicted in paintings and statues with a pig at his feet, and in parts of rural England the smallest piglet in a litter used to be called Saint Anthony's pig, or 'tantony' pig for short. But Mallorca maintains a much more generous association with the saint. The purchaser of the winning raffle ticket in Palma will neither acquire a runt nor even just any old pig in a poke, but will become the proud owner of the *biggest* pig on the island. Don't be deterred from trying your luck if you haven't a handy pigsty of your own, though. Prospective winners can opt to pocket the market value in lieu of taking home the giant porker itself.

Modest in size compared to the Palma city version of the same event, and less well-publicised than the ancient, eel-pie-eating happenings that take place concurrently in the town of Sa Pobla in the north of the island, the Andratx Sant Antoni's Eve Fiesta is held in the market place, Es Passeig de Son Mas. Every Wednesday morning, this long, open area near Son Mas Castle on the eastern outskirts of town swarms with hundreds of locals and thousands of tourists, all keen to respectively sell or buy bargains from the multitude of colourful stalls set up specially for the day.

When we arrived on that chilly January night, Sant Antoni's bonfire was already blazing briskly at the end of the *passeig* closest to the edge of town. The number of people assembled there was less than on market days, but the atmosphere was just as vibrant, though in a markedly different way. The gathered revellers were silhouetted against the fire's inviting glow. Above them, tongues of flame licked the night sky, while showers of rising sparks enjoyed glorious moments of dancing among the stars before disappearing into oblivion over the inky outline of the surrounding mountains.

The strident blare and clattering thump of bugles and drums faded with the sparks, as the local children's marching band exited the scene and headed off into the darkness, no doubt to go their separate ways until reassembling for the big church parade in the morning. Their departure would have answered the prayers of any of Saint Anthony's four-legged charges that happened to have been in the market place during the band's recital, if the whimpers of relief from Bonny, our boxer dog, were anything to go by. She had my fullest sympathy. Yet I could also empathise with the keen young musicians. In my own pre-adolescent youth in Scotland, I'd been a bagpiper in a boys' pipe band, so I knew how easy it can be, when enveloped in the magical (and deafening) process of making music in the company of equally enthusiastic and unaccomplished rookies, to be oblivious to the pain your raw efforts can inflict upon those unfortunate enough to be within earshot.

With her hearing once again unmolested, at least for the moment, it was now the turn of Bonny's sense of smell to be tortured, but to be tortured in the most pleasant of ways. As a symbolic (though somewhat backhanded) compliment to Sant Antoni's hallowed pigs, whose contribution to the island's agricultural and culinary history can never be overestimated, the eating of Mallorcan pork sausages, called, according to their individual recipes, *llonganissas* or *butifarróns*, is a time-honoured custom on the night preceding the saint's day. The toothsome aroma of these savoury morsels being barbecued at the Andratx bonfire was irresistable. Bonny licked her chops – and so did we.

We, on this occasion, amounted only to Ellie, Charlie and me, Sandy having gone off to football training at the ground of the junior team he played for over at La Real, a little town just a few kilometres north of Palma.

Emerging out of the crush of spectators surrounding the bonfire was Toni, a young Spanish lad of Charlie's age from Sa Coma hamlet at the end of the lane near our farm. The two youngsters had struck up a friendship shortly after we arrived on the island, and Charlie's impressive command of Spanish swear words had been credited mainly to Toni's tuition. However, I'm sure the gesture had been reciprocal, judging by the string of curses in faltering English I'd overheard coming from Toni on the occasions he thought he'd been as safely unheard as he was hidden up our trees when helping Charlie with his fruit-picking chores. But Toni was a decent and truly likeable kid, one of a large family, who, like Pablo Gomez, had originally come to the island from mainland Spain. Toni and his brothers and sisters had been born in Mallorca, and were regarded by their contemporaries at the local school as being just as *mallorquín* as those whose island lineage stretched back for countless generations – a demonstration of acceptance that wouldn't necessarily have been afforded his parents or grandparents when they first settled in the area. Mallorcan country folk, like their counterparts anywhere, can take a while to fully accept incomers into their close-knit communities. For example, 'white settlers', as they're unflatteringly dubbed in parts of rural Scotland, may well be looked upon with suspicion by the locals until they've proved that they deserve to be regarded otherwise. I'd witnessed it happening often enough in Scotland myself to realise that we'd have been seen in exactly the same light by our new neighbours when we settled in Mallorca. Now, if old Pep's ostensibly negative reaction to our having a swimming pool built was anything to go by, it was possible that the degree of local acceptance we'd managed to achieve to date was about to be wiped out in one fell splash.

But at least Charlie and Toni displayed the kind of uncomplicated friendship that comes naturally to boys of that age. Charlie seemed to have been accepted by his generation of local kids, although not without having to work at it first. He'd had to go through an intial period of being ribbed about being a foreigner by the village youngsters, and had even had the virtue of his mother called into question when passing through Sa Coma on his bike one day. That was all part of the initiation process, though; the law of the juvenile jungle, and he appeared to have passed muster all right. He'd shown that he could take it *and* give as good as he got, as witness the black eye he'd given the boy who'd dared call Ellie a whore. However, even that episode did have an upside, in that it had taught Charlie yet another useful phrase for his steadily growing vocabulary of Spanish obscenities.

Armed with sufficient *dinero* from my pocket, he and Toni headed cheerfully off through the throng to fetch us a selection of barbecued pork products.

A temporary stage had been set up on trestles at a safe distance from the bonfire, yet close enough to the two market-place bars to allow their patrons a reasonably uninterrupted view of the entertainment from their chosen positions indoors. It *was* a chilly evening, which made it all the more surprising to see old Maria Bauzá, our immediate farming neighbour in the valley, sitting at a table *outside* the Bar Ca'n Toniet. Elflike and ancient, Maria was a loveable character. She was both generous and helpful to a fault, although capable of being every bit as crotchety as Pep.

However, the breadth of her distinctive two-teeth-up, three-teeth-down smile showed that she was in fine fettle on this occasion.

A Mallorcan folk troup in traditional costume had just taken to the stage, and the prospect of watching their familiar dances and listening to the lilting accompaniment of flute, fiddle and guitars clearly appealed to her. For Maria, there was nothing to match her beloved 'old days', and I knew from past experience that this point of view applied as much to ploughing with a donkey instead of a tractor as it did to her preference for the simple customs of yesteryear, compared to the *vulgaritát* that television and the influence of mass tourism had brought to present-day island life. This reminded me that she hadn't paid us a visit since work started on our swimming pool, so I still had her opinions on that to face. Something told me I'd better be prepared for a roasting.

At present, though, the only roast I was interested in was of the pork sausage variety, and the boys duly returned toting a full selection, each one sandwiched hotdog-style between chunky slices of *pan payes* (Mallorcan country bread). They'd brought an extra *butifarrón* for Bonny, and she wolfed down the black-pudding-type treat in one greedy gulp. The ensuing smile on her upturned face confirmed that Charlie and Toni had chosen well for her.

'It's the pig's blood that she likes. *Sí*, that is why all dogs love *butifarróns*.' It was Bernat, a young tanker driver with Pujol Serra, one of the local drinking-water supply companies. Bernat had delivered water to our *aljibe* a few times, so he knew Bonny well and they got on famously. He bent down and patted her head. 'But only a *butifarrón* for you on special occasions, *muchacha* – otherwise maybe you get fat, eh.'

Given a choice, I'm sure that was a risk Bonny would have been glad to take. But she'd just have to thank Sant Antoni for small mercies. There would be no more sausages for her tonight. The onstage folk music was blissfully gentle on the ears compared to the bugle band, so while I started to talk to Bernat, Bonny lay down happily at our feet, her twitching nose still savouring those drifting sausage smells.

Bernat was in his late twenties, a Mallorcan through and through, and fortunate to possess an abundance of the elegantly handsome looks so distinctive of many of the island men. Above all, though, he was a down-to-earth chap, born into an Andratx farming family, but now having to supplement his income by driving a water truck, simply because the family farm, like the one we'd left in Scotland, had become too small to be viable in these changing times. Anyway, I reckoned that he must have filled up a few swimming pools during his career with Pujol Serra, so I thought I'd pick his brains about how much water we'd have to buy for ours. I started to tell him what the final dimensions of the pool would be, but he immediately held up a silencing hand.

He already knew exactly what the dimensions were to be, he told me. He'd known since the morning after the excavations were started, in fact. Old Pep had winkled the information from Groucho in the lane the previous evening, and had told Bernat all about it outside the agricultural merchants' warehouse next to Pujol Serra's garage. 'Pep was telling everyone he met that morning,' said Bernat. '*Sí*,' he laughed, 'and he seemed to be going out of his way to meet as many people as he could!'

So, my suspicions had been well founded. Pep had known all along about the pool, and his theorising about trout and anchovy farms and the rest had all been part of the old rascal's premeditated scheme to wind me up. All I could do was shake my head and laugh along with Bernat.

Ellie had gone over to join Maria, while Charlie and Toni had stationed themselves at the front of the stage to watch the folk show – or, more likely, to ogle the girls' legs and exchange smutty comments about their underwear as their full skirts billowed up during the many twirls and whirls that typify the old Mallorcan dances.

'So, Bernat,' I said, 'how many truck loads of water will it take to fill this pool of ours once it's finished?'

'Six, but you can save money by ordering only five, if you top it out with water from your field well – provided the building of the pool is complete before you start irrigating your land at the start of the dry season, *naturalmente.*'

That appended qualification of his was an impromptu and perfect example of a Mallorcan farmer's natural concern for the needs of his plants and trees before anything else that his precious water might be used for. However, the thought of drawing water from our well for the pool had never even crossed my mind, though not for quite such agriculturally altruistic reasons as Bernat's. It was more because the well shaft was uncovered, so there was no telling what else its depths contained in addition to water. You certainly wouldn't want to drink the stuff, so swimming in even a much diluted quantity of it surely wouldn't be too wholesome an idea either. I put this point to Bernat.

His response was merely to shrug and say one word: '*Cloro.*'

'Chlorine? You mean chlorine will kill all bugs that are in the well water?'

'*Sí,*' he affirmed with another shrug. After all, that's what the chemical was for. He then added that if chlorine could neutralise the effects of all the pissing that went on in hotel swimming pools, it would cope easily enough with the residue of any dead leaves and things that happened to be floating in our well.

I told him that it was the 'and things' part of his observation that bothered me slightly – particularly if those 'things' happened to be dead mice, or even rats.

But Bernat would have none of it. '*Cloro*,' he repeated. '*Mucho cloro – no problema.*'

Well, time enough to learn all about such technical things when the time came, I decided. For now, I was more interested in knowing what other farmers in the area thought of Pep's news of our proposed swimming pool. And who better to ask than Bernat, since he chatted to them all on his daily rounds?

His reaction was to flash me a knowing smile and tell me not to feel guilty about adding a bit of luxury to our property. People of his generation knew only too well that if they ever had to sell their small farms, perhaps in hopes (no matter how forlorn) of moving on to a bigger spread, then in all probability it wouldn't be another farmer who'd buy their *finca*. It'd be a foreigner, whose only interest would be to enjoy the place's amenities for retirement or holiday-home purposes. So, the more of the right kind of amenities that had already been put in place, the better the price that would be realised for the properety when put on the market. That was an unquestionable fact of life in Mallorca these days, and, he assured me, I'd be surprised if he told me just how many of the island's small farmers had seen the light years ago and had done just what we were doing now. It was a form of insurance – nothing more, nothing less – and I certainly shouldn't be concerned about the opinion of anyone who couldn't appreciate the sense of that.

Suddenly, I felt a lot better about our thinking regarding the swimming pool project, and I judged our decision to proceed with it even more vindicated when Bernat went on to tell me about a related experience of his own...

His great-grandfather, a local sheep farmer, obliged by lack of capital to operate on a very modest scale, similar to that still followed by a rapidly dwindling band of old-timers like Pep, had established the fate of future generations of the family by making just one wrong business decision. It had been long before anyone had even dreamt of the upsurge in tourism that would one day change the fortunes of Mallorca beyond belief. And therein lay the hook to Bernat's story.

Struggling, as ever, to make ends meet, his great-grandfather's already parlous financial state had been exacerbated to near breaking point by the inability of another small farmer to pay him for a number of sheep he had sold him some months earlier. The man simply didn't have the cash to clear his debt, but he did eventually come up with a suggestion of two ways by which the situation might be resolved. It would be for Bernat's great-grandfather to decide. He could either have his sheep back, or he could have the title deeds to a block of land a few kilometres along the coast. Well, the choice was easy to make. He knew the piece of land that he was being offered – a stretch of scrubby dunes and rocky slopes covered in pine trees skirting the shore. It was good for nothing, and no farmer in his right mind would swap even one lamb for it. He'd have his sheep back, *muchas gracias*.

That piece of 'worthless' land, Bernat revealed with a rueful smile, was eventually to become one of the most valuable chunks of real estate on the island – the site on which much of the now flourishing holiday resort of Peguera would be built. And the irony of it was that, in time, penniless incomers like Pablo Gomez would make their fortunes by building the hotels and apartment blocks that now rose from those same dunes and hillsides, while Bernat drove a water truck for a living.

He gave me the customary parting slap on the shoulder. 'So,' he said, 'go ahead and have your swimming pool built, *amigo*. And if old Pep says that you'd be better buying sheep with the money it costs, tell him to go find a sand dune and bury his head in it!'

In one way, it was a relief to learn that a young Mallorcan fellow took the same practical view of things as we had, but in another it was sad to hear confirmation that his generation were resigned to seeing so much of the island's small-farm heritage slip out of their hands. But, as in his great-grandfather's time, money – the lack of it or the pursuit of it – was at the root of everything, and few, when the opportunity arose, could resist entering into a pact with that persuasive devil.

With Bernat having gone off to talk to someone he'd noticed in the crowd, I strolled over to join Ellie and Maria on the little raised terrace in front of the Bar Ca'n Toniet. Just as well to get that roasting about the swimming pool over with while the old woman was in a good mood, I reckoned. I broached the subject as soon as pleasantries had been exchanged.

'I suppose you've heard that we're having a swimming pool built, Maria.'

Instead of answering me, she enthusiastically drew Ellie's attention to the particular dance the folk troup were now launching themselves into. It was the Parado de Valldemossa, she explained; one of the most graceful of all the age-old Mallorcan dances. And the performers were from the Mallorcan town of the same name, she added. 'A very famous group. Well-known all over the world. *Sí claro.*'

I sensed that we were in for one of Maria's reverse-leapfrogging conversations, in which she had this weird habit of answering your last question but one. The routine took a bit of getting used to, so to get the ball rolling, I decided to slip a second question in quickly.

'Aren't you cold sitting outside here, Maria? Look, there's an empty table by the window inside the bar. Why don't we all go and sit in there?'

'Swimming pools are a waste of good water,' she replied, without taking her eyes off the dancers. 'But it's your water, so you can do what you like with it.'

'Well,' I told myself, 'that was a much less chastening reaction than I'd expected.' But I'd jumped to the conclusion a tad too quickly.

'*Españoles*,' Maria muttered, her eyes still on the dancers, but the smile ominously wiped from her face.

I'd heard old Maria sounding off before about how she disliked and mistrusted mainland Spaniards, but I couldn't understand what she was on about this time. '*Españoles?*' I queried. 'But I thought you said the folk troup came from Valldemossa, right here on the island.'

'The builders of your swimming pool,' she grunted. '*Españoles* every one! You should have given the job to a proper Mallorcan builder – like Toni Ensenyat, a good Andratx man born and bred. *Sí claro!*'

Fair comment, since I'm all for supporting local businesses. What's more, I knew Toni, as he'd done some work for us before. He was indeed a good man, an excellent tradesman as well, and he had actually been the first person I'd approached about building the pool. But building swimming pools is a specialist job, and he'd freely admitted that it was one that he'd had no previous experience of. Accordingly, he had politely advised me try another builder. There was no point in explaining all this to Maria, however.

The verbal exchanges with her were shaping up to get complicated enough without that, so I decided to repeat my previous question to see if the manoeuvre would head her off at the conversational pass. But Maria was one step ahead of me – or behind me, depending on your point of view.

'Cold?' she said, the grin returning to her face, as she spun her head round to look me straight in the eye. 'Cold? Me?' She let rip with one of her tinkling little laughs. 'I am never cold, not when I have my *maridét* with me!' At that, she lifted up the hem of her long black skirts to reveal a little brazier glowing away merrily between her feet.

This was her *maridét*, her 'little husband', a charcoal-fired personal comforter, whose use, I'd heard, had died out in Mallorca years ago. The introduction of shorter skirts in the 1920s would probably have set the trend. But here was Maria, still holding on grimly to another relic of her precious 'old days', and she was patently delighted to be doing so.

'At my stage of life,' she told Ellie with a wink, 'this little husband does more to heat me up than the real thing could, no?'

Ellie frowned, clearly concerned for the old woman's safety. 'But aren't you afraid you'll set your clothes alight?'

Maria wagged a gnarled finger at her, a mischievous smile lighting her face. 'In my time, I have had hotter things than this up my petticoats, *señora*, and I have never once had the need to send for the fire brigade yet. *Nunca*! Not ever!'

We were left to take what we wanted out of that, as Maria released another cascade of cronely cackling. Little was she to know then, however, that her suggestive little wisecrack may just have tempted fate a smidgin too far on this particular saint's eve.

We were spared the problem of trying to find a more delicate topic of conversation by the most unearthly noise exploding from the stage. The folk troup had been replaced by what, at first glance, looked like a quartet of survivors from the heyday of punk rock. But closer inspection revealed that they were only school kids, who had obviously gone to a great deal of trouble to make themselves appear as horrific as possible for their big break. They'd succeeded, and they produced music to match. Their attempt at playing 'heavy metal' came over more like a distorted recording of a high-speed rail crash mixed with the sound of one of Saint Anthony's pigs being castrated.

Bonny raised her muzzle to the heavens, puckered up and joined in the vocals with a blood-curdling yowl.

'*Españoles!*' Maria shrieked, stabbing an accusing finger in the band's direction. 'Sons of *españoles*! Mallorcan boys would never make such an ungodly row on the eve of a holy day!' She crossed herself with her accusing finger and stood up to leave, inadvertently kicking her 'little husband' off the terrace in the process. When it hit the ground, the *maridét*'s lid fell off, and the glowing charcoals spilled out onto a small heap of cardboard fruit trays which, presumably, had been abandoned there on market day.

Fanned by one of those breezes that can suddenly swirl down from the mountains as the temperature drops at night, the trays rapidly took light and were blown across the ground to come to a blazing rest against the tarpaulin that was draped round the front of the stage. Maria, we noticed, was swift to take advantage of the general confusion that followed by making good her exit from the market place before the fire brigade arrived. The pseudo-punk rock group were also spurred into rapid action, falling over themselves in a frantic rush to bundle their instruments and amplification gear off the stage as the flames spread.

Its screaming pack of schoolgirl groupies may have been disappointed that the band's big gig had been so rudely cut short, but at least Bonny was happy. For her, Saint Anthony couldn't have kindled up a more merciful fire. I offered up a grateful 'Halleluja' on her behalf – and my own!

Sandy, on his way home from football training, drove into the market place just as the firemen were giving a final hosing to the charred remains of the stage. We waved him down.

'I spoke to Charlie round the corner there,' he said. 'He was chatting to his school chum Dec O'Brien. He says Dec's folks have invited him to stay at their place tonight, seeing as how it's a school holiday tomorrow. Charlie's been looking for you to ask if it'll be OK.'

Right on cue, a big American sports car rolled onto the scene and pulled up beside us. It made the little SEAT Panda that Sandy was driving look like a matchbox toy in comparison. Charlie was sitting regally in the back of the gleaming red Ford Mustang, with Dec in the front passenger seat, and Mick, one of his older brothers, behind the wheel. We knew the O'Brien boys well enough, and although they belonged to one of the most flamboyantly rich families on the island, they were quiet, mannerly lads, who had a reputation for being well behaved and never causing their parents any anguish. Consequently, we didn't worry about Charlie being in their company, except for his increasing attraction to their family's hedonistic lifestyle. But we were doing all we could to keep his feet firmly on the ground, and we had to trust in his own common sense. Enjoying an occasional taste of the unattainable is one thing, but aspiring to it is quite another, and we were sure Charlie was aware of that. It would have been churlish of us, therefore, to regard his friendship with Dec as being any less wholesome than his friendship with young Toni, who just happened to come from one of the *less* well-off families on the island.

Toni was now conspicuous by his absence, however, so Ellie asked what had become of him. She obviously didn't like to think that Charlie might have dumped him as soon as the O'Brien boys had arrived. But she needn't have worried. Charlie assured her that Toni had gone off to the Cine Argentina on the main street with a bunch of other local boys just before Mick's Mustang growled into town. There was nothing to worry about. It was simply that Toni had fancied going to the local movie house tonight, and Charlie hadn't, so it was no big deal. Well, so Charlie said. But I suspected that, when away from the sheltered community of his international school, he still felt himself to be very much the outsider when in the company of more than one or two local kids, whose native language wasn't his own and who had known one another and every detail of their surroundings all of their lives. I assumed that Sandy felt exactly the same way when training and playing with La Real's football team. That was only natural. But time and the inevitable sense of growing familiarity with their new social circles would resolve things like that. Or so Ellie and I hoped.

'Cool new car,' Sandy said to the proudly grinning Mick. 'Last time you brought Charlie home you were driving that rattly, old beach buggy of yours.'

'Yeah, well, you know how it is,' Mick replied, lowering his eyes and raising a smile in an attempt to cover an obvious twinge of embarrassment. 'My nineteenth birthday and all that. Dad just sort of… well, you know how it is.'

Without looking at Sandy, who had also had his nineteenth birthday recently, I could tell that his facial expression would be saying that, no, he didn't know how it was. Not bloody likely he didn't! Box-like old Pandas and sleek new Mustangs could hardly be farther apart on the league table of street-cred 'wheels' in the eyes of any virile nineteen-year-old. The fact that Sandy had also had to blow his own savings to buy the little SEAT runabout wouldn't have helped him 'know how it is' either. And it would have been no consolation to have been told just then that old Maria had said he would be better getting around with a donkey and cart than poisoning the air of the island with that fume-spewing *máquina* of his. Yet, ironically, he had actually bought that little car more to act as a present-day donkey and cart than for any other reason. If he had wanted to go for even a modicum of show-off value in his chosen car, he could have bought, for no greater an outlay, something like the very Volkswagen beach buggy that Mick had just 'graduated' from. But of what practical use would a pose-mobile like that have been? Sandy's main concern had been to buy a vehicle that would double up as a means of transporting crates of oranges, and, with its rear seat folded flat, the boxy little Panda fitted the bill perfectly. In buying it, he'd thought more about contributing to the family business effort than to his own image, and for that Ellie and I were proud of him. Modest though his little car was compared to young Mick's dream machine, at least he had bought it with the fruits of his own endeavours. He may not have appreciated it at that moment in time, but such independence of nature was a character-asset that could never be attained by being lavished with all the extravagant birthday gifts in the world. However, like Bonny and her fattening *butifarróns*, I'm sure that, given the choice, Sandy would have taken his chances with the more immediately-attractive option. That was only natural as well.

'Fancy coming along for the ride, big brother?' Charlie asked him. 'We'll be going for a burn-up along the *autopista* to Palma, then popping into a coupla flash nighclubs for a boogie. Loadsa chicks. You'll have a ball, honest.'

'Yeah, right – in your dreams, Charlie,' Sandy mumbled. 'It's already way past bedtime for sprogs like you, don't forget!'

Dec gave an edgy little laugh.

Mick was quick to quell any apprehensions that this little bit of brotherly banter, and Dec's reaction to it, may have caused Ellie and me. 'Don't worry,' he smiled. 'I'll be taking this pair straight home, and I'll be driving *very* carefully on the way. Dad's already warned me about treating a powerful car like this with respect, and he's told me he won't warn me twice.'

While I had no reason not to take Mick at his word, I couldn't help but wonder why his father had bought a nineteen-year-old a fast car if he didn't expect him to be tempted to use its speed. It seemed a bit like laying a plate of six *butifarrón* sausages in front of Bonny, leaving her on her own for a while, and believing that she'd only eat one.

'Yes, well, your dad's given you sound advice, Mick,' I nodded. 'Just think of the boy-racers who end up in hospital casualty departments every weekend.' I was inclined to make my point much more graphically than that, but Mick did seem to be a level-headed young chap, so I decided not to overstate the obvious. Instead, I thought I'd try to appeal to his sense of responsibility. Attempting to sound as casual as possible, I added, 'Make sure you keep these two younger guys here under control, eh. Pair of reprobates. We don't want to be getting any complaints about Charlie's behaviour from your folks, right?'

Mick started up the Mustang's motor, gave me a reassuring smile and said, 'You can rely on me. Charlie'll be OK, I promise.'

'Wait a minute!' Ellie piped up, as Mick released the hand brake. 'Charlie! You haven't got a change of clothes with you! What about clean underwear?'

'Aw, relax, Mum,' Sandy groaned. 'I mean, he's only been wearing his current pair of underpants for a fortnight, so another couple of days won't make them smell any worse.'

Charlie's response was to raise the middle finger of his right hand to his brother and silently mouth something which *could* have been lip-read as, 'Four coffees!'

'It's OK,' Dec shouted to Ellie over the departing snarl of the Mustang's exhaust, 'he can borrow some of my kit if he needs it. Not a problem.'

Although Ellie acknowledged his offer with a brave attempt at a smile, I suspected that, like me, she was recalling the last time we saw Charlie dressed in clothes that Dec had provided. It had been at the O'Briens' over-the-top house-warming party in their new Hollywood-style mansion a few months earlier, when the two boys made a late-night entrance wearing tuxedos and bow ties 'borrowed' from the wardrobe of Dec's brother-in-law, a Spanish soccer star with more money than height. They joked to us that they'd also borrowed the brother-in-law's white Mercedes to drive into Palma to 'do a bit of boogying' at Tito's Palace, the swankiest nightspot in town. We knew that they had to be pulling our legs, as neither of them was old enough to drive, and even if they had managed to get into Palma somehow, there was no way that a sophisticated establishment like Tito's would allow a couple of kids like them past the door. Also, Charlie, as ever, was broke, which made the whole yarn even more preposterous. Yes, they'd only been pulling our legs. Of course they had... *hadn't* they?

Ellie and I exchanged glances of doubt as the big red Mustang cruised out of the market place and on into the night.

Sandy's parting quip didn't do much to allay our nagging feelings of disquiet either. 'I wonder which one of the O'Briens' fleet of flash cars Charlie and Dec will be hitting the highspots in tonight,' he said dryly, then crunched the little Panda into gear and took off for home.

Ellie and I looked at each other, then at the departing Panda, then at each other again. We shook our heads. 'No, he's only pulling our legs as well,' we said in unison.

'Of course he is,' I said.

'Yes, of course he is,' agreed Ellie, that brave attempt at a smile returning to her face.

I gave her a nudge with my elbow. 'Come on, let's get another sausage before the bonfire dies out.'

Bonny, pricking up her ears at the sound of the 'sausage' word, barked her approval and, with typical doggy optimism, led the way. Maybe, just maybe, Saint Anthony's Fire would magic up another little treat for her before the night was over.

– FIVE –

SICK AS A DOG

'Water? You being drink the baster *water*?' Jordi almost choked on his beer. 'Bloody 'ell, man, being drink the Mayorky water be going kill you. Is ridickliss!'

I was sitting with Jordi in the Bar Son Mas, overlooking the market place, on the morning after Sant Antoni's bonfire night. The local animal-blessing formalities, complete with procession-leading bugle band, had already moved on to Port d'Andratx, down on the coast about five kilometres away. Meanwhile, the good citizens of 'inland' Andratx town had taken over the site of the previous night's celebrations for the purpose of staging their annual agricultural show.

As a spectacle, it was a fairly low-key affair. There were none of the grand parades of coiffured prize cattle or the spectacular equestrian events that are the norm at the larger country fairs in Britain, for example. Neither were there endless ranks of farm equipment stands flaunting extravagantly proportioned (and priced) tractors and all the other high-tech paraphernalia of modern, large-scale farming. The livestock and machinery on show at the Andratx fair reflected a much more modest and, in some ways, a refreshingly more old-fashioned type of husbandry.

In a single line of little pens and stands running down the centre of the market place were the animals and working tackle indicative of a community of small family farms. Yet, the old man standing beside his fold of more-practical-than-pampered sheep and the young boy with a cage containing a couple of nervous-looking 'table' rabbits could not have been more proud of their charges had they been champion Aberdeen Angus bulls. Neither was the implement salesman, who was trying to attract buyers for a basic, mule-drawn reaper, being any less convincing than his counterpart in another place would have been while pitching the merits of a state-of-the-art, satellite-guided combine harvester, costing about as much as we'd paid for the entire farm of Ca's Mayoral.

On show here were the goods and chattels of people facing a future being made increasingly unreliable in a farming world where big was becoming ever more beautiful. The cruel irony of this was that the root of their problem was the selfsame 'family' aspect of their businesses that had sustained their forebears through thick and thin for centuries. But, far from letting such uncertainties depress them, the Andratx small farmers were intent on enjoying their annual fair to the fullest. Their heritage of frugality and make-do-and-mend had bred into them a toughness of character and, just as importantly, an ability to take and relish their pleasures whenever the opportunity arose.

Jordi Beltran was, in marked contrast to the size of his *finca*, the biggest local upholder of this admirable trait.

'Water?' he gasped again. 'You saying me you only want drinking baster *water* today?' His bony frame shook in time with his 'tee-hee' sniggers. 'Bugger Jordi for a game of dominoes! Mayorky water? You been going off your forking nuts, man?' He looked round to the crush of farmers milling noisily round the bar, then, still laughing, pointed at me as if I were an exhibit in a circus freak show. Fortunately for me, none of the bar room gathering had understood Jordi's English-language jibes, and in any case, they were all more interested in comparing one man's pen of pigs or goats with another's than in heeding Jordi's incoherent ramblings about his *loco extranjero* of a companion.

He gave me a playful punch on the chest. 'Don't being such a pin in the arse! She being a fiesta day today, so be having you a *real* baster drink!' He made to stand up. 'Jordi go telling the barman to putting you a beer.'

I laid a restraining hand on his arm. 'No, honestly, Jordi. Thanks all the same, but I really think I'd better stick with water today. Sorry.'

Jordi's look of utter dismay as he slumped back in his chair made me feel almost as sorry for him as I was feeling for myself that morning. I'd had a dull backache for a couple of weeks now – not all the time, but frequently enough for it to have started to annoy me, *and* to worry me as well. At first I'd thought it was just a throwback to a pulled muscle I'd sustained the previous year when digging irrigation channels round our trees with one of those short-handled *aixada* hoes that Groucho was currently using to excavate our pool. But this was a different kind of pain, and the longer it went on, the more convinced I was that it wasn't coming from a muscle at all, but from my kidneys. A chill, maybe – or a slight infection at worst. Anyway, drinking water, and plenty of it, seemed the sensible thing to do. That had been the vet's recommendation for Bonny when she'd had a kidney problem a month or so before, and, combined with a course of prescribed tablets, she'd quickly recovered.

I related all of this to Jordi.

He slapped his knees and burst out laughing again. 'Pins in the kiddilies?' he chuckled. 'Bloody 'ell! No wonders you being have the damn bugger pins in the kiddilies! I telling you, is the baster Mayorky water!'

'Sorry, you've lost me, Jordi.'

'*Cal*!' he shouted at me, his expression suggesting that, if I didn't immediately grasp the significance of that one word, then I should get my head examined instead of worrying about my kidneys.

'*Cal*?' I queried, clueless.

'*Cal*!' he repeated.

'*Cal*? Who's *Cal*?'

'Is no baster *who*, is baster *what*!'

'OK, so what's *cal*?'

Jordi closed his eyes in exasperation. 'You know,' he sighed wearily, 'the bloody stuff what being make socks in your kettles.'

'Socks in my... *kettles*?'

'Yes!' he barked. '*Cal*, I telling you! Socks in the kettles!' He paused. He held a finger to his forehead, thinking. Then, inspiration glowing in his eyes, he exclaimed, 'The hairs of the dog up your pipe!'

I was well accustomed to being exposed to Jordi's improvisational skills when he was stuck for a word in English. He never allowed himself to be stumped for long, and it was his speed of coming up with an ad lib alternative that usually resulted in confusion – certainly for me, though clearly not for Jordi. He knew *exactly* what he meant, and he invariably had a plausible (to him) line of thought to back up his choice of substitute word. Feeling every bit the moron he obviously believed I was, I looked blankly at him and awaited the delivery of his latest etymological hypothesis. I didn't have to wait long.

'OK, be listening to Jordi and be looking at this,' he said with an air of pained patience. He hitched up one threadbare trouser leg and swung his foot onto the table. Pointing to his sock, he said, 'Socks, right?'

I nodded my head.

'And the socks being made from?'

'Cotton?'

Jordi threw his arms in the air. 'Forking 'ell!' he shouted, the volume of his outburst causing a momentary outbreak of silence at the bar. 'Is no baster cotton, is baster – is baster – is...' Spluttering in frustration, he pointed out of the window to a nearby pen of lambs, '... is baster shirts of the sheeps.'

'Oh, *wool*! Right, got it. Woollen socks.' I pondered that for a moment, before admitting that I still didn't see what a kettleful of socks, whatever they were made of, had to do with the pain in my kidneys. Before Jordi could get another word in, I swiftly blurted out that his cryptic clue about hairs of the dog up my pipe had left me even more flummoxed.

Jordi was squinting accusingly at me now. '*Crap*tic?' he queried. 'Hey, you be telling Jordi he being speak crap?'

There was no point in going down the rocky road of trying to explain what I'd actually meant by 'cryptic clue', so I just said 'No' and took a sip of my water.

Jordi took a deep breath. He then took a deep gulp of his beer – thinking again. He pointed to his jacket. 'Jordi's gherkin, right?'

'Jerkin.'

'Right – this exacaly what Jordi been saying, OK?'

'Right.'

'OK. So what you be calling the gherkin your lady being wear in winter?'

I thought for a second or two. 'Ehm, her winter coat?'

That did it. His patience exhausted, Jordi threw his arms in the air again and demanded to know what kind of shit English they speak in bloody damn Scotchland anyway. Didn't I even know what the hairs of the dog were called when made into a lady's gherkin to keep her warm, for fork's sake?

'Ehm, well… no.'

'Eskymoos!' he yelled at me. He drew an imaginary circle round his face. 'The hats of the baster Eskymoos!

The penny finally dropped. 'Oh, *now* I get it,' I laughed. 'Fur! You're talking about fur, right?'

'Furs!' he shouted, leaning over the table and glaring at me. 'Furs – hairs of the dog – same baster thing! This what Jordi been bloody tell you, Crisakes!' He rolled his eyes, patently amazed at my dim-wittedness, then slouched back in his chair again. Huffing and puffing and muttering 'Ridickliss' and 'Forking Mormon', he pulled a cigarette from his shirt pocket and lit up.

I waited until a few inhalations of smoke had produced their calming effect on him, then I crossed my fingers under the table and broke the news that I still didn't understand what wool and fur had to do with my having sore kidneys.

'Fork the pope and stone the bleedin' crows, mate!' he piped. 'It being the bloody *cal*, I telling you!' Realising that I was still none the wiser, he raised his right arm and thrust a finger in the direction of Juan the plumber's shop on the other side of the market place. 'Wools – kettles – furs – pipes – water – troubles in the kiddilies! THE BASTER *CAL*!'

Just then, Ellie walked into the bar after a leisurely wander round the shops, and joined effortlessly into our conversation.

'*Cal*? Oh, I know – it can be a real a nuisance in the water, furring up the pipes and everything. In fact, I've just been over at Juan's buying some more of those Brillo Pad thingies that soak up all that woolly gunge the *cal* leaves in the bottom of the kettle.' Ellie's tone couldn't have been more matter-of-fact.

My puzzlement couldn't have been more acute. How the hell did she know what Jordi was on about?

Jordi stood up and gave Ellie a courteous little bow. 'Hello, lady,' he smiled. He extended a hand towards a vacant seat at our table. 'Please, lady, be depositing your arse down here, thank you very much please.'

This was Jordi's version of chivalry, and none the less genuine for the use of a mild swear word. Ellie knew from previous encounters that 'arse' would be the strongest profanity she'd hear while in Jordi's company. As Jordi himself might have said, he was a forking gentleman in the presence of baster ladies.

Ellie was quick to notice the perplexed look that her easy understanding of the '*cal*' topic had planted on my face. 'Just a matter of horses-for-courses again,' she told me. 'Vocabulary, you know. You've picked up Spanish words that are common in farming. I mean, you know the Spanish for things like dung and worms and mildew and everything, while I've become more familiar with, well, domestic words – like *cal*, limescale. Yes, it's all to do with the limestone where the Mallorcan water comes from. Subterranean caves and things.' She shrugged her shoulders. 'Every woman here knows about *cal*. If you don't use a softening shampoo, for instance, the water plays havoc with your hair.'

Jordi keenly nodded his agreement. 'It also be playing hammocks with the kiddilies as well, lady.' He cocked a thumb in my direction. 'Jordi just being try explain him this.'

Ellie raised a quizzical eyebrow. 'The, uh… *kiddilies*?'

Forestalling another of Jordi's elucidatory onslaughts, I quickly interjected and gave Ellie the highlights of his theory about the cause of my back pains.

'Is very, very trueness, lady,' Jordi sagely confirmed. 'I tell you, Jordi been knowing it from the personal experiences, with much pins in the tripe from the many Mahatma Gandhis drinking, oh yes.'

Fortunately, Ellie had heard all about this horrific blot on Jordi's health record before, so I didn't have to risk offending him with an attempted translation. In a nutshell, he had once damaged his liver (or, because of the onions connection, 'tripe' in Jordi's word stock) during a marathon boozing session with Wayne, his occasional Aussie mate. Between them, several bottles of brandy (Mahatma Gandhi) had been consumed, resulting in Jordi being hospitalised. The doctors had advised him to drink nothing stronger than water from then on. Not surprisingly, however, Jordi had soon opted for beer, his contention being that drinking water was giving him 'bad comforts in the large incestines'. He'd conveniently ignored the technicality that his preferred brand of Mallorcan beer was brewed, in all probability, using the very same water that he professed had irritated his innards when drinking it in its purest form.

Looking solemnly at Ellie, he leaned an elbow on the table, cupped a hand to his cheek and confided, 'Oh yes, lady, with the water drinkings, Jordi been crap through the eye of a needle from the fifty metres distances.'

Feigning a coughing fit, Ellie tried to look suitably serious while struggling to stem the flow of giggles that Jordi's confession had triggered. 'Really?' she warbled. She pulled a hankie from her handbag and dabbed her eyes. 'Imagine – fifty metres!'

Jordi smiled in a way that suggested he was satisfied that at least one of his audience of two had proved capable of understanding plain English. He stood up and gave Ellie another little bow. 'Jordi must to leaving, lady.' Then, ever the gentleman, he asked her, 'Drink for you before Jordi be going?'

Ellie, equally graciously, declined with a demure little dip of her head.

Swept along in this flood of etiquette, I stood up myself, shook Jordi's hand and thanked him for his valuable advice about the dangers of drinking water.

'Is the *cal*, man, I telling you,' he reiterated. 'The limeys in the Mayorky water.' He pointed to the approximate location of his liver. 'Worse for Jordi's tripe than the Mahatma Gandhi, oh yes.' He then gestured towards my midriff. 'Boulders,' he said. Then, with more grave nodding of his head, he added, 'The pins in the kiddilies? Is the boulders in the kiddilies – from the *cal*. Is ridickliss!' With that, he was off, shouting his hearty farewells to all and sundry in the bar as he left.

'He could be right, you know,' Ellie opined. 'Could be that's what's giving you all the nagging pain. Kidney stones. They say drinking hard water can cause them.'

'I'm not exactly noted for the amount of water I drink,' I pooh-poohed. 'Let's face it, this is the first glass of water I've ordered in a bar in my life.'

'Hmm, I'm surpised the shock to your system didn't bring on a heart attack, never mind kidney stones.'

I looked at my cheerless glass of water, then at all the fun-inducing drinks being downed by the farmers at the bar. 'Be fair, Ellie – I'm suffering agonies here. It's hardly a laughing matter, you know.'

Ellie couldn't resist a little titter anyway. 'Well, if it's all that bad, you should go to the doctor. Going about feeling sorry for yourself won't cure anything. All it does is make the rest of us feel down as well.' Then, just in case I hadn't got the point, she added, 'You're a complete misery when you're like this. The original bringer of doom.'

'Florence Nightingale strikes again,' I grunted, taking a verbal swipe at Ellie's nursing background and at what I considered to be her accompanying lack of compassion for the afflicted. 'For a former angel of mercy, you can be really hard-hearted at times, you know.'

'Yes, well, giving bed baths to dirty old men and slopping out bedpans in the middle of the night does eventually dilute the milk of human kindness.'

It was obvious that I wasn't going to get any mollycoddling here. At the same time, Ellie was absolutely correct in what she said. I should have been paying a visit to the doctor instead of angling for sympathy in the vain hope that getting some would make the problem go away. And it wasn't as if medical advice would be hard to come by. We had taken out private health insurance with a renowned Spanish company called Mare Nostrum when we arrived on the island, and they'd registered us with a doctor down in Port d'Andratx. He had an excellent reputation locally, so I had no real reason to be apprehensive about contacting him. That said, the fact that his name was Jesús did make me feel just a wee bit uneasy. Doing conjuring tricks with loaves and fishes, no matter how miraculously benevolent, didn't quite square with my idea of what a modern medical practictioner should be about.

But I was only deluding myself. The real reason for my delay in making contact with Doctor Jesús was a disinclination to converse with him on the telephone. I'd been warned that the good doctor spoke no English, so, as part of the process of making an appointment to see him, I'd have to be able to create a very accurate word picture in Spanish of what was ailing me. His response and, consequently, my future health would depend on it. A serious matter. The snag was, though, that I still found conducting a conversation on the phone in Spanish much more difficult than doing so face-to-face. Perhaps it was because of the inability to exchange facial expressions of understanding or, more crucially for me, of confusion. Even when doing something relatively simple like calling the Pujol Serra depot to order a truckload of water, I was liable to trip myself up with a stammered string of 'uhms' and 'ahs' if an unexpected question was fired back at me. Talking on the telephone with the doctor, therefore, would be even more of a verbal booby trap, particularly since my Spanish vocabulary didn't include much that was even remotely medical in context. My restaurant-speak *Riñones al Jerez* (Kidneys in Sherry Sauce) was about the strength of it, and I didn't see myself getting very far with that. All things considered, then, I decided it would be easier to put a brave face on things and procrastinate. My diligently-acquired aptitude for *mañana*ness was coming in handy again.

'No, Ellie,' I said, 'what you say about going to the doctor is fair enough, but I think I'll persevere for a while yet. I mean, it's more than likely only a slight chill in the kidneys I've got. So, whatever Jordi says, I'll just keep drinking plenty of water, and everything will be fine in a day or two. Yup, plenty of water – that's the thing.'

'Oh yeah? Anything to avoid making a phone call to the doc, eh?'

I made no comment, but took a doleful sip of water instead.

Ellie tittered again. 'OK, be a martyr,' she shrugged. 'They're your kidneys.'

What I hadn't told Ellie was that I'd actually been treating myself for a kidney *infection* for the past three days. As a sort of trade-off against my feelings of inadequacy regarding phoning the doctor, I'd decided that taking a leaf out of the *vet*'s advice book might be a sensible compromise. Someone had once assured me that, while doctors aren't ethically supposed to treat animals, the opposite is the case for vets in relation to people. Not, I hasten to add, that Gabriel Puigserver, the Andratx vet, had actually given me any advice about *my* complaint, but he had treated Bonny for *her* kidney infection, and he'd told me at the time that the tablets he was prescribing were exactly the same as those given to humans. At least, I *thought* that was what he'd said, and my painstaking efforts to translate from Spanish into English the directions-for-use inside the packet of pills didn't reveal any warnings for humans *not* to take them.

The trouble was that, after several days on the dog's medicine, I wasn't feeling any better. In fact, the pains had become more frequent *and* more acute. Maybe I'd have to pluck up courage and make that call to Jesús after all. Then again, what would happen if I got the explanation of my symptoms all wrong? I could easily end up talking myself into a vasectomy or something! The more I thought about it, the more I became convinced that I'd probably be doing myself more harm than good by dialling the doc.

Yes, I'd keep taking Bonny's tablets and drinking plenty of water for another day or two yet.

For all her implied indifference to my plight, the truth was that Ellie hadn't really committed the legacy of Florence Nightingale to the waste bin of nursing cynicism. Although I'd been too wrapped up in myself to notice, she'd been watching me closely, and her concerns about my wellbeing had increased apace with my mood of despondency. Knowing me as well as I knew myself, she realised that even attempting to cajole me into making an appointment with the doctor would have no more positive an effect than calling me a gutless wimp, and a stupid one into the bargain. Yet she wasn't prepared to leave me to the fate of my own shillyshallying. If there was indeed something wrong with my health, then the sooner it was attended to by the doctor the better. Ellie had devised her own way of bringing matters to a speedy conclusion…

It was two days after the Andratx Agricultural Fair, and I had just come into the kitchen at Ca's Mayoral after delivering the morning's consignment of oranges to Jeronimo's warehouse in Peguera. My facial expression must have reflected the pain in the small of my back. Ellie was preparing lunch. As I slumped down at the table with a weary sigh, she walked over to me with a wry smile.

'This is for you,' she said, presenting me with a small polythene bag containing what looked like a mixture of dried leaves and little flakes of tree bark.

'What's this?' I frowned.

'It's a mixture of dried leaves and little flakes of tree bark.'

'Yes, I can see that, Ellie, but what the hell's it for?'

'I got it from Netherlands Nelly.'

'Who the hell's Netherlands Nelly?'

'Her real name's Nelleke van Something-or-other. It's one of those long Dutch names, but everybody just calls her Nelly. I've bumped into her a few times when I've been shopping in town. Really nice person. Really interesting. She packed in a high-flying career in Amsterdam and came over here to escape the rat race. She's house-sitting for a German family down near S'Arraco at present.'

All of this conjured up crystal-clear images in my mind's eye. The village of S'Arraco, slumbering in a valley midway between Andratx and the little coastal resort of Sant Elm, did have a reputation for attracting a certain bohemian element to the anonymity of its sleepy environs.

'S'Arraco, eh. Hippy, is she?'

'Well… sort of, I suppose.'

'Amsterdam, eh.' I glanced askance at the packet Ellie had given me, then dropped it onto the table. 'Smokes this stuff, does she?'

'Don't be silly,' Ellie tutted. She picked the packet up and handed it back to me. 'You're supposed to make a brew with it!'

'Whatever. I'm not into any kind of brain-blowing trip that some of those meusli-eating drop-outs round S'Arraco are rumoured to go for.' I shoved the packet back over the table. 'Thanks all the same, but give me a bottle of *vino* any day.'

'Which is precisely why Nelly gave me this for you. Unless, of course, you think Doctor Jesús would be better than her at turning all the water you're drinking into wine.'

I shook my head impatiently. 'You're talking in riddles, Ellie.' I looked at the plastic bag again, considered its implications, then shot Ellie a sceptical scowl. 'Here, you haven't been sampling any of these *loco* tea leaves yourself, have you? Get a grip, woman!

Ellie's response was to loftily inform me that suspicious minds always think the worst of everything and everyone, and my mind was clearly in the major league in that respect. Not only would she never even *dream* of taking a dodgy substance of the type to which I was alluding, but neither was her friend Nelleke van Thingy-ma-whatsit interested in tempting *me* to. Netherlands Nelly, she stressed, was only trying to cure my kidney problem (if indeed that's what it was) by 'alternative' means. In short, getting me off the water and back on the wine, without having to go through the linguistic hoops of consulting the doctor.

'Yeah, yeah, yeah, and why would she want to help a perfect stranger like me?' I lifted the packet and flipped it over. 'Hmff! She's charging you plenty for this bag of woodland sweepings, I take it?'

'There you go again – thinking the worst. There are *some* unmercenary souls left in the world, you know, and if you can stop your feeling-sorry-for-yourself grouching for a few minutes, I'll tell you why I think Nelly's one of them.'

With my ill-humoured lip duly buttoned, Ellie proceeded to relate how Nelly and her partner, Piet, had given up their executive jobs in Dutch advertising to follow their dream of starting a new life together in Mallorca. As both were mad keen on yachting, they'd sold their respective homes and had invested much of the proceeds in buying a wooden-hulled ketch, the *Sandpiper*. Sea-going and big enough to live in, the old boat, though requiring some tender, loving care, was just what they'd wanted for the charter business they planned to set up in the Med. They'd sailed away from Amsterdam flush with excitement and full of great expectations, and, despite almost foundering in a violent storm while crossing the Bay of Biscay, they eventually arrived safe and sound off Mallorca. They'd put into Port d'Andratx, still varnishing deck rails and buffing up brass fittings, but otherwise all set and more eager than ever to get their new venture up and running.

They'd anticipated that it would take some time to complete all the formalities required by the Spanish authorities before they could put to sea with paying customers, and they hadn't worried unduly when they eventually realised that it was all going to take a bit longer than they'd hoped. After all, this was Spain, the land of *mañana*. Besides, wasn't getting out of the hurly-burly push-and-rush of their previous lives why they were here in the first place? Suddenly, time was something they had plenty of, and while they waited for receipt of the required permissions and licenses, life on the quayside served only to confirm to them that they'd made the right decision by risking all to come here.

It was magical enough just waking up every morning in the snug comfort of their old boat, with its timbers creaking drowsily on the gentle swell, and with the warm Mediterranean waters lapping against its hull. But an even greater thrill awaited them when they climbed up on deck to be greeted by the sun rising over the pine-clad mountains that enfold the wide sweep of Port d'Andratx Bay. This was a scene that they knew they'd never tire of savouring.

And there was the social life. Tied up cheek-by-jowl along the length of the stone pier that juts out at right angles from the old harbour wall were the boats of their new neighbours – a few permanent berth-holders, others transient visitors, some of them local fishermen. However diverse their backgrounds, though, the essential things that all of the folk in the port shared were their love of the sea and the boats they sailed. This was a small, enclosed, but lively and happy community, which Nelleke and Piet become part of with consummate ease. The unhurried chats with like-minded friends on the pier; happy nights spent carousing in Tim's Bar, the mecca for yachties in Port d'Andratx; the nods and smiles of recognition from local characters; envious glances from day-tripping tourists strolling along the quayside; the endless days of balmy breezes that cheer the northern seafarer's heart.

Their dream had come true. What more could you want than to cast off whenever the urge took you to explore another little cove somewhere round the spectacular

Mallorcan coast, or even to cross the closer reaches of the Med to one of the neighbouring islands of Menorca or Ibiza for a few days? This, surely, was the life they had been born for.

But it's a life that doesn't come cheap, and the cost to Piet was soon to be counted in more than purely financial terms. Skippering and crewing a heavy, old vessel like the *Sandpiper* with only Nelleke to help him required not only doing the tasks of two or three men at times, but taking the consequent risks as well. Sailing short-handed all too often results in taking short cuts in matters of safety. One day, while clambering up the rigging during a fierce squall, Piet lost his footing and fell to the deck, sustaining spinal injuries which turned out to be both severe and potentially permanent. He wasn't insured.

The cost of essential surgery to Piet's back, followed by long months of hospital treatment, all but completely exhausted their savings. On top of that, the constant need to stoop when moving about a sailing boat, whether on or below deck, meant that Piet could no longer live aboard the *Sandpiper*. Strapped for cash as they now were, the only solution was to hire themselves out as 'housesitters' for absentee property owners in the vicinity, until such time as Piet's mobility improved. But at least they still had their cherished boat, and if fate was kind to them, perhaps, in a year or so, Piet would recover sufficiently for them to be able to launch their dreamed-of charter business after all.

Their hopes may have been dented, but certainly not crushed. Yet, no matter how positive their thinking for the future, the harsh financial realities of the present would take more than optimism to resolve. One thing more than any other hung like the Sword of Damocles above their heads – the outstanding harbour dues for their mooring in Port d'Andratx. They were substantial, and would wipe out every last cent of what money they still had left. But there was worse to come. The charges for berthing in Port d'Andratx were set to rise, and if they weren't paid promptly from then on, Nelleke and Piet risked losing their boat, their home, their everything. With no prospect of a means of earning money, the future looked bleak. The dream of two more starry-eyed sailors seemed doomed to perish on the rocks of the Mediterranean's siren shores.

Of a sudden, my own physical aches and financial pains felt a lot less severe. Intrigued by this tale of true misfortune, I asked Ellie what the outcome had been. As she was about to reply, the nasal rasp of a motor scooter coming down the lane drew her over to the window.

'Well,' she smiled, 'you can ask Nelly yourself. That's her coming now.'

'Coming here? But why?'

Ellie cast me a chastening look. 'That's hardly the hospitable attitude I'd expect from someone who's just been given a herbal escape route from having to phone the doctor.'

'Yes, well, that's just the point. I really don't want to get involved in all this weird hippy malarky. You know, magic mushrooms, opium poppies and all the other dopehead stuff they say grows wild here.' I tapped the plastic packet with the back of my fingers. 'I mean, not so long ago, she'd have been burned as a witch for peddling quack cures like this.'

But Ellie wasn't listening. She walked towards the door. 'Hmm,' she mused, 'I hope Nelly remembered to bring her hypodermic syringe.'

What the blazes was Ellie up to now! 'A hypodermic sy*ringe*?' I squawked.

'Yes, that's right,' she murmured airily as she exited the kitchen. 'I'm going to teach her how to inject.'

– SIX –

SAFE IN THE ARMS OF JESUS, MD

Whatever troubles Netherlands Nelly was carrying on her slender shoulders, she certainly wasn't letting them weigh her down. She breezed in like a walking advert for anti-depressant tablets, which I immediately took for granted that she'd been popping, despite reminding myself of Ellie's assertion about my suspicious mind. Could anyone, particularly someone whose world was threatening to come crashing down round her ears, look this infectiously carefree without some sort of chemical assistance? Nelleke van Thingymajig could, as I would find out.

Dressed in an ankle-length denim frock embroidered with guitar and treble-clef motifs, and with her long, blonde hair woven into beaded dreadlocks, she looked like a cross between a 1970s Nashville queen and an albino Masai princess. Slim as a tulip stalk, she'd have been about thirty-five, I estimated, though her peach-smooth skin and laughing eyes gave you an initial impression of her being half that age. While she clearly made no particular effort to accentuate any physical attributes that nature had bestowed upon her, Nelly's face did radiate a sort of serene prettiness, of almost the same demure type with which church images of the Madonna are depicted. Almost, but not quite. In Nelly's case, there was a certain twinkle in her eye and a mischievous lopsidedness to her smile that suggested a character somewhat more wordly-adventurous than the Virgin Mary's – or any other virgin's, for that matter. But that aside, hers was a face that exuded a zest for life and an open invitation to be friendly. Indeed, only the most terminally-surly would not have been uplifted by Nelly's presence. She certainly made me feel a lot more chirpy than I'd done for days.

As soon as introductions were out of the way, she got straight to the point. 'So, you are suffering from a sore back, *ja*?' she asked me in flawless English, though sounding the letter 's' as 'sh', in that soft-lisping way that many Dutch people so engagingly do.

'Yes, well, a little bit… but, ehm, I think it's just a chill in the –'

Interrupting me with a raised hand and a sympathetic smile, Nelly told me that Ellie had already explained everything. She pulled up a chair beside me at the table. 'May I sit here?' she politely enquired.

I nodded the affirmative, silently hoping that she really had been lisping that particular letter 's'.

She picked up the packet of dried bark and leaves, patted it with her hand, then looked me in the eye. 'I think this will quickly cure you, but if not, you must go to see the doctor right away, *nee*?'

'Yes, well, no offence, but I think I'll just persevere with the water and –'

But Nelly would have none of it. She was clearly a woman accustomed to getting her own way. From what Ellie had told her, she said, it seemed possible that I was suffering from kidney stones, just as Jordi had maintained. If so, drinking infusions of the mixture in the packet might just 'flush them out', according to the nuns in Palma who had advised her.

'Nuns? Did you say *nuns*?'

Nelly looked miffed. '*Ja*, of course nuns! And why not?'

For the sake of good manners, I tried not to appear totally dismissive, but I couldn't prevent a little snigger of derision escaping my nostrils. I muttered that the last time I'd had anything to do with nuns was in that underground car park in Palma, and I'd come away from the encounter a lot worse off physically than before I'd driven into the last available space ahead of them.

But Ellie was quick to jump to Nelly's defence. For my information, she bristled, those same nuns had probably saved Nelly's Piet from spending the rest of his life in a wheelchair. With no money to pay for continued hospital treatment, Nelly had been obliged to rely on the kindness of the nuns and the benefit of their advise on how best to help Piet recover. And it was working – slowly but surely.

Nelly confirmed this to be the case, adding that I shouldn't be so quick to belittle the ability of the holy sisters to administer medical guidance. Theirs was knowledge gained through centuries of selflessly caring for the poor, with nothing more to sustain their success than access to the curative qualities of the things of nature – flowers, seeds, herbs, leaves and the bark of trees. And now, unless I had any objections, she would put their ancient skills to the test again… on me. Before I had a chance to draw breath, never mind even attempt an objection, she added that, in any case, the brew she was about to make wasn't poisonous, so it wouldn't kill me, even if it didn't effect a cure.

Nelly and Ellie had put forward a robust case. So, suitably reprimanded, if not entirely convinced, I shut my mouth again and opened my ears. Ellie set the kettle to boil, while Nelly, without any prompting from me, proceeded to fill in the time by continuing from where Ellie had left off with the account of her and Piet's troubles…

Just when they had been clinging, ever more forlornly, to the final straws of hope of *somehow* being able to find the money to continue paying the mooring fees for their boat, they discovered that expensive maintenance work on her hull would have to be carried out below the water line – and urgently. All now appeared to be lost. The *Sandpiper* would have to be sold, but with her keel in need of repair, they'd be obliged to accept a price substantially less than they'd paid, and they still owed the bank for much of that. Having burned all their metaphorical boats back home in Holland, a distruptive and insecure lifestyle of going from one Mallorcan house-sitting job to another appeared to be the best they could hope for, at least in the short term. Then, once Piet was fit enough not to require Nelly's near-constant attention, they would both just have to swallow their pride and get back into the cut-and-thrust world of advertising, rent a little apartment, and start from scratch all over again.

Then Lady Luck stepped in. She appeared in the guise of an affable American couple they met during a final, sorrows-drowning session in Tim's Bar. The couple, Bud and Amy, came up with the ideal solution. As they had only recently sold their own ocean-going yacht and were on their way to visit friends who owned a little boatyard near Valencia on the Spanish mainland, they would sail the *Sandpiper* over there to have the necessary repairs done. Their friends owed them a few favours, so wouldn't charge any more than the bare minimum, which they, Bud and Amy, would be glad to pay – just for the thrill of sailing an old, wooden-hulled ketch across the Med. This would all take a few months to complete, so, by the time they returned to Mallorca, maybe Piet would be fit enough to get that charter business going, which, in turn, would get rid of their worries about how to cover future harbour fees.

It all seemed too good to be true, but it did present them with a way to both keep the *Sandpiper* and to have those essential repairs done. The straw the Americans had held out wasn't just the best one Piet and Nelly had to grab at now, it was the only one. To keep things right with the maritime authorities, the boat's registration-of-ownership papers would have to travel with it, Bud had pointed out at the time, and neither Nelly nor Piet had had a problem with that. OK, they'd be trusting their worldy all to people they hardly knew, but Bud and Amy *were* boat folk, they were members of that exclusive quayside fraternity, and they came over as being as honest as the day was long. Thoughts of possible chicanery never seriously entered Nelly and Piet's minds, therefore, and they cheerily waved goodbye to their benefactors as they sailed the Valencia-bound *Sandpiper* out of Port d'Andratx a few days later.

That had been almost a year ago, and it was the last Nelly and Piet saw of their cherished old boat. Subsequent enquiries revealed that no such boatyard as the one Bud had given details of existed on the Spanish mainland. Neither were the names of Bud and Amy and their alleged home address in the States recognised by the American Embassy in Madrid. They, whatever their real identities were, and the *Sandpiper*, whatever it was called now, had simply disappeared, and Piet and Nelly were obliged to accept that they'd never clap eyes on them again. They had fallen victims to pirates while sitting drinking with them in a yachties' bar, and had been marooned on the nearby pier with not even a splinter of lovingly varnished timber to keep as a memento of what they'd once seen as their passport to a new life.

'A mug,' Nelly said to me as she tore open the packet of dried leaves.

'Yes,' I sighed, 'I'm afraid you were.'

'No, I meant for you to *give* me a mug – you, know, so that I can soak this stuff in it for you to drink.'

Ellie gave me a 'think before you open your clumsy mouth' glare while bringing a mug and the kettle of boiling water to the table.

I duly apologised to Nelly, but I couldn't help thinking that she and Piet had indeed been complete mugs to entrust everything they owned to total strangers like that. Yet, here was I, about to hand over the welfare of my innards to someone who was a total stranger to me. 'The gullible guiding the credulous' appeared to be the order of the day. But what the hell? She'd said the concoction wouldn't kill me, so I might as well give it a go.

No sooner had Ellie dowsed Nelly's carefully measured quantity of nun-mix in boiling water, however, than I began to have second thoughts.

'Hell's teeth!' I gagged. 'That stinks like something that shot out of a skunk's anal glands!' I shied back from the table, pointing at the steaming brew. 'And you expect me to drink *that*?'

'Here, swallow it all down,' Nelly said blandly as she handed me the mug. 'They say it tastes better than it smells.'

'They told you a bloody lie then,' I spluttered after taking only one thimbleful. 'Believe me, not even a skunk would admit to anything as foul-tasting as this coming out of its backside!'

'No pain, no gain,' said Ellie, po-faced. 'Go on – do as you're told and drink it all up.'

With that, she thanked Nelly for kindly donating the herbal 'cure' without accepting reimbursement of its cost. But a deal was a deal, Ellie conceded, and she would now keep her side of the bargain. She took a plump orange from a bowl on the sideboard and, quite matter-of-factly, asked Nelly if she'd remembered to bring her hypodermic syringe.

'*Ja*,' Nelly replied. She dipped into her copious canvas shoulder bag. 'And I also have the dope. Which,' she added with a casual glance in my direction, 'I obtained from the nuns as well.'

By now, I was too busy trying not to throw up when taking each disgusting sip of Nelly's woodland infusion to be bothered asking what the hell the pair of them were about to get up to. But I needn't have worried. As I already knew (certainly as far as Ellie was concerned), they weren't preparing to start mainlining spiked orange juice or anything as daft as that. No, the dope that Nelly had referred to turned out to be nothing more sinister than a phial of painkiller, which needed to be given to Piet as an intramuscular injection – ideally, to the fleshiest area of his buttocks. But, try as she might, Nelly just hadn't been able to even think about stabbing that needle into poor Piet's rump. Hence ex-nurse Ellie's imminent demonstration with the hypo and the orange.

She explained to Nellie how she would have to pierce the phial's diaphram, draw out the required measure of liquid, squirt any air bubbles out of the syringe, then, having wiped the target area with some surgical spirits…

Nelly winced as Ellie took the orange and plunged (with slightly *too* much enthusiasm, in my opinion) the business end of the hypodermic deep into the symbolic human butt she held cupped in the palm of her hand.

'Easy as that,' she told Nelly through a confidence-inspiring smile. Ellie then adopted a nursey nonchalance. 'Act positively and quickly,' she advised her squirming pupil, 'and there's no pain at all.'

'Not unless you get your finger in the way of the needle,' I cynically suggested.

Ellie treated that remark with the silent contempt she clearly felt it deserved. She handed the orange and syringe to Nelly. Now it was her turn to have a go, she said, still smiling.

But Nelly simply couldn't steel herself to puncture the skin – not even of an orange. Ellie, she confessed with a pleading look, would have to inject Piet for her.

And this kicked off a routine that was played out every time Piet's backache became too much to bear. On receipt of Nelly's phone call, Ellie would drive down to S'Arraco, Piet would drop his pants, and Ellie would do the necessary needlework to his naked nether regions.

'He's got a low pain threshhold, that man,' she would offhandedly tell me on returning home. 'From the squeals he makes, you'd think I was inflicting some terrible torture instead of just jabbing him in the bahookie.'

To most people unfortunate enough to be thrown to the cold-blooded mercies of some members of the nursing profession, I would archly remind her, being darted in the arse truly *is* a form of torture. I countered her scandalised objections to any suggestion that she might actually be deriving some sort of sadistic pleasure from stabbing a needle into this hapless bloke's bum by reminding her of a certain incident that had occurred during her time as a novice nurse…

Before going off duty one Christmas Eve, Ellie had been instructed by the night sister to dispense a teaspoonful of laxative to each of the bed-bound patients in the male surgical ward – as a means of preparing them for the 'seasonal dietary variations' of the following day. The sister's written 'Tsp' abbreviation for 'Teaspoon' had been mistakenly – and unfortunately for the ward's inmates – read as 'Tbs' by her keener-than-careful trainee. Brimming tablespoonsful of purgative (every individual dose sufficient to clear the colon of a constipated rhinoceros) had consequently been administered by young Nurse Ellie to her trusting victims.

'If your ears weren't burning during the night,' the patients' spokesman growled at her when she walked into the ward next morning, 'they damn well should have been! Honest, you'd have thought a dysentery epidemic had broken out in here!'

As ever, Ellie would react to my repeating of this true story with a coy little smile which, in my view, hinted more at being tickled than ashamed.

Trusting that she didn't share Ellie's sense of 'humour', I promised Netherlands Nelly that, despite being filled more with trepidation than optimism, I would faithfully drink the nuns' potion for the next three days. If my condition hadn't cleared up by then, Nelly told me, I'd have to go to the doctor without further delay. After just one mugful of the disgusting brew, I already knew that I'd be delighted to do just that. Ellie's cunning plan was already working. But, as events would have it, she wouldn't need to wait for three days to see it through.

I felt so awful the following morning that I didn't even get out of bed. The pain in my lower back was worse than ever – incessant now and becoming more concentrated to one side. But I still resisted the call of common sense to visit the doctor. For some unfathomable reason, I even continued to force myself to drink Netherlands Nelly's brew at the recommended intervals, despite suspecting that taking it may have been the cause of the rapid deterioration in my state of health. As the hours passed, I began drifting in and out of consciousness, not sure whether I was actually hearing the sounds of Groucho digging outside or only dreaming it. I eventually awoke from one particularly fitful slumber to find the bedroom in darkness. The pain in my left side was excruciating. It was as if someone had plunged a red-hot knife into me and was twisting it mercilessly this way and that.

I crawled out of bed and crept on all fours along the corridor to the living room, every laboured move producing yet another torturous thrust of that burning blade. Ellie was watching TV. Her face fell when she looked round to see me struggling through the door on my hand and knees. Even Bonny's expressive boxer features were wrinkled in concern as she came forward and gently licked my forehead. But it was going to take more than the sensitive ministrations of Bonny's tongue to relieve a pain like this – a pain that even my taking the self-prescribed course of Bonny's kidney tablets had failed to stem – a pain so violent that it eclipsed the agonies that I still remembered suffering during a near-fatal attack of appendicitis in childhood.

'Please, Ellie,' I panted, a cold sweat burning my eyes. 'The doctor… take me to the doctor, *please*.'

'But it's after midnight. His surgery's been closed since –'

'Well, take a carving knife and cut out whatever's causing this bloody pain. I mean it, Ellie – I can't take any more.'

Ellie could see that I wasn't exaggerating. This wasn't a silly act designed to test her Florence Nightingale qualities. She began to help me to my feet. 'Palma,' she said. 'Can you hold on 'til we get to Palma? I'll drive you straight to the Mare Nostrum hospital.'

'Too far,' I gasped, every word an effort now. 'Peguera. Only ten minutes away. The main street – there's an all-night clinic there.'

As Peguera is a resort that caters predominantly for German clientele, it was no surprise to discover what the Spanish duty doctor's second language was.

'*Was ist das problem*?' he asked the moment he saw me inching into his surgery, holding my side, my face ashen and contorted with pain. He guided me over to an examination couch and indicated that I should lie down. '*Wo ist die schmertzhaftigkeit*?'

My own command of German being limited to the ability to order a *bier* and a *bratwurst*, the doctor's question was well beyond my powers of comprehension. So, after delaying for so long, I was now finally left with no alternative other than to explain my problem as best as I could in Spanish. And it's surprising, when the chips are down, how much can be conveyed with a word or two and some frantic pointing.

'*Riñon*,' I grunted, indicating my left kidney. '*Dolor*' (pain). 'Bloody *terreeblay*!' (no translation required).

After some urgent prodding and poking around the area of discomfort, the doctor took a close look at my eyes, walked over to a wall cabinet, then came back and told me to roll up my shirt sleeve. He didn't say what he was injecting me with, but simply advised me to lie back and relax. Almost instantly the pain began to recede, and within a few minutes I was feeling absolutely fine again. In fact, I was feeling better than fine. The racking agony had transmuted into a strange but wonderful sensation of total wellbeing. The doctor, having come across as a fairly stern chap when I first saw him, now appeared as smilingly benign as a stained glass saint. Ellie, too, seemed to exude a kind of angelic bonhomie. Hey, I could get used to this, I told myself. Wow!

The doctor told me that the injection should keep the pain at bay for several hours. After taking an x-ray of my back, he said that I should now go straight home and try to get some sleep, then visit my own doctor first thing in the morning. But sleep was the last thing I was thinking of now. I was feeling so high that an all-night party seemed a much more attractive proposition. Back out in the street, I felt as if I was walking on air. I felt like singing and dancing. I was Gene Kelly in the umbrella sequence from *Singing In The Rain* – except it wasn't raining, and instead of singing Gene's song I was lah-lah-lah-ing 'Happy Days Are Here Again'. Ellie was embarrassed, as were a few German holidaymakers, making their wee-small-hours way homeward, when accosted by this grinning Scotsman insisting on giving them Hogmanay handshakes and 'Auld Lang Syne' hugs and kisses. If a police car had been passing, I'd probably have been arrested for disturbance of the peace – if not indecent assault.

I remember nothing more until waking up in my own bed next morning, noticing no after-effects of the euphoria-inducing injection, and, even more delightedly, feeling not even the slightest trace of the pain that had driven me to the brink of despair just a few hours before.

At breakfast, Ellie passed me an envelope. 'That's a note the Peguera doctor gave me. He said you've to hand it to Jesus when you see him this morning.'

Doctor Jesús Lopez Viejo's surgery was located in a ground floor room of a house in one of the narrow little streets that rise steeply from the waterfront of Port d'Andratx. I remember thinking the backdrop of those pine-clad mountains that look down on the bay had never appeared more beguiling than they did when I parked the car outside the doctor's house that morning. Although, in all probability, the intoxicating effects of the previous night's injection had already worn off, the pain in my kidney hadn't returned, so I couldn't have felt more elated in myself or well-disposed towards the entire world.

Doctor Jesús turned out to be a neatly-built, clean-shaven, grey-suited man in his forties. He had a gentle smile and kind eyes, but that was where any visual similarity to the popular image of the biblical Jesus ended. However unintentionally, though, he did show a divine turn of phrase.

'*Es un milagro*,' he said after reading his Peguera colleague's case notes.

He'd said it was a miracle, and I reckoned he was right. In fact, I felt so jubilant that, if I'd had the vocabulary, which (fortunately) I didn't, I'd probably have told him that I'd even heard the 'loud hosannas' ringing in my ears as I floated out of that clinic in Peguera during the night.

Doctor Jesús' considered reaction to events was, however, much more pragmatic. His response to my broken Spanish was also much more reassuring than his reputation for being unable to speak English had led me to expect. In our respective versions of Spanglish, therefore, we managed to make ourselves surprisingly well understood.

It would be necessary to have the appropriate analyses done in order to ascertain *exactamente* what had caused me so much pain, he told me. No chances could be taken regarding the function of the kidneys. He informed me that he'd take a blood sample from me there and then, and if I'd be so good as to provide a urine specimen in a *bote estéril* (a sterile container), which I could purchase from the local *farmacia*, I could then deliver both items personally to the *laboratoria* in Palma.

As luck would have it, I was already familiar with this do-it-yourself way of processing medical samples in Mallorca. A couple of months earlier, I'd had to go to the same Palma lab with a little cyst the vet had removed from Bonny's front leg. The understanding was that I'd return a day or two later to collect the results of the analysis, which, in turn, I would take back to the vet for interpretation. It was a quick system, and efficient too.

Bonny's cyst, incidentally, proved to be benign, as did Doctor Jesús' expression when eventually reading the lab's report on my two analysed specimens. I'd tried to decipher the details before delivering them to him, but the combination of technical medical terms and their related score lines would have meant little enough to me if they'd been in English, so I'd given up the challenge of translating them after a cursory flick through.

I would be relieved to know, Doctor Jesús smiled, that there was no evidence of any infection or stones in my kidneys. Indeed, he assured me, they appeared to be functioning *perfectamente*, according to the lab's findings. He ran a finger down one of the reports, nodded his head as he concentrated on one entry, then asked me bluntly: 'What is your preferred drink – *alcohólico*, I mean?'

In the happy-go-lucky frame of mind I now found myself revelling in, I had an urge to reply that, at barely nine o'clock in the morning, it was a bit early for me, thanks all the same, but if he fancied a snifter himself, he should go right ahead. I realised, though, that this was neither the time nor the place to be making such wisecracks – partcicularly one that he, like every other doctor, had probably heard a hundred times before. I stole a glance at the paper he was referring to. It was headed *'Higado'* – 'Liver'. Hmm, under the circumstances, definitely *not* a time for corny quips.

'Wine?' the doctor prompted. 'I take it you drink *vino*, no?'

'*Sí, sí,* I do like a glass of *vino* occasionally,' I confirmed with a casual air, quickly adding, 'I seldom touch spirits, though, and usually only drink beer in the summer when it's very hot or –'

'OK, OK,' Doctor Jesús cut in, 'so how much wine *do* you drink each day?'

My resultant spasm of fidgeting, uhm-ing, ah-ing, head-scratching, leg-folding and chin-stroking was stemmed by the doctor's blunt question: 'Look, do you drink more or less than a litre of wine a day?'

This was like being awarded a PhD for giving my name and address, and with a built-in concession of being allowed to get half the answer wrong. 'Less,' I grinned, promptly considering myself a paragon of virtue. 'Oh, yes – *def*initely less than a litre a day!'

The doctor's look could either have been interpreted as mildly amused or quietly relieved. Still, it didn't seem to be totally sceptical, and that suited me fine. He closed my file, stood up and offered me his hand. '*Ésta bien,*' he smiled. 'That's fine. No more than a litre of wine a day and you won't do yourself any harm. But,' he added as I turned to leave, 'always make sure you do as we Spanish do.'

'*Qué*?' I queried, hoping that there wasn't going to be a sad sting in the tail of this happy litre-a-day bullseye that I'd already set my sights on.

'When you are drinking your wine, *amigo*…' He hesitated, his smile fading into a little frown of caution.

'*Sí, sí, sí*?' I urged. 'When I'm drinking my wine…?'

'Always make sure you eat something with it – even if only a few olives or some almonds.'

I flashed him a relieved smile. '*No problema*, Doctor Jesús. *Sí, sí*, always a little to eat with wine.' That, I firmly assured him, would be *absolutamente no problema*.

He stepped forward and opened the door for me. 'The food, you see, acts as *un filtro* to protect the function of your... of your...' He paused again, patting the area of his liver with his fingers. 'Uhm, how do you call this *órgano* in English?'

'Tripe,' my mouth said of its own volition, mischievously slipping into Jordi-speak without taking time to heed the tempering influence of my brain.

The doctor gave me a grateful nod. '*Sí*, to protect the function of your... tripe.' He smiled and nodded again. '*Gracias, señor*. Tripe – I will remember that when talking to my English patients in future.'

I drove home to Ca's Mayoral feeling euphoric at having been given a clean bill of health, but also praying to his celestial namesake that I wouldn't have to visit the good doctor again for a very long time, or, better still, that he'd be blessed with a bad memory for newly-learned English words.

On the way out of his surgery, I'd asked him why he originally referred to my sudden recovery as a miracle. I felt strangely disappointed when the doctor explained that, if, as he suspected, a kidney stone had indeed been present, the chances were that it would have been no larger than a split grain of rice. Drinking plenty of water, he advised, did sometimes result in an ostensibly miraculous cure, the sufferer 'passing' the tiny object without even being aware of it.

I preferred to believe, though, that the foreign body had actually been a 'boulder', as suggested by Jordi, and that the nun's mixture had inexplicably blitzed it. Surely the tortures I'd suffered hadn't been caused by something not much bigger than a grain of sand. On the other hand, as Ellie dryly suggested, maybe I just had a low pain threshold… like Piet, the Dutchman!

Her predictable assertion that I must have misunderstood Doctor Jesús' generous litre-of-wine-a-day limit may or may not have been correct. Equally, Jordi's claim that drinking limey Mallorcan water would kill me had probably been a gross exaggeration. All the same, I decided to hedge my bets by making a point of diluting my water fifty-fifty with wine from then on. As a further precaution, I resolved to rigidly follow the doctor's food-with-wine advice, while also heeding a reminder from 'Nurse' Ellie on the subject of 'moderation in all things'.

So far, the regime appears to be working well (fingers crossed), although I do seem to be going through a helluva lot of olives and almonds!

– SEVEN –

SCHOOL DINNERS – FOR ADULTS

As it had become Ellie's custom, since arriving in Mallorca, to grab any excuse to celebrate by eating out, my release from the agonies of the kidney complaint amounted to ample justification for indulging the habit today. It was a Saturday and the boys were off doing their own respective things, so she suggested that a drive towards Palma would be a good idea. We could stop for a leasurely lunch en route, then continue into town to catch the shops when they opened again after their siesta break. The second part of the deal didn't appeal much to me, but I realised that, as my good fortune was the reason for Ellie's suggesting the former, it would have been selfish of me to show unwilling to go along with the latter.

If today's weather conditions were anything to go by, it appeared that *Las Calmas de Enero* were over for this year.

Gone were the clear blue skies and unseasonably warm, limpid air with which the island had been blessed for the previous week or so. In their place, a wash of leaden clouds had diffused the sun's rays into a film of watery light that hung over the landscape like a shroud. As we left Andratx and cleared the mountain pass of Coll d'Andritxol, the summits of the Costé de Na Mora ridge on the northern skyline were obscured under a blanket of drifting cloud. The deep, vertical clefts that scar the craggy brow of the ridge were filled with slowly descending flows of mist, reminding me of scenes in remote, drizzly glens of the Scottish Highlands.

The effects of the recent temperate conditions were much in evidence, nonetheless. On the *autopista* motorway that forms the final fifteeen kilometres of the Andratx-to-Palma road, the oleander bushes occupying the central reservation were already making preparations for spring. Among their rabbit's-ear leaves, buds were appearing – tiny green bombshells that soon would burst into an explosion of colour to cheer the travellers' way throughout the months of summer. Birds, too, had recognised the signals given by *Las Calmas de Enero*. Sparrows and finches were flitting about industriously in the pine groves that border the road, picking up beaksful of dry grass to line their nests for the busy breeding season ahead. The flora and fauna instinctively knew that spring was just around the corner, and even the dismal weather of this late January day could do nothing to hinder the reproductive drive of nature.

Half way along the *autopista*, the castellated outline of Bendinat Castle suddenly appears to the right of the road. The name Bendinat derives, according to legend, from the year 1229, when the armies of the Christian King Jaime I of Aragon, intent on ending the three-century Moorish occupation of Mallorca, fought and won the vital first battle of their campaign nearby. The king celebrated the victory by resting and taking food in a tented encampment on the site of the present castle. Although the meal was of necessity frugal, at the end of it the thankful king is said to have declared (in Catalan), '*Bé hem dinat*' – 'We have eaten well'. Tenuous as this conjecture about the derivation of the Bendinat name may seem, it's still an attractive notion and a harmless anecdote that has become part of the island's folklore.

Beyond and below Bendinat Castle you catch a first glimpse of the wide sweep of Palma Bay. Today, the colour of the water had changed from its usual saphire blue to reflect the murky tones of the sky. Yet, there was still something joyously Mediterranean about the view…

Two tall palms, silhouetted on the near horizon, framed a moving picture of a *crucero*, a cruise liner, steaming majestically out of far-off Palma harbour. The pristine white of the great ship's profile extended into its wake, which drew a line over the surface of the water as straight as a rulered chalk mark on a slab of slate. Surrounding the liner, the sails of a flotilla of little yachts swayed slowly this way and that as they waltzed among the white horses dancing over the broken surface of the sea. Where else but in the Mediterranean could a palette of grey and white appear so colourful as this? And where else but in Mallorca would we be so spoiled for choice of good-value, atmospheric places to eat on the fringes of the capital city?

The village of Génova clings to the slopes of Na Burguesa Mountain just beyond the western outskirts of Palma, the views over the bay afforded by its elevated position and its wide selection of eateries making it a popular destination for Palmesanos seeking a handy alternative to the epicurean delights of the city. Once just a scattering of modest cottages dotted around the entrance to caves that are one of the area's tourist attractions, Génova has grown into a bustling residential area, with houses and apartment blocks huddled together amid a confusing network of narrow, one-way streets. About the nearest thing to a centre that Génova can boast is, paradoxically enough, a set of traffic lights at its northern edge, where the road from Palma, the Carrer Rector Vives, crosses the end of the village's main street. As an indication of what Génova has to offer the itinerant gourmand, the first three buildings you encounter after the crossroads are restaurants, and one of those, the Meson Ca'n Pedro, was our destination on this occasion, as it had been many times before.

Over the past thirty years, Pedro Estevan has turned his little establishment into a veritable mecca for those who enjoy traditional Mallorcan food. So successful has he been, in fact, that there is now a second Meson Ca'n Pedro a few hundred metres farther up the hillside – a purpose-built restaurant of grand proportions, yet retaining a relaxed, rustic ambience, and specialising in the same wholesome Mallorcan cuisine that has made Pedro one of the most successful restaurateurs on the island. And it's a talent that runs in the family, for Pedro's brother Jacinto runs two equally popular restaurants in the village – both called, appropriately, Meson Casa Jacinto. The Estevan brothers, it could be claimed, have set the standard to be followed by the many other restaurants (seventeen at the last count!) that now aspire to share their prosperity in and around Génova.

We had been keen patrons of the Estevans' places since first being introduced to their simple, value-for-money qualities by no less a dedicated gastronome than Jock Burns. It was at the original little Meson Ca'n Pedro along from the traffic lights that we had decided to eat today, though.

There was just something irresistably appealing about its cosy atmosphere on an overcast day like this, although you'd never guess it from the decidedly plain look of the exterior. The moment you walk through the door, however, you're enveloped in a feeling of unpretentious hospitality.

A long bar area separates the restaurant into two *salós*, or dining areas, each with a corner *parrilla*, an open, log fire that serves both as a grill for meats cooked *a la brasa* and as a cheery focal point for the customers. Fortunately, we had arrived about one-thirty, fairly early for lunch in Spain, so there was still a reasonable selection of tables available. Pedro himself, a neat little man with a shiny pate and a convivial – though unobtrusive – manner, ushered us to a table comfortably close to one of the fires.

La señora, he said with a gracious smile in Ellie's direction, would appreciate a warm *sitio* in which to eat on such a *día inclemente* as this.

It struck me then that we had grown surprisingly sensitive to relatively insignificant drops in temperature after only fifteen months' living in this most gentle of climates. Although Mallorca was reminding us that her winter wasn't *quite* over yet, the slightly misty conditions that prevailed today were kind in the extreme compared to those accompanying the marrow-chilling *haar* fog that occasionally rolls in from the sea on our native east coast of Scotland, even during summer. Yes, we had become soft. And did we feel ashamed? Absolutely not – just extremely grateful for having had the opportunity to be so! As one old cattleman once told me, 'Show me a bullock beast that prefers the cold and wet to a bit o' sunshine on his back, and I'll show ye an early candidate for the knacker's yard.' Wholeheartedly concurring with that admirable truism, I sat back, lulled by the crackling of the olivewood fire, and surveyed our surroundings in new-found, softie contentment.

The dusky patina of Ca'n Pedro's walls is testament to years of smoke drifting from those homely fires, on whose barbecue grids the first beefsteaks of the afternoon were now gloriously sizzling. Chunky, red-pine furniture reflects the warm tones of the exposed ceiling beams, from which ranks of whole hams and a tantalising variety of plump pork sausages hang like palatable stalactites along the length of the bar. On the subject of those hanging hams, it's worth noting that Pedro prides himself in keeping only the very best in his restaurants. If you ever visit one of them, try the *Jamón Ibérico de Bellota*. Known as the monarch of Spanish hams, it's made exclusively from the ancient breed of black Ibérico pigs that have fed free-range on acorns in the mountain oakwoods of the southern mainland for a whole season prior to meeting their maker – or, more accurately, their curer. Robust of colour and flavour, yet melt-in-the-mouth tender in a pleasantly chewy sort of way, *Jamón Ibérico de Bellota* is truly unique. Ask for it by name, because there are many alternatives, which, according to some ham buffs, are noticably inferior. They say it's all to do with that crucial diet of acorns, the very *bellotas* that distinguish this ham's name from all others.

However, as with most things epicurean, it ultimately comes down to personal taste, so why not decide for yourself if the '*de Bellota*' denomination is worth its premium price by tasting as many Spanish hams as you can? In Palma de Mallorca, one of the best places to go for sample morsels is the city's oldest deli, La Pajarita, situated at No 4 Carrer Sant Nicolau, one of a maze of streets between 'the Born' and the Plaça del Mercat.

Alternatively, do as we did that January day – find a little place that's popular with the locals and rely on the landlord's recommendation. On the counter of even the humblest of *tascas* (taverns) in Spain you'll see a *jamónera*, a ham-carving frame. By ordering a little slice of the house's best, accompanied by a sliver of, say, *Queso de Mahon* (cheese from the island of Menorca), you'll treat yourself to an appetiser fit for a king.

To complement his display of fine porcine products, Pedro has adorned one wall of his restaurant with the 'trophy' head of a wild boar, flanked by those of curly-horned, black mountain goats. While the goats manage to look aloof to the point of appearing quite proud of their fate, the rueful expression on the face of the boar seems to say, 'Dammit, if only I'd turned a quick left at the foot of the mountain instead of galloping straight on into this bloody wall!'

'Well, hello there, Pedro, ye darlin' man!' The raucous, cackling laughter of Colleen 'Col' O'Brien rasped through the restaurant like a buzz saw. 'Come and give me a great, big hug, ya little-wee Spanish leprechaun that ye are!'

We looked over to the entrance, where a patently embarrassed Pedro Estevan was being smothered in kisses and cuddles by a one-woman compilation of the world's greatest fashion gaffes. Mallorca's queen of Irish eccentrics was dressed today in typically bizarre style – if 'style' isn't a total misnomer when relating to the get-ups Col invariably managed to put together. The mother of Charlie's school chum Dec and his several siblings, Col hadn't allowed her fabulous wealth to change her from being, as she described herself, 'a common-as-spuds owld Irish tart'. But, according to Sean, her lanky, laid-back and likeable husband, it was surprising how much Colleen had to spend in order to look as cheap as she did. Dolly Parton, he said, would be proud of her. He'd been known to stress that his wife's clothes might look like shite, but it was the best shite that money could buy.

Today, Colleen's sartorial excrement consisted of a rainbow-striped silk headscarf arranged turban-like over her bleached beehive hairdo, a white mink poncho dotted with 'ermine' tails, and scarlet jeans tucked into emerald green thigh boots, complete with Davy Crocket fringes running down the outside of the legs. Sean, with what seemed like an endless succession of O'Briens and their various cohorts, followed his wife into the restaurant.

'Holy mother,' she bellowed on catching sight of us, 'it's yerselfs, so it is! Talk about yer happy coincidences!'

'So much for a quiet, leisurely lunch,' I muttered to Ellie, while flashing Col a welcoming smile. I stood up and braced myself for a repeat of the physical onslaught that little Pedro had just endured.

Beanpole-thin as she was, Col still possessed prodigious cuddling power. I feared for the state of my ribs as she locked me in a vice-like clinch, which only ended when one of her hands wandered downwards to pat my backside, while the fingers of the other gave it a playful pinch. 'Yer arse has gone as tight as a crab's,' she whispered in my ear. 'Yeah, and that's feckin' watertight!'

After another blast of cackling, she turned her hugging attentions to Ellie. 'Ah, sure but ye're lookin' radiatin'!' she declared. Then, with a suggestive wink and chuckle, she added, 'Heh, it's obvious yer man here knows how to put a smile on *your* face, eh?'

More grating laughter. Col was in fine fettle.

I'd noticed a whiff of gin melding with the aura of pungent perfume that always followed her about like an asphyxiating shadow.

'It's me birthday!' she grinned. 'Well, it *was* yesterday. Ah, yeah, a grand celebration we had last night, so we did.'

She winked again, then confided sotto voce, 'This is just a wee kinda *recovery* party we're havin' today, like. Ya know what Oy mean?'

Sean then approached us, and it was clear that he was already as recovered as a newt.

He shook hands with me. 'Nice – hick! – nice t' see ya again, George,' he slurred, his glazed-over eyeballs doing chameleon manoeuvres behind half-closed lids as he tried to focus on my face. 'How – uhm – how'z yer oz-oz-ostrich-farmin' goin'?'

Obviously, Sean hadn't a clue who I was, as I'd never been near an ostrich in my life, but I reckoned it would be easier just to say, 'Yes – ostriches all fine, thanks', and that seemed to satisfy him. He smiled vacantly, patted my shoulder, hiccupped again, then toddled over to the bar to order up a swift shot of recovery juice.

Although the present generations were enjoying its fruits, it had actually been the business acumen of Sean's late father, the 'common-as-spuds' but 'banjaxingly-shrewd' Paddy, that had sown the seeds of the family's fortune. Scrap had been his main game, and he'd proved himself a winner at the highest level. The huge house that Sean and Col had recently had built on a private promontory on the south-west coast of Mallorca wouldn't have looked out of place on the most exclusive slopes of the Hollywood Hills. It was a film-star palace on which no expense had been spared – a white marble and gold-adorned edifice that exuded opulence and dodgy taste in equal measure. Even the blank-cheque freedom that had been afforded the world-famous designers responsible for the house's décor hadn't proved enough to protect their talents from the stamp of Col's personal input. Classy understatement wasn't a term that figured in her idea of 'style'.

Having met Col and Sean through Charlie's school friendship with young Dec, Ellie and I had already been given a guided tour of Chez O'Brien, and had even been guests at the house-warming 'hooley' shortly afterwords. The colourful expat set they belonged to wasn't a community that we were particularly attracted to being part of, no matter how much we liked the individual members of the O'Brien family themselves. Theirs was, frankly, an unashamedly extravagant lifestyle that was just too rich (in every sense of the word) for our comparatively simple tastes and modest resources.

Charlie, on the other hand, positively loved being involved with that echelon of Mallorcan 'high' society. It wasn't a surprise, therefore, to see him trooping into the Meson Ca'n Pedro with Dec and the other young O'Briens, particularly as he'd been staying overnight at their place again, as he frequently did at weekends. It shouldn't have been any more of a surprise to see Jock Burns and his wife Meg breezing into the restaurant right behind them. I'd already noted that several tables had been placed together in a long row down one side of the *saló*. My initial assumption had been that they'd been arranged in this way to accommodate the members of a wedding party, perhaps. But now that I thought about it, it was equally likely that Jock, presumably having been at Col's birthday party the previous night, had been the driving force behind this whole 'recovery' junket today. He had a schoolmasterly flair for organising school-dinner-sized get-togethers, and he promptly took charge of supervising the seating arrangements in Ca'n Pedro.

'You'll be joinin' our mob,' Col told us. 'No point in ya sittin' here on yer own like a coupla spares.'

Ellie slipped instinctively into excuse-making mode. 'Well, we'd love to,' she said, 'but we're just having a quick snack before heading off to the shops.'

'Away wit' ya now!' Col pooh-poohed. 'It's Saturday afternoon, so it is. Most o' the shops is closed 'til Monday!'

Ellie's face fell in conjunction with my rising spirits. We'd both forgotten about the weekend shopping hours in Spain.

'Oh dear, what a shame, Ellie,' I lied. 'Still, never mind, eh. At least Col's saved us a wasted journey into town.'

Ellie said nothing, but the look on her face spoke volumes. Apart from the disappointment of missing out on a shop-touring binge, she knew how Jock's 'school dinner' sessions could sometimes end, and she clearly didn't fancy the way this particular one was shaping up.

It didn't take Jock long to notice us. 'Wow, well met, pardners!' he shouted in a mid-Atlantic twang, beckoning us over and instructing me to sit beside him. 'And, Ellie honey, you'll be here next to Meg. Charlie and Dec,' he called out, 'you and the rest of the junior dudes'll be down at the far end of the table in the corner there. Yeah, and before we go any further, any clowning and you'll be on detention after school all next week. Let's have some goddam decorum in here, right!'

I noticed that, as soon as Jock turned his back to continue sorting out the rest of the table places, Charlie and Dec gave him barely-concealed V-signs, accompanied by smirked mutterings of dissent. They did as he'd told them, though. The laws of the classroom were being upheld, no matter how grudgingly. Too bad, however, that such adherence to discipline wasn't about to extend to many of the older members of the company.

Another wave of 'morning after' recoverers filed in, and soon the O'Briens had assembled a lunch gathering to outnumber even the largest of the extended Spanish families now starting to occupy the neighbouring tables. What's more, it didn't take long for the O'Brien clan to outdo even the noisiest of them with their cross-table banter and associated hilarity. Such conversational clamour is one of the delights of eating out in Spain. Spanish families have an enviable predilection for it. It's a practice that's part of their culture. But there was something different about the O'Briens' version – something altogether more wild and unrestrained. Celtic chaos was descending upon the Meson Ca'n Pedro, and even schoolteacher Jock's efforts to control it were proving futile. Eventually conceding defeat in the battle of seating arrangements, he concentrated instead on attempting to organise what was, for him, the much more serious business of ordering food.

Standing up, he banged a spoon on the table several times. 'Hey, listen up here, people!' he yelled over the hubbub. 'All right, I'm suggestin' that, for openers, we share some plates of –'

'Aw, shut yer cakehole!' Col shouted at him. 'Sure, we're able enough to read the feckin' menu ourselfs!' She grabbed the arm of one of a quartet of waiters trying valiantly to make sense of the torrents of Spanglish already gushing at them from all directions.

'*Para empezar, señora*?' he asked her. 'To start, madam?'

'Oy'll have a gin,' she told him. 'Yeah, wit' ice and lemon. Oh, and a *botella* o' tonic water an' all. A *botella*, mind. None o' yer bulk pish out o' yer little-wee hose behind the bar there!'

Sean grinned in nodding agreement. 'Same for me, *amigo*,' he keenly verified. Then, lest there had been any misunderstanding on the waiter's part, he pointed to his current glass of gin and tonic. '*Sí*, a *nuevo* one o' them, *por favor*.'

It appeared that at least the adult members of the O'Brien family hadn't bothered to learn much more than the basic essentials of the language of their adopted country. 'Money talks' was, no doubt, their maxim, the theory being that the donation of a fat backhander transcends the most daunting of linguistic barriers. As if to prove the point, Sean produced a banknote from his breast pocket and slipped it into the waiter's hand. 'Yup,' he affirmed, 'another one o' yer *grande* G-and-Ts, *grassy ass*. Yeah, *amigo*,' he winked, 'and keep 'em comin', eh.'

Despite Jock still doing his utmost to take control, the food-ordering process rapidly descended into total disorder, so Charlie took advantage of the situation to temporarily escape his designated place at the 'junior dudes' end of the table. He was all smiles as he came up to us.

'Fancy seeing you here,' he said.

Although Ellie hadn't mentioned anything since seeing Charlie arrive as part of the O'Brien entourage, I could tell that she was uncomfortable about the effect that such juvenile antics by so-called grown-ups might be having on an impressionable kid like him.

'I hope you behaved yourself at Dec's house last night,' she said with a wary look.

Charlie read her mood perfectly. 'Don't worry, Mum,' he smiled. 'Dec's folks aren't always like this. They're just having a birthday fling, that's all. It's Dec's old lady's fiftieth. Gotta be a good enough excuse for letting their hair down, no?'

'Hmm, well, just so long as *you* didn't get up to anything you shouldn't have at the party.'

Charlie chuckled. 'Nah, you needn't worry, *madre*. Us kids weren't even at the shindig.'

Ellie jumped to the expected conclusion. 'You mean,' she said, a note of panic in her voice, 'Dec and you weren't in the house last night?'

Charlie laughed now. 'Are you asking if we took one of the cars and drove along to Tito's Palace in Palma?'

Ellie, like me, still wasn't totally convinced that he'd only been pulling our legs when he'd told us that he and Dec had once 'borrowed' one of the O'Briens' cars to go boogying, tuxedo-clad, at Tito's, one of Mallorca's top night spots. Caught off-guard by Charlie's incisive response, she was all of a fluster. 'Well, no, I – I mean, I wasn't actually suggesting, you know, that...'

'Uh-huh?' Charie prompted mischievously.

Cornered, Ellie ditched her discretion and came right out with it. 'OK,' she said, 'did you really go nightclubbing with Dec last night?' Her qualms container now uncorked, the evidence of her misgivings came pouring out. 'I mean, Charlie, you're only *just* thirteen – not even old enough to be going to such places. Not that you can afford to – not off your pocket money, anyway. So, I hope you're not sponging off Dec. I mean, I'd hate to think that his parents have been given the impression that your father and I are skinflints or anything. And if I thought you'd been breaking the law by helping Dec steal one of his family's cars... I mean, Dec's not even old enough to learn to drive, and, and –'

Charlie held up a hand, traffic-cop-style. 'Pull over, lady,' he said. 'You're breakin' the speed limit here.'

Ellie looked at him, apprehension and confusion writ equally large on her face.

Charlie gave her a reassuring smile. 'It's OK, Mum. Dec and me were at home all last night – playing snooker with his brothers, watching videos, playing computer games, all that kinda stuff.'

Ellie held him in a sceptical stare. 'Playing snooker? But didn't Col use the games room for her party? I mean, that's where they had their house-warming, so…'

'Last night's party wasn't in the house.'

'It wasn't?'

'Nope.' Charlie pulled a subject-closing shrug. 'They held it in some posh hotel or other. The Son Vida, I think it was.'

But Ellie's misgivings motor was still revving. 'And the videos?' she probed.

'The videos?' Charlie queried. 'What about the videos?'

Ellie fidgeted. 'Well, I – you know – I hope…'

Charlie sniggered. 'Porn. You're asking if we were watching porno movies, aren't you?'

It was time to get Ellie off the hook before she got herself totally tied in knots. 'Look, Charlie,' I said, 'your mother isn't accusing you of anything. She – we – yes, *we* just want you to know that we depend on you to be a credit to us when we're not there to keep an eye on you.'

'No probs, *padre*,' Charlie grinned. 'I'm cool to all that stuff. And, hey,' he continued with a roguish wink, 'it's not as if I haven't seen one or two of *your* house parties before, huh?'

'Hmm, the words stones and glass houses come to mind,' Ellie said under her breath.

That really was a subject-closer, and I made no attempt to counter it.

'Touché, Charlie,' I conceded. 'On you go and enjoy your lunch. Better get back to your place at the table before Jock starts hitting you with a detention notice.'

Charlie headed off, but he stopped after a couple of paces and called back, 'Oh, and incidentally, Mum – when we go clubbing in Palma now, Dec and me tend to borrow his big brother Dermot's motorbike instead of the Merc.' He winked again, pseudo-confidentially this time. 'Two wheels are more fun than four for a burn-up on the *autopista* – get my drift?'

'Tell me he's just kidding, Peter,' Ellie groaned. She put on an assurance-bolstering smile for Charlie's benefit. '*Please* tell me he's only kidding.'

'Your Charlie did well to pick one of the O'Brien lads for a mate,' Jock said right out of the blue. He was taking his seat again now that the food had started to arrive. His natural inclination to control communal matters had suddenly been supplanted by the more powerful urge to get his teeth into his quota of the shared 'picks' he'd eventually succeeded in ordering up for everyone. Now that he was talking only to us, he had reverted to his natural Scottish accent. 'Aye, great kids, those O'Brien youngsters,' he said while drizzling olive oil over a slice of crusty bread that he'd already smeared with the flesh of a tomato. 'Never had the least bit o' trouble at school with any o' them since they came to the island. Model students, that lot.'

Ellie cleared her throat. 'So, ehm,' she began hesitantly, 'you, uh, you wouldn't say that Dec would be prone to, say, under-age driving, or anything like that?'

Jock speared a small shoal of deep-fried anchovies with his fork. 'Under-age drivin', did ye say?'

'Yes, you know – *borrowing* one of his family's cars to drive into Palma when his mother and father were… well, when they're…'

'Pissed?' Jock suggested.

Ellie smiled uneasily. 'Well, yes, I suppose you *could* put it that way. But what I really mean is –'

'Listen, hen,' Jock butted in, 'I know what ye're gettin' at. But, hey, believe me, for all their rent-a-party lifestyle, the O'Briens have never missed a trick as far as bringin' up their pot lids is concerned.'

'Pot lids?'

'Kids, darlin'.' Jock popped a couple of stuffed olives into his mouth. 'Rhymin' slang, ye know.'

'Dead right,' Meg agreed. 'Ace bevvy artists they may be, but take it from me, flower, that pair are right on the ball when it comes to keepin' their family in line.' She poured herself a glass of wine from one of a platoon of assorted bottles now paraded along the line of tables. 'Under-age drivin'?' She wagged a finger at Ellie. 'No danger, petal, and that *is* the truth.'

'Aye, and you better believe it, by the way,' Jock affirmed, as he dipped a few winkled-out snails into a dish of garlicky *all-i-oli*. 'Top parents, the O'Briens are. Yeah, and top hosts as well.' He grabbed a bottle of red wine, filled his glass and raised it to anyone who might be looking or listening. 'Cheers! Here's to Col's fiftieth!'

But everyone was too busy chatting, swapping jokes, laughing, eating and drinking to pay attention.

'Bunch o' bloodsuckin' hangers-on,' he mumbled. 'Freeloadin' bastards, every one o' them. Like bloody vultures when there's a freebie feed and booze-up on.' He downed his glass of wine in one gulp, poured another, then devoured a couple of large grilled prawns, taking care to suck out every last drop of juice from their severed heads. 'Come on, son,' he said to me. He indicated the array of 'picks' and bottles laid out before us. 'Make hay while the sun shines. Get yer gnashers round some o' this grub and get quaffin' the Calvin Klein before these greedy buggers scoff the lot!'

Soon, shoulders and legs of lamb, suckling pig cutlets, T-bones of veal, fillet and entrecôte steaks, breasts of chicken, baby rabbits, loins of pork and several varieties of fish were served up from the grill and consumed with gusto by their respective recipients the length of the table. Platters of boiled, roast and fried potatoes, along with bowls of salad also came and disappeared down more than thirty eager gullets, all of this food washed on its way by a tide of wine.

As the afternoon wore on, cleared plates made way for even more bottles of *vino tinto*, *blanco* and *rosado*, which, in turn, were replaced by coffees of various hues and strengths. The arrival of the latter wasn't intended as an antidote to any surfeit of *vino*, however, but rather as an accompaniment to the munificent Pedro Estevan's on-the-house provision of a selection of liqueurs, to be self-served at will by his esteemed clients.

In all of these respects, with the possible exception of the volume of alcohol drunk, the O'Brien crowd's extended lunch had more or less mirrored what had been happening at those neighbouring tables occupied by Spanish families. Significantly, where the main difference lay was in the areas of decibels and bread…

The din emanating from Jock's 'school dinners' assembly increased apace with the passage of time, the banter and wisecracks becoming correspondingly more undignified and risqué as one hour drifted into two and beyond. The commotion climax was reached when Jock, returning from a visit to the loo, appeared behind Col's seat with a large, red, leather-bound menu, lifted from the bar in passing and held aloft in the crook of his arm.

'Collen O'Brien – wife, mother, common-as-spuds old Irish tart and piss-artist *par excellence*,' he announced, dramatically aping a well-known television presenter, 'THIS IS YOUR LIFE!'

An outburst of cheering, clapping, whooping and hollering provided more than enough encouragement for Jock to launch into an outpouring of good-natured insults and trumped-up scandals about Col's past. It was a bit like a typically smutty and suggestive best man's speech at a wedding, and Jock's version was up there among the most indelicate imaginable. Still, Col delighted in being the centre of attraction, and the ribald comments contributed at the top of their voices by her gathered entourage only set her off in ever louder cascades of cackling laughter.

My own relative sobriety, stemming from the recently-adopted and Ellie-incited resolution for 'moderation in all things', allowed me (for once) to assume something of a 'holier than thou' attitude towards such rowdiness, particularly when perpetrated by people old enough to know better. Indeed, it was interesting to note that the most decorum-observing members of our group were Charlie and his chums, the teenage O'Briens.

Even they, despite their youth, resisted joining in the school-dining-hall bread fight that then broke out between some of Sean's regular drinking buddies. One of them, Stan, was also employed, bizarrely enough, to act as Sean's chauffeur on occasions when 'himself' was too inebriated to drive his gold Rolls from one watering hole to another. The flying bread episode, however, drew nothing worse than a few disapproving glares and tutted brickbats from other Ca'n Pedro customers in the immediate vicinity – until, that is, one over-energetically chucked heel of baguette missed its target and hit the ear of a bulky German-speaking gentleman who was sitting with his wife at an adjacent table. The shock of the blow was nothing, however, compared to the outrage provoked by the offending missile ricochetting off its victim's head, landing in a bowl of *arroz brut* soup and causing an eruption of snails, rice, assorted vegetables and saffron-tinted broth to splatter all over the front of his white Ralph Lauren shirt. The designer garment's little polo-horse logo didn't look quite so prestigious when embellished by a soggy slice of wild *seta* mushroom with a small pendant of French bean dangling from it.

'*Himmel!*' the German gentleman boomed. '*Mein hemd!*'

Ellie leaned towards me and whispered, 'He said, *Heavens! My shirt!*'

Ellie, you see, was born in Germany and lived there until moving to Britain with her parents when she was five. Although she claimed not to remember much of her mother tongue, she could usually be depended upon to dredge up items of vocabulary pertinent to such potentially interesting situations as this.

Spinning round in his seat, the bespattered German selected Stan as the likely culprit, glared at him and bellowed, '*Dummkop! Unvorsichtig, kindisch lümmel!*'

'He said, *Blockhead! Careless, childish lout!*' Ellie hissed in my ear.

The puzzled expression on Stan's face suggested that he didn't understand the actual words being hurled at him, although it was patently obvious to him, and to every other non-German-speaker within earshot, that he wasn't being complimented on his grasp of the finer points of etiquette.

'*Unbeholfen Englisch idiot!*' was the irate German fellow's next verbal arrow, and he released it with a vengeance.

'*Unbeholfen,*' whispered Ellie, '– that means clumsy, I think.'

But no-one, least of all Stan, needed a translation of the remaining two words in the sentence.

'Here, mate,' he growled, standing up and pointing threateningly, 'who the hell are you calling an English idiot? How dare you!' Stan gave the impression of being as much hurt as insulted. 'I'm fucking *Welsh*, boyo!' he proudly declared.

Pulling himself up to his full height, Stan drew in his stomach and adopted a pose intended to best show off his substantial physique. True to the rugby-playing heritage of his native land, he was built like a cross between a weight lifter and the proverbial brick shithouse.

'I'll punch your bloody lights out, Erik!' he barked at the justifiably-fuming German, following up his threat with a tirade of inflammatory abuse, which culminated in an open invitation to 'settle this right now out in the street!'.

The self-congratulatory smirk that Stan flashed his surrounding chums was quickly transformed into a look of dropped-jaw amazement, however, when Herr Erik stood up himself. He was revealed to be not just bulky, but more akin to a bouncy-castle version of the Incredible Hulk. Stan, in comparison, looked like Tom Thumb on steroids. This was a veritable giant of a German, big enough to have Stan for his main course, and looking intent on doing just that.

A hush spread throughout the room.

'*Mein* shirt, it is ruin-ed!' Herr Erik thundered in broken English. '*Ja*, it is now *kompleteleesh kaputt!*' He glanced at his soup-dripping Ralph Lauren, then eyeballed Stan menacingly. '*Und* zo,' he growled, 'vot about it vill you be doink, *mein freund*?'

Stan blanched, all signs of his previous bravado suddenly gone. 'Sorry,' he gulped, 'but, uhm, it wasn't actually me.'

'VOT?'

'It – it wasn't m…'

Stan's voice trailed away as his adversary stomped over and glowered down at him, fists clenched, his eyes oozing intimidation.

'VOT?' he repeated.

Stan's expression was beginning to resemble that of the wild boar's head on the wall. He realised he'd made a grave mistake and now deeply regretted it, albeit too late. 'The, ehm, bread – the soup – the shirt,' he quavered, '– it w-wasn't me.'

This timorous pleading of innocence was of no consequence to Herr Erik, though. He lifted a glass of water from the table and proceeded to pour it slowly over Stan's head. '*Ja*,' he snarled when the deed was done, '*und* zat voss not me alzo!'

Just when things were starting to look distinctly bleak for Stan, none other than Sean, three sheets in the wind though he was, struggled to his feet, wobbled over and patted the big German on the arm. He smiled and said, 'Ah, now then, sir, don't you be goin' worryin' yer good self about them little details, eh.' He then pulled out his wallet and handed over a few notes. 'Sure, and this should cover the damage – no matter who done it.'

From what I could see, Sean's peace offering would have been sufficient to buy a whole rack of expensive shirts. Nevertheless, to make doubly sure that his chum Stan would no longer be in danger of physical liquidation, he hailed Pedro, who had been standing by the bar, no doubt poised to phone the Civil Guard if things got really out of hand.

'A bottle of yer finest bubbly for me German friend here,' Sean shouted. 'Yeah, make it a magnum of yer best *cava* for Erik and his missus, why don't ya!'

Pedro, ever the professional, not only promptly relayed Sean's order to his barman, but also dispatched a waiter to do what was necessary to clean up the shirt of Sean's new German friend.

All of this generosity finally brought a smile to the face of its much-maligned beneficiary. He thanked Sean and Pedro individually. Then, after thumbing through the money he'd been given, his smile widened and he thanked Sean yet again. With a courteous little dip of his head, he turned away to rejoin his wife. Before sitting down, though, he took a moment to address Stan one last time.

'*Und* for your information, *mein freund*,' he sternly announced, '*mein* name is *nicht* Erik. *Nein*, it is Fritz.' He stood to attention and clicked his heels before closing with a grinned, '*Ja, und* I am a fuckink Austrian!'

This pithily-apt riposte drew a round of applause combined with an outbreak of relief-induced laughter from the O'Brien army. Party time was here again, and more wine was ordered up to celebrate the event.

Col leaned across to Ellie, gestured obliquely towards the 'junior dudes' end of the table and shouted over the hullaballoo, 'Now, ye see, that's the good ting about them youngsters livin' in a place like Mallorca here.'

Ellie cast her a quizzical look. 'Sorry, I'm not sure what you mean.'

Col heaved an exasperated sigh. 'Oy'm talkin', don't ya know, about yer international population and yer multi-lingo cultural exchanges like what ye've just seen. It's mind-widenin', so it is.' She settled back in her chair, took a swig of gin and declared, 'Nah, nah, ye can't feckin' whack this kinda life for yer sprogs, darlin'!'

While Ellie took a contemplative sip of her water, Meg nudged her and said in all seriousness, 'See what I mean, flower – always thinkin' about the upbringin' o' her kids, her.'

At that, Meg got up and joined Jock in a back-slapping walkabout of the entire restaurant. Everyone was being given the same hearty treatment, and it was only when I noticed money and bits of paper being exchanged that it dawned on me what they were up to. They were cashing in on the widespread feeling of euphoria engendered by the end of Austro-Welsh hostilities to embark on a promotional drive for Jock's forthcoming Burns Night extravaganza.

'Like I say, son, make hay while the sun shines,' Jock advised me, while edging his way past to try his ticket-flogging spiel on Fritz and his *frau*. 'It's the only way to survive on this island, by the way,' he chuckled. 'And, hey, you better believe it!'

Meg, now in characteristic one-woman-Rio-Carnival mood, was conga-dancing along behind him. 'Yeah, strike when the iron's hot,' she giggled, waving her book of Burns Night tickets above her head. 'Opportunity knocks but once, folks' she pronounced, her kaftan of many colours billowing breezily as she glided towards her next victim like a square-rigger in full sail.

Ellie gave me a philosophical look and quietly observed, 'Hmm, and while the proverbs are flying about, you could add that it's an ill wind that doesn't blow *some*body a bit of good.'

– EIGHT –

SOCIAL SNAKES AND LADDERS

Although Col O'Brien's opinion of the 'mind-widening' quality of certain aspects of cosmopolitan Mallorcan life was open to debate, it seemed that her own offspring hadn't been harmed by regular exposure to it. Jock had maintained that they'd all been model students at school, and the same could be said for the way they'd conducted themselves during that memorable lunch date for delinquent grown-ups at the Meson Ca'n Pedro. Perhaps seeing, during their formative years, the older generation making frequent exhibitions of themselves had taught them a lesson on how *not* to behave in public. It was similar, in an obverse kind of way, to Spanish kids being brought up to regard the drinking of wine at the table as perfectly normal, resulting in their ultimate abuse of alcohol being extremely rare, compared, for instance, to certain of their northern European counterparts. We continued to hope that our two boys – impressionable Charlie in particular – would treat with due respect their new-found access to such 'free' social attitudes.

Charlie was certainly making the most of the new friendships he'd formed at school to help him enjoy life in Mallorca to the full. To be fair, though, by no means *all* of such relationships involved the children of rich folk. His chums, representing a fair cross section of the pupils at the Sant Agustí school, came from diverse family backgrounds. Most had parents who had to work hard for a living and, like ourselves, were consequently obliged to look after the pennies much of the time. Inevitably, however, some families that Charlie mixed with did have more monetary resources than others, and a few were able to boast material assets that only the seriously well-off could afford. Although, on balance, Charlie probably spent more of his free time with kids of relatively modest means than he did with those more financially favoured, he made no attempt to hide his liking for the 'better' things in life. There were plenty of those in Mallorca, and never any lack of foreign residents with the wherewithal to enjoy them. And there's no mystery there. 'Dream islands', the world over, do attract the rich.

Where a mystery does occasionally occur, however, is in the murky area of how some of these rich 'settlers' manage to sustain such blatantly lavish lifestyles without any apparent means of earning the money to do so. According to Meg, who knows just about everything about everyone in her patch of Mallorca, most of the super-affluent set, like the O'Briens, were quite open about how their fortunes were won or inherited. Some even liked to brag about it, given half a chance. But there was always the odd character, the archetypical mystery man of Spanish 'expatland', who kept the procurement details of his prodigious stash of pelf very much to himself. One such enigma was a stylish English chap, who, for reasons of discretion, we'll simply call Mr X.

He was in his mid- to late-thirties, athletic-looking and always impeccably turned out, no matter how casual his dress. His son Tim, an only child and a quiet, shy boy, was about a year younger than Charlie, but had established a strong bond with him since first meeting at school. Despite, or maybe because of, the disparate nature of their personalities, Charlie had become something of a big brother figure for Tim. Indeed, if it hadn't been for Charlie's regular out-of-school involvement with others in his wide circle of friends, I'm sure Tim would have had him spending *every* weekend at his house. And what a house it was.

Whilst in no way as outlandishly ostentatious as the O'Briens' Hollywood-style pile, Tim's home could still be counted among the most impressive of the large villas on the Son Vida golfing estate on the north-western fringes of Palma. The list of owners of properties on this most exclusive of the island's urbanisations reads like a page from the who's who of the rich and famous. Not, however, that all are both rich *and* famous. Some, like Mr X, are only rich. He, for one, made no bones about being determined to remain anonymously so, and no-one would deny his entitlement to do just that.

Naturally, though, this cloak of secrecy soon cast a shadow on the integrity of Mr X's character, at least in the eyes of the covetously suspicious – and there are always plenty of those about on an island with such a long social ladder as Mallorca.

'Son o' a multi-millionaire arms dealer,' was Meg's confidential word on the subject. 'Dead illegal, by the way.

Livin' here as an outlet for his old boy's laundered money. Use it or loose it – see what I'm sayin'?'

She'd been made privy to this information 'on the best of authority' by one of her beauty salon clients, who claimed once to have been a close friend of Mr X's parents back in Britain. Meg was quick to point out, however, that she doubted the veracity of this allegation, for the simple reason that its perpetrator had been as skint as a church mouse before winning the UK lottery just a few weeks before moving to Mallorca. Meg, you see, had subsequently heard from another of her clients that, although claiming to have been 'well plugged into' the London society scene in which the X's figured prominently, this woman had actually only been a cook in an all-night transport café. The nearest she'd have got to London society, in Meg's considered opinion, would have been a snog and an alfresco knee-trembler from the occasional Cockney truck driver round the back of the greasy-spoon kitchen where she worked. That chin-waggin' bitch, Meg accordingly deduced, would have known dick about where Mr X's spondulicks came from!

For all that, the rumour that had been started about Mr X Senior's shady involvement in arms dealing soon spread, the way such juicy bits of gossip do, and the scandalous speculation didn't stop there.

'All the kids reckon Tim's dad's a big-time drugs baron,' Charlie told us one afternoon when we picked him up from school. 'Carries a loaded revolver in his car.' Then, in anticipation of our likely rubbishing of this assertion, he promptly tagged on, 'I've seen it! No kidding!'

I shook my head wearily. 'Yeah, yeah, Charlie,' I droned, '– just like you and Dec drive about in a big Mercedes and burn rubber along the *autopista* on a powerful motorbike at weekends. Yeah, yeah, yeah, we all know about your sense of imagination.'

Charlie, for reasons best known to himself, decided to pursue the subject no farther.

We had just waved goodbye to Tim and his mother, who had asked us if we'd allow Charlie to sleep over at their house the following Saturday night. She was an exceptionally pleasant young woman – shy, like Tim, but also with a timid, almost cowed, look to her pretty face. We'd had no hesitation in telling her that we were perfectly happy for Charlie to spend the night with them. He'd already done so on a few occasions, and he'd enjoyed the experience, despite having told us that Tim's home, for all its five-star amenities, had a 'strange' feeling about it. Unlike the happy-go-lucky atmosphere that always pervaded the O'Brien household, the X family's privileged equivalent was, in Charlie's words, a bit like an adult playpen, containing the most costly toys imaginable, but with the fun-making batteries removed. It was all to do with Mr X's sullen disposition, said Charlie. He had lavished every imaginable extravagance on himself, from the flashiest of cars to the most expensive of Swiss watches and handmade Italian shoes. And he did nothing except play golf, swim in the house's huge pool, work out in his private gym, wallow in his jacuzzi and go off occasionally on what he called 'business trips' – alone. Yet, for all his leisure time and self-indulgent ways, he never came across as being happy. He always seemed to have something weighing heavily on his mind, and this down-in-the-dumps feeling permeated every corner of the family home like neglected dust.

Ellie's first, and only, encounter with Mr X was on the following Saturday morning, when he arrived at Ca's Mayoral with Tim to pick up Charlie. Instead of driving into the yard and coming to the door, he chose to park his open-top BMW in the lane, remain seated behind the wheel and sound the horn repeatedly until someone came out. Charlie was first on the scene, cheerfully running over the yard exchanging shouted greetings with his young friend. Bonny the boxer was trotting along behind, and no sooner had Charlie clambered into the back seat of the car than she leapt in beside him. Like most dogs, Bonny loved going for a car ride, and she couldn't resist what she considered to be an open invitation like this one. After all, she didn't even have to wait until someone opened the door for her.

'Get your damned mutt out of my car!' was the angry yell directed at Ellie when she walked round the corner of the house.

Her intention had merely been to introduce herself to Mr X and to say a courteous thanks for inviting Charlie to his house. Instead, she found herself making an embarrassed apology for what had been no more than a family pet's impulsive reaction to what, in her doggy mind, had seemed a friendly situation that she naturally wanted to be part of.

'Filthy brute! Just look at what it's done to my good leather upholstery!' Mr X was clearly in no mood to accept Ellie's olive branch.

Taken aback, Ellie summoned a confused Bonny out of the car, then looked inside to inspect the damage. From the frantic way Mr X was going on about it, she'd expected to see at least some scuffed claw marks, but the only evidence of Bonny having been in the car was a tiny smudge of dry mud on the cream-coloured hide of the back seat. It was such an insignificant blemish that Ellie could have flicked it away with a finger. However, realising that Tim's father was genuinely infuriated, she thought it prudent to ask if he would like her to fetch a damp cloth to wipe the leather clean. To her utter surprise, he not only confirmed that he would indeed like her to do just that, but said that, if she didn't, he'd be sending her a bill for having someone else do it.

Ellie related all of this to me when I drove back into the yard after delivering the day's consignment of oranges to Señor Jeronimo's warehouse.

'You mean to tell me he sat on his arse and let you traipse all the way over the yard to the kitchen and back just to wipe a tiny smudge off his car's back seat?

Ellie nodded her head. She was still looking understandably stunned, and I could tell that she also felt hurt at having been treated with such contempt by someone she was only trying to be polite to.

'The arrogant bastard!' I raged. 'No wonder his wife looks so browbeaten!' I opened the car door again. 'Right – that does it! I'm going straight along to Son Vida to give that spoilt upstart a sharp lesson in manners.' I was really fired up now. 'Yes,' I went on, 'and Charlie will be coming back with me. I don't want any kid of mine exposed to the influence of some pampered bighead who abuses my dog and shows a lack of respect to my wife.'

'In that order?' Ellie asked, a mischievous twinkle in her eyes.

'What?' I barked.

Now, Ellie knows that I'm not easily riled, but she also knows that when something does get my dander up, sparks are liable to fly – and not always with my having given due thought to the possible consequences. A little smile spread over her face. 'What you're saying is that you're more upset by Bonny being insulted than by me being taken for a dogsbody, is that right?'

This was Ellie's way of pouring oil on potentially troubled waters. I realised that, but while I commended her good intentions, I wasn't about to back off that easily from what I saw as a justifiable reason for raising pure hell with this guy. 'Take your pick,' I said. 'Bonny, you – it doesn't matter which of you comes first. Either way, he owes you both an apology, and I'm going to make sure he gives it – prefereably in front of his butler, his housemaids and whatever other domestic drudges he's in the habit of treating like muck. So, come on – get into the car with Bonny. We're going to Son Vida!'

Ellie shook her head. 'And what good would giving a dressing down to Tim's dad do?'

'It'll bring the stuck-up git down to earth, that's what!'

'Hmm, maybe, but *he* may not be the one to come off worse if you do have a barney with him.'

'Don't be daft,' I scoffed. 'Don't tell me you believe all that baloney Charlie gave us about him having a gun.'

'You're missing the point. What I'm saying is that creating a scene in his own house may not be the best way of going about things.'

'And why not? He insulted you on *your* own property, didn't he? Yeah, so he'll only be getting a taste of his own medicine!'

Ellie laid a hand on my arm. 'And who do you think will suffer most if you belittle him in front of his own wife and kid?' Ellie didn't wait for me to reply to that, but instead proceeded to point out that, as Mr X was obviously the bully boy type, the revenge for any embarrassment he was subjected to would almost certainly be taken out on those closest to him. It was the classic way of the coward, and the manner in which this man had treated Ellie and Bonny had made it plain that he slotted firmly into that category.

I had to concede that what Ellie was saying made perfect sense. The red mist was already fading from my eyes. 'Hmm,' I said, 'and there's Charlie's friendship with young Tim to consider, I suppose.'

'That's right. Believe me, Charlie would much rather have jumped out of that car with Bonny this morning. His immediate reaction would have been to give Tim's father a good tongue-lashing for the way he'd treated me, but he was thinking more about Tim's feelings than his own. He could see that the kid was absolutely mortified by his father's performance.'

'And Charlie didn't want to make him feel even worse, right?'

'Precisely. And that says a lot for him.' Ellie closed the car door. 'Come on – let's go inside and have a cup of coffee. You'll get your chance to make your point to Mr X, never fear – but at the right time and in the right place.'

As usual in matters for which a cool head is required, Ellie was absolutely right in everything she'd said. Except in one respect. I never did get that chance to make my point. A few days later, Mr X was found dead in his car, which had careered off an *autopista* near the city of Barcelona over on the Spanish mainland. According to the newspaper report, although the police had no immediate evidence to establish the true cause of the 'accident', foul play wasn't being ruled out. No such evidence has ever been forthcoming, though, so the mystery of the demise of at least one expat mystery man remains unsolved. What was revealed in that initial press report, however, was that a loaded revolver was found in the glove compartment of Mr X's car.

'Maybe,' I remarked to Ellie on reading this, 'just *maybe* we should take Charlie's claims about Dec driving him around in a big Mercedes a bit more seriously in future.'

Ellie pouted pensively, but said nothing.

As Sandy's off-farm activities were pretty much limited to midweek training sessions and a game each Sunday with the local league football team over at La Real, we knew that the height of his social week would normally be nothing more profligate than an after-match beer and a few *tapas* with his teammates in a little bar near the team's ground. Ellie and I had been in it a couple of times after watching him play. The place had a friendly enough atmosphere, but it was essentially a no-frills, small-town Spanish bar – a workaday men's den, in which female visitors are silently eyed up and tolerated, rather than welcomed with spontaneous gestures of chivalry. Sandy was hardly likely to get hooked on a hedonistic lifestyle there, nor was he liable to meet, within its male-chauvanist walls, the *señorita* Ellie forever hoped would become the catalyst that might lead to his long-term commitment to living in Mallorca.

I'd mentioned this to Ellie a few times, but her stock reply was invariably along the lines of: 'Love will find a way, no matter how impossible the odds.' I automatically put this point of view down to the latest overdose of the sugary romances that Ellie read – no, devoured – with all the nail-nibbling fervour of an incurable schmaltz junkie. Barbara Cartland had a lot to answer for.

Imagine my surprise, then, when Sandy arrived back from his football game late one Sunday afternoon with an extremely attractive girl sitting beside him in his little car. She looked more the 'brand-new Ferrari Modena' than the 'second-hand SEAT Panda' type to me. Her flowing raven tresses, immaculate make-up and trendy clothes seemed more representative of a supermodel adorning the bonnet of a shiny new sports car at the Geneva Motor Show than of a likely partner for a struggling fruit farmer's son in a back-of-beyond Mallorcan valley.

But Ellie didn't see it that way. She, Charlie and I had just finished picking Señor Jeronimo's quota for the following morning when Sandy pulled into the yard. After spending a couple of hours clambering up ladders, rummaging about in the foliage of trees and lugging fruit crates about, we were looking typically unkempt and smelling heavily of orange peel – not the most attractive of odours when blended with the sweat of honest toil.

Ellie wiped her sticky hands on her jeans. 'Oo-ooh,' she cooed as she watched the answer to her match-making prayers slink out of the car at the other side of the yard, 'isn't she just *gor*geous!'

'Wow, what a babe!' Charlie gasped. He took an appraising eyeful of his big brother's stunning companion, then concluded, 'Yeah, I reckon there's only one way he could have pulled a looker like that. But...' (He paused to make an even keener inspection) '... I don't see her guide dog.'

'Nonsense,' Ellie scolded, too excited by the prospect of cupid's little arrows darting everywhere to realise that Charlie was only being Charlie, '– your big brother's a *very* attractive young man. A great catch for any girl, I've always said.'

'Or guy,' Charlie muttered.

Ellie's eyes blazed at her younger son. 'I *beg* your pardon!' she warbled.

Charlie knew that he had his mother nicely wound up now, so he gave the handle another crank. 'Well, you have to admit,' he shrugged, 'the local chicks haven't exactly been lining up at the gate for a date with him since we came here, have they? I mean, the only admiring glances I've seen him getting lately have been from Pep's mule.'

Ellie covered her outrage with a sweet smile as she prepared to welcome her unexpected guest. 'That's rubbish, Charlie!' she snapped as an aside. 'And anyway, Pep's mule is a female!'

Sandy got out of his car. 'This is Linda,' he casually informed us across the yard.

'Well, well,' I discreetly commented to Ellie and Charlie, 'a *very* spectacular young lady! Mmm, quite the dark horse, our Sandy is!'

'Which is probably why Pep's mule has the hots for him,' Charlie quipped.

Ellie chose to ignore that one. She nudged me and whispered, 'Linda – that's Spanish for pretty, isn't it? Oh, and she *is!* I bet she's a beauty queen.' She wiped her hands again and stepped forward to welcome the girl I suspected she was already visualising as her future daughter-in-law. '*Hola!* I'm Ellie,' she gushed. 'Ehm, *bien… bin… benveni…* uhm… *bonvendo…*' She let out a nervous laugh. 'Oh dear, I'm sorry – my Spanish – really *terr*ible. What I want to say is welcome to my house – eh, you know, to my *casa*.' Tittering self-consciously, she went on, 'Yes, as you *españolos* say, *mi casa* is, uhm-ah, what is it again? My house is your house, isn't it? *Sí*, that's it – *mi casa es su casa…* or something.'

Linda smiled and said, 'Aw my, that's awful nice. Awful kind, so it is.' Her accent was broad west-of-Scotland, her vowels as long as a Saturday night saunter along Glasgow's Sauchiehall Street. 'Aye, and ye don't need tae apologise about yer Spanish tae me, cos Ah cannae understand a word o' it anyway.'

Unconcerned by her mistaken assumtion of Linda's nationality, Ellie gave her a hug and the customary two-cheeks Spanish kiss of greeting.

Close up, Linda's features appeared not quite so delicate as they had from a distance, her make-up a bit less carefully applied, her clothes more bargain-basement than *haute couture*. But she still looked a lot more chic than the three of us orange-pickers did at that moment. In any case, her friendly disposition immediately negated such superficial considerations – at least as far as Ellie and I were concerned.

'She – I mean Linda – missed her plane back to Scotland,' Sandy somewhat apprehensively informed us.

Charlie immediately chipped in with, 'Well, it's a long swim home!' His offhand attitude indicated that his early admiration of Linda's looks had already disappeared down the fickle plughole of adolescent babe-evaluation.

'They're going to get her on another flight tomorrow,' said Sandy, 'but…' He hunched his shoulders and gave Ellie a decidedly sheepish look.

Ellie tilted her head enquiringly. 'But?' she echoed.

Sandy shuffled his feet. 'Well, ehm, you see, it's just that she's been turfed out of her apartment. Another bunch of holiday punters moving in tonight and all that. You know how it is. So…'

Charlie was revelling in the awkward situation his brother had got himself into. 'So?' he taunted.

'Belt up, Charlie,' Sandy grunted. 'Kids should be seen and not heard.'

Charlie adopted a camp posture, one hand resting on his hip, the other raised and hanging limply by the side of his head. 'Oo-oo-oo-ooh!' he goaded in mock astonishment. 'In one of your masterful moods, are you, big brother?' He winked at Linda. 'He's *really* sexy when he's like that, hmm?'

There was no way for the poor girl to answer that leading question without either appearing forward to Ellie and me or derogatory towards Sandy, so I stepped in by telling Charlie to mind his manners.

To her credit, though, Linda then responded by good-naturedly informing us that she had a younger brother just like Charlie at home, so she was well used to such schoolboy wind-ups and put-downs. She returned Charlie's wink and teased, 'Goin' steady yerself, are ye, wee man? Or are ye open tae offers?'

Charlie tried to dismiss that pawky parry with a shrug and a smirk, but the truth was that he'd been taught a sharp lesson in the delivery of the verbal counter punch, and he knew it. He duly kept his mouth shut. But Ellie was quick to head off any risk of a deterioration in the atmosphere by taking Linda by the arm and shepherding her towards the house.

'Poor thing,' she cooed maternally. 'What a terrible experience – missing your plane like that, and being stranded in a foreign country and everything. Really awful. Never you mind, though – you're welcome to stay here tonight. *More* than welcome, in fact, so don't you worry about it any more.'

Sandy, Charlie and I looked at each other in silence for a few moments after Linda had followed Ellie indoors. Sandy still showed signs of being ill at ease. Charlie was patently delighted about that. I, on the other hand, was more curious than anything else, as this was the first time that Sandy had ever brought a girl home.

'La Real's a bit far flung from the tourist belt,' I eventually said to him, while flashing a mischievous wink at Charlie.

'Certainly is,' he replied, giving nothing away.

'I mean, I'm assuming Linda was here on holiday, right?'

'Correct.'

'At the seaside, right?'

'Right again.'

'Yes, well, I'm not being nosey or anything, but I was wondering how she came to be so far inland at your football match this afternoon?'

'She wasn't at the game.'

'She wasn't?'

'No.'

'So, she was on a bus tour or something and just happened to get off at La Real and wander into that scruffy little bar you go to with your mates after the match. Is that what you're saying?

'No, I'm not saying that at all.'

It was abundantly clear that Sandy wasn't about to be easily pumped, so I decided not to press the matter farther. But no so Charlie.

'I get it,' he grinned after a moment or two of creative thought. 'There's a dog sanctuary near La Real, as I remember. So the lovely Linda was chucked in there after being captured running loose on El Arenal beach with the rest of the strays. Yeah, then you saw her in the pound on your way past, felt sorry for her, had a word with the dog warden and –'

'Shut it, Charlie,' Sandy snarled.

'It's not that I want to pry, Sandy,' I said, my curiosity getting the better of me again, 'because it's really none of my business. But it's just that, well, your mother sort of hoped you might meet a Spanish girl through your football, and –'

'OK, OK,' Sandy cut in, his initial reticence now veering rapidly towards irritation, 'I met her in Sinky's Glasgow bar in Magalluf, if you must know!'

Charlie and I looked at each other. 'Magalluf?' we gasped in unison.

'But surely Magalluf's a bit out of your way when you're driving from La Real to Andratx,' I suggested.

'Maybe,' Sandy said, 'but you get highlights of the top Scottish football games on big-screen telly in Sinky's on Sundays, so I occasionally make the detour for that. Anyway, Sinky's bar is a kind of home-from-home for Glasgow holidaymakers, and that's where they go if they need any info on the local scene.'

'Like what to do if they've missed their plane home?' I ventured.

'That's it,' Sandy confirmed. 'I saw Linda in there and I overheard her asking Sinky if he knew where she could find a room for tonight, as she was flat broke. The rest, as they say, is history.'

'Ah well, that would explain the physical attraction,' Charlie piped up. 'Sinky's place is well known for its dim lighting. You could mistake Quasimodo for Sharon Stone in there, they say.'

If looks could kill, the one that Sandy fired at Charlie then would have seen him transported straight to the morgue.

Now it was my turn to pour oil on potentially troubled waters. 'Pay no attention to Charlie,' I said. 'The main thing is that Linda seems a really nice girl, and your mother's obviously taken a shine to her. Spanish or Scottish, English, Irish or Chinese – it really doesn't matter to her.'

Sandy shook his head, his impatience rising. 'Listen, Dad, I know what Mum's game is, but she may as well forget about all that lovey-dovey bollocks. The girl needed a roof over her head for tonight, that's all. There's nothing more to it, OK?'

I gave him a paternal pat on the shoulder. 'Yeah, I know that. But, well, put it this way – it was nice of you to offer her a bed.' I tried to cover Charlie's smutty snigger by swiftly adding, 'What I'm saying is, you can't tell when you might be in a similar situation yourself, so you should never hesitate to help a lame dog over a stile.'

'Absolutely,' Charlie agreed. 'And in this case, with the emphasis on the word dog. I mean, Mum said Linda looked like a beauty queen, but if that one ever wins a contest, I reckon it'll be at Crufts!'

I could see that Sandy was about to have Charlie by the throat, so I rapidly put up a verbal barrier between them. 'Right, Charlie, that'll be enough dog gags for today, thank you very much! And, Sandy, I think you should go into the house and help your mother make Linda feel at home. She's your guest, after all. In the meantime, Charlie, you can give me a hand to finish stacking these crates of oranges here.'

If Ellie harboured any notions that there might still have been romantic reasons for Sandy having brought Linda home to Ca's Mayoral, they *should* have been well and truly dispelled at dinner in the kitchen that evening. Neither of the two young people paid any heed to the other, apart from little courtesies like passing the salt. In fact, if it hadn't been for Linda's gregarious dispositon (a well-known attribute of the good folks of Glasgow), the atmosphere at the table could have become laboured in the extreme. But she never let the conversation flag, and soon proved herself to be a really entertaining character. Even Charlie was eventually won over by her bubbly nature and have-fun-while-you-can outlook on life. They were on the same wavelength in that respect, and ended up getting along famously.

'Cool chick,' Charlie discreetly told me before he went to bed. 'I like her style. Definitely one of the boys.'

But Linda being even a metaphorical boy clearly wasn't what was on Ellie's mind when I half opened my eyes during the night to see her lying wide awake beside me. Ellie seemed preoccupied, as if listening intently for something. That 'something', I surmised, would have been the sound of doors opening and closing between Sandy's room and the guest bedroom where Linda was billeted. The customary rasp of snoring echoing along the corridor from Sandy's room should have been sufficient to reassure her that no such moonlight liaison was likely to happen, however.

'Forget it, Ellie,' I muttered. 'Barbara Cartland didn't write the plot for this one, so go to sleep, for God's sake!'

My reading of the situation was validated the following morning. When we went downstairs, there was a note on the kitchen table from Sandy to say that he'd gone off to do some ploughing for Pep on the farm of one of his old *compesino* friends further up the valley. Would we, the message asked, please drive Linda to the airport?

'Well, Ellie,' I said, mustering as much enthusiasm for things as I could, 'at least he was showing more kindness than self-interest when he invited her here.'

'Mm-hmm,' Ellie stoically sighed, 'just as Charlie did when thinking more about young Tim's feelings than his own when his father insulted Bonny and me.'

'A very commendable trait,' I willingly acknowledged, while offering up a silent prayer to the gods of selflessness that they wouldn't subject us to the presence of any more pistol-packing big heads or free-bed-seeking strays in future.

Yet, for all of Charlie's gibes about his big brother's main source of amorous interest coming from mules and dogs (of either sex!), it wasn't to be too long before Glasgow Linda made sure her path crossed with Sandy's again. And the outcome would prove to be even less Barbara Cartland-like than that of their first encounter.

Tim and his mother, meanwhile, were to move out of their Son Vida mansion and quietly disappear from Mallorca forever, taking with them the mystery that had surrounded them for so long. Consequently, it was open season again for the expat chinwags to select the next target for their idle tittle-tattle.

– NINE –

DREAM DEALS ON ELM STREEET

Such social shenagigans wouldn't have played any part in the down-to-earth life of little Groucho, the Gomez construction company's 'small digger', of that I was sure. And down-to-earth is literally how it was, at least in the part of his life that concerned us. In a few short weeks, he had single-handedly excavated the gaping, eight-by-four-metres hole in the ground that would eventually be transformed into our swimming pool. On the day that he heaved his last bucketful of subsoil onto the perimeter heap, I took him one final glass of *coñac* to mark the occasion. His boss, Pablo Gomez, had also turned up on site, both to ensure that Groucho's part of the work had been completed to his satisfaction, and then, without ceremony or undue delay, to see the little fellow off to his next job. Time, in Pablo's book, was most certainly money.

'*Perfecto!*' he grinned, when looking down into the neatly excavated void. He confirmed his obvious delight by informing me that Groucho's was the biggest one-man hole he had ever seen. This observation was followed by a bawdy chortle, which even the normally-doleful Groucho allowed himself to accompany with a faint smile and a droll grunt. Little did we know, however, just how that off-the-cuff wisecrack would eventually come back to hurt Pablo where it hurt most – in his wallet. For the moment, though, my only thought was one of gratitude that this first phase of the undertaking had been completed, and on time, at that.

'*Gracias*, Groucho,' I said. 'And feel free to come by and help yourself to some oranges and snails any time you want.'

'*Usted es muy amable*,' Groucho replied with a characteristic little dip of his head. I was very kind, he said, and assured me that he would certainly take me up on my generous offer.

He never did, though, and I wasn't really surprised. I'd come to know Groucho as a proud man, and while he didn't mind receiving token handouts when they were linked directly to his work, he'd have seen it as demeaning to take anything outside of that without paying for it. This, for Groucho, would have been tantamount to accepting charity, and his self-respect, no matter how humble his station in life, was too great to allow him to entertain the thought. To me, that little fellow was worth more as a human being than all the pompous, self-indulgent Mr Xs in Mallorca put together. And there were more than enough of them on the island, although not, fortunately, in the Sa Coma valley. Their prodigal ways would have been given short shrift by the likes of old Maria and Pep, I'm certain.

Mind you, the thought was still nagging at my conscience that, from their point of view, I may well have been entering into that very category myself. That said, by no stretch of the imagination could it be perceived that our improvement work on the farmhouse at Ca's Mayoral was transforming it into an O'Brien-style Hollywood palace. Far from it. But it *was* lifting it out of the purely-practical, bare-essentials mould that exemplifies the typical house on a small, working Mallorcan farm. Deep down, and despite what Bernat the young water-truck driver had said to convince me of the contrary, I still felt that I was turning into something of a turncoat within the simply-living little community into which we had now been accepted.

Not that our creating of the barbecue area had been done at any cost to the agricultural integrity of the farm. We'd purposely designed it in a way that didn't interfere with the tending or harvesting of the little grove of almond trees that lay between the house and the ancient wall at the foot of which the actual barbecue 'grill' was located. Accordingly, the access pathways were laid out to compliment the stand of trees in the form of flagstone ribbons winding their way between. We'd chosen the spot for the crazy-paved dining area with equal care. Furnished with a big, rustic table and matching wooden benches, it was situated in a tiny clearing where the overhanging almond branches afforded it some dappled shade in daytime, and from where at night we could best see the effects of the concealed lighting we'd installed to gently illuminate the trees and the face of that rugged old wall.

So, while managing to protect the output of that small corner of the farm, I believe we'd also added considerably to its charm. The pleasure we derived from completing that particular project was all the greater for having done the work ourselves, and for a minimum of outlay on materials. And even if it wasn't a task that old-timers like Pep and Maria would have bothered undertaking, times and people's fancies change, and our new barbecue area was merely an illustration of one example of that. I really shouldn't have been feeling guilty about it at all. But I was – just a little.

Converting the big *almacén* workroom/store that occupied much of the ground floor of the house into a games room was also something that I feared many an old Mallorcan farmer would have frowned upon. Traditionally, the *almacén* was the heart of a Mallorcan country household during working hours. It's where the produce of the farm was brought to be sorted and stored or prepared for sale; it's where hand tools and other items of agricultural paraphernalia were kept and maintained; it's the laundry where the woman of the house would scrub and wring the family's washing; it's a pantry in which she'd keep her home-made sausages and preserved fruit; and it's even where, in many cases, the donkey or mule would be stabled. It might even be a milking parlour for the farm's goats.

The thing was, though, that we'd never used the *almacén* for any of those purposes. Our system of marketing the fruit by selling most of it 'direct-from-the-trees' to a wholesaler, instead of at the farm gate or from a stall at the Andratx market on Wednesdays in the way that Francisca Ferrer's forebears had done, meant that we didn't need the *almacén* for storage. Having the tractor meant (thankfully!) that we had no need for a donkey or mule. Neither did we possess, nor intend to possess, any goats. Although, in common with our Mallorcan neighbours in the valley, we were hands-on small farmers, our own practical experience before coming to the island had allowed us to leapfrog their age group's natural inclination to be self-suffient to the extent of producing their own eggs, meat and milk. We had become, to a large extent and for better or for worse, members of the get-it-from-the-supermarket generation.

Subsistence farming, purely for the sake of compliance with those old island practices, had never been our intention. We weren't aiming to be refugees from reality, but rather to make a decent living for ourselves while balancing, we hoped, the up-to-date methods we were accustomed to with due regard for the time-honoured ways so highly valued by older Mallorcans. For example, Ellie's automatic washing machine, though much decried by Pep as a water-waster, wasn't about to be replaced by the antiquated, washboard-pummeling facilities that he claimed to favour.

All in all, then, the *almacén* was simply surplus to our particular requirements, both agricultural and domestic. This fact, however, still didn't stop me from feeling that we'd be judged by our elderly neighbours to have shown scant respect for centuries of Mallorcan country life by turning the hub of the house's workaday past into a place of relaxation and amusement. To complicate matters, our decision to retain as wall decorations relics of bygone times, like various items of donkey harness, three-pronged wooden pitchforks, a gap-toothed crosscut saw, leaky fireside bellows, as well as less wholesome things like rusty rat traps and pig-castrating 'pliers', seemed to lend more tweeness to the atmosphere than an authentic echo of what the *almacén* had once been.

That, anyway, was my own initial feeling. But Ellie and the boys begged to differ. Their unanimous verdict was that, if *we* weren't going to use the *almacén* as a workplace or storage area any more, there would be precious little chance of anyone else doing so in the future. At least we'd left the room intact and had been sensitive enough to put on display a few mementos of days that would never return. This, surely, was a lot more respectful than a tinselly conversion of the type that the O'Briens, for instance, might have chosen.

To further convince me (as well as encourage me to get on with the work), Ellie added that, once I'd built the planned bar in the corner, only the most glum spirits of Ca's Mayoral's past would fail to approve of what we'd done to an indoor area that many of them might well have seen as a haven of pure drudgery at times. Contrary to what old Maria always advocated, not everything about the 'old days' was worth leaving unchanged. Ellie gave me a wry smile and said that my own refusal to work with a donkey had underlined that, so why should I get all sentimental about an inanimate thing like a redundant *almacén*?

A good question, and one for which I had no logical answer. I readily admitted this.

'Right,' she replied, 'so get your sleeves rolled up and set about building that bar before the hot weather returns and another bout of your hard-won *mañana*ness kicks in!' Ellie has a highly individualistic approach to man-management. But it's usually extremely effective, at least when applied to her own man. 'In my book,' she stated in a way that indicated no fear of contradiction, '*mañana* was yesterday's tomorrow, *not* today's! OK?'

I dutifully rolled up my sleeves.

The discarded *persianas* (louvred wooden shutters), which I'd salvaged from outside the workshop of Juan Juan the *carpintero* in Andratx, were to form the basis of the bar front. I'd wondered at the time just why the ever-thrifty Juan Juan had decided to dump these particular examples. They'd seemed in surprisingly good condition to me when I loaded them into the back of the car. Here was a real stroke of luck, I'd thought. *Persianas* from heaven, even. Only when I started to strip off their onion-like layers of paint did I realise why Juan Juan had been so ready to let me have them for nothing. It now struck me that he'd probably thought I was moonlighting for the municipal refuse-collection department. The paint was virtually all that was holding them together. Worse than that, those many coats of green and brown had been concealing a massive infestation of woodworm. Maybe their widespread presence in Mallorca has something to do with the warm, often-humid atmospheric conditions of the island. Whatever the reason, those voracious little blighters are the scourge of Mallorcan timberwork, and if you once allow them a tooth-hold in your house, look out. Eventually, they'll be burrowing into everything from your ceiling beams to your floor boards and even your toilet seat.

However, once I'd treated the *persianas* thoroughly with the recommended bug-killer, I was confident enough that this particular colony of wood-devouring parasites had been snuffed out. Then, following the liberal use of glue and and some discerning restoration work with plastic wood, it seemed that the old shutters *might* just pass muster. Indeed, after a final sanding down, they were starting to look not too bad at all. An application of dark beeswax gave the wood the desired mellow look, and even the peppering of those dreaded woodworm holes added to the 'distressed' effect that manufacturers of expensive reproduction furniture go to great lengths to fake. I was pleased with the results of my labours, even if there had been times during the recycling process when I'd been solely tempted to smash the whole caboodle into smithereens.

'He conquers who endures,' said Ellie, casting an approving eye over my handiwork. 'Yes, now all you have to do is put everything together.'

Amazing, I thought, how exasperatingly simplistic Ellie could be at times like this.

'You're about as perceptive as the three blind mice,' I bristled. 'You've no grasp of the amount of work that's involved in practical things, that's your trouble, Ellie. Tell me, is that a gift of nature, or do you get up early and practice?'

It had been a long, boring and often finicky process transforming several items of potential firewood into something worthy of gracing the front of the bar, and I knew that this was only the start of what would be an even more testing series of challenges for me.

'I'm not a professional bloody bar-fitter, Ellie! I mean, building one from scratch isn't as easy as just "putting everything together", you know!'

Ellie's response was that you never know what you can do until you try. She pointed to the plan for the bar that I'd drawn up and pinned to the wall in the appointed corner of the *almacén*, reminding me that I'd said at the outset – somewhat cockily, in her opinion – that the key to success is in the preparation. She then indicated the neat stack of new timber, already dressed and cut to size, that I'd bought from Juan Juan for making the framework of the bar.

'Plan,' she said, pointing to my sketch again. 'Wood,' she said, gesturing towards the pile of timber. 'Plan – wood – wood – plan.' Her pointing finger was rocking back and forth like the pendulum on a metronome. 'Plan – wood – wood – plan,' she reiterated. 'All meticulously prepared. So go to it and put it all together!'

Ellie sensed, of course, that my tetchiness hadn't been generated, on this occasion, by an attack of *mañana*ness, but rather by a lack of confidence in my own ability to satisfactorily complete something that I'd earlier suggested I could do with ease. This flush of hubris had been brought on by the eupohoria that swept over me the day the boys and I first sweet-talked Ellie into agreeing to our turning the *almacén* into a games room. However, the time had now come for me to put my bar-building expertise where my mouth was, and Ellie knew how to goad me into doing just that.

'Mind you,' she said, poker-faced, 'if you think you're not up to the job, I can quite easily ask Juan Juan to do it for you. Admittedly,' she shrugged, 'it'll cost, and it'll mean you going back on your promise that you'd do all the work yourself. But, hey,' she sweetly smiled, 'we all have to face up to our limitations eventually, so don't feel too bad about it, hmm.'

Grimacing, I rolled up my sleeves again.

Outside, in the meantime, work on the pool was going ahead swimmingly. Pablo Gomez had replaced his 'small digger' with another solo performer, this one a tall, swarthy and sinewy Andalusian, whose distinctly Moorish appearance prompted us to give him the nickname of Abdul. If anything, he was a man of even fewer words than Groucho. He obviously knew what he had to do, and his only concern appeared to be to get on with it without indulging in irrelevant chitchat. To my surprise, he wasn't even interested in my offer of an early-morning *coñac* to get his metabolism going.

Abdul's first task was to create a huge 'basket' of steel reinforcing rods to fit exactly within the walls and over the sloping floor of the pool. This really was a painstaking job of epic proportions, as he had to cut and bend every single rod by hand. Then, each intersection of every one of the hundreds of criss-crossing lengths of metal had to be securely tied with wire. And it was starting to get very hot when the midday sun was beating down into that yawning hole in the ground. Day after day, Abdul worked on with only the briefest of pauses to slake his thirst. What he was taking in his stride without a murmur of complaint made my bar-building efforts in the relative cool of the *almacén* seem pretty puny in comparison, both in terms of scale and in the level of skill required.

One of the most intriguing aspects of his method of weaving that metal latticework was that he seemed to judge all the measurements by eye. He trusted that the dimensions of Groucho's excavation were exactly right, which was all very well, except that I'd never seen Groucho using a measuring tape, or spirit level either. And it wasn't as though it was simply a matter of Abdul making a big rectangular cage, for the bottom of the pool had been dug in a way that it emulated the configuration of a stretched letter 'S', sweeping down in two gentle curves from the shallow to the deep end. I wouldn't have been surprised to see some sort of laser contraption being used to check the contours and calibrations. But the skills that Groucho and Abdul possessed clearly pre-dated such high-tech gadgetry by centuries, and rendered it, as far as they were concerned, superfluous. More importantly, the fastidious Pablo Gomez was obviously happy with this method of going about things, and who was I to question his judgement? It all looked fine to me, excellent progress was being made, and I was more than happy to let the experts carry on with the work in whatever way they saw fit. I had enough to occupy my thoughts for the moment...

'Very attractive,' said Ellie on the morning I was fixing the assembled base of the bar to the floor of the *almacén*. 'See – I said you could do it.' Still looking closely at my 'creation', she folded her arms, put a finger to her cheek and nodded approvingly. 'Yes, and it fits in perfectly with all the old farming bits and pieces round the walls.'

I stood back and took a good look for myself. I had to agree that Ellie wasn't wrong in what she'd said, although I couldn't help wondering if she was merely humouring me.

For my own part, only modesty prevented me from saying that I reckoned a darned fine job had been made of building the bar. Well, it *almost* prevented me, but I said it anyway. Yet, deep down, I felt there was still something missing; still that little touch that would make it into a *proper* bar.

'Mmm, it's all right,' I said after a few moments of silent deliberation, 'but it looks a bit – I don't know – a bit bleak.'

'How do you mean?'

'Well, a bar needs to be cosy-looking – welcoming. OK, the old shutters have turned out nice and rustic and everything, but it's all a bit bare-looking. It could be the counter in a newspaper shop, or the baker's – anywhere like that, but –'

'Yes, I see what you mean now,' Ellie interjected. She stroked her cheek, looking carefully at the bar and thinking. 'Hmm, maybe it'll be better when you put some shelves up for bottles and things on the wall behind. You know – a sort of gantry, with an old mirror and a couple of tankards and all the usual pub-type clutter.'

Ignoring the 'clutter' crack, I said, 'Yeah, I already had that in mind. And I can visualise it. But no…' I shook my head. 'Nope, it needs something else as well.'

All of a sudden, Ellie pointed her cheek-stroking finger at the bar. 'Lights!' she exclaimed with near-eureka excitement. 'You could put concealed lights under the overhang of the counter thingy there. Diffused ones – amber coloured, maybe – glowing down over the louvres of the old *persianas* – just sort of highlighting them. *That*'d look really warm and welcoming!'

I'd already thought of that too. But, not wanting to dampen Ellie's enthusiasm, I told her it was a great idea and said I'd definitely get round to doing it. I was still far from satisfied that we'd found that elusive 'something' I was looking for, though.

Ellie caught my mood without my having said a word. 'Well,' she sighed, 'if *you* can't put your finger on what's missing, what chance have *I* got? You've doubtless been in more pubs than I've had hot dinners, so you'll just have to fathom it out for yourself.' She wandered over to the window and gazed out, a faraway look in her eyes. 'What a glorious, sunny morning,' she murmured. Then the sound of bits of metal clanking together attracted her attention. 'Poor Abdul,' she said, 'toiling away in that hole in the ground. Must be like a cauldron in there.'

'Yeah,' I agreed, 'I take my hat off to him. Only a bloke whose forefathers spent their lives herding camels in the desert could work for hour upon hour in those conditions.'

Ellie nodded her head absentmindedly. 'Hmm, that's as may be, but I still feel like taking a parasol out to him.'

'That's it!' I beamed. '*That's* what we need to add the final touch to the bar!'

Ellie spun round and looked at me as if I'd taken leave of my senses. 'A *para*sol?' she frowned. 'You want to turn it into a *beach* bar now?'

'Nah, nah, nah,' I laughed, 'you've got it all wrong. I don't mean an actual umbrella type of parasol. No, no, I'm talking about a canopy.'

Ellie's frown deepened. 'You mean one of those stripy sheets they wind out over shop windows to keep the sun off?'

I gave a little chuckle. 'It's called an awning, I think.'

I was about to go on, but Ellie cut me off by shaking her head and tutting loudly. 'No, no, no,' she objected, 'that would look totally silly – completely out of place! If that's what you've got in mind, you might just as well pitch one of those trendy canvas gazebo thingies round your little bar, for all a shop-window sunshade would do for the rustic look you're going for!'

I tutted this time, even more loudly than Ellie had done. I had a feeling that, for all her back-patting and idea-floating, she wasn't taking this seriously enough. 'You're always too quick to jump to conclusions,' I retorted, '*that's* your trouble, Ellie!'

'Only trying to help,' she pouted with a 'suit yourself' shrug.

'Yes, well, If you'd let me finish, what I was about to say was that what's needed is a canopy made out of that brushwood stuff you get here.'

Ellie looked at me blankly.

I tutted again, even more impatiently now. 'You know the stuff – it comes in rolls, about a metre wide. It's brown. It looks like long, spindly twigs of broom, all matted together.'

Ellie's vague expression morphed into a smile of enlightenment as the penny finally dropped. 'Ah-h-h-h, *now* I know what you're on about. They use it to make screens above garden walls and things, don't they? Sort of thatch-type fencing, right?'

I gave her an exaggeratedly patronising smile. 'She's got it! By George, she's got it! And I couldn't have put it better myself. The canopy will look *just* like a thatched roof above the bar.'

I could see Ellie trying to picture all of this in her mind's eye, and judging by the little smile that started to tug at the corner of her lips, it appeared that the image appealed to her. That, however, didn't prevent her from getting a little dig in about the same 'thatch-thingy-stuff' being used to make umbrella-type parasols on Spanish beaches. I allowed her that one without comment.

She took a deep breath and, for the first time since the games room idea was mooted, she cast what seemed like a genuinely interested eye round the old *almacén*. She stroked her chin and pouted again – this time pensively. 'So,' she said, still slowly surveying the empty room, 'apart from a snooker table and the bar, what exactly *did* the boys and you have in mind for kitting out this big playpen of yours?'

I could hardly contain my delight; so much so that I couldn't think of a worthwhile answer. I'd always hoped that Ellie might lend some of her flair for interior design to the refurbishment of the former workroom-cum-store. She'd already applied her decorative talents to the rest of the house, and to great effect. I'd assumed, though, that her interest in such things wouldn't stretch to getting too involved in 'tarting up' what she doubtless saw as essentially a lads' den. And to her credit, she'd already mucked in with the boys and me on the tedious task of restoring and painting the cracked and flaking plasterwork, which was now looking as good as new. But for all that, if the converted *almacén* was to join the barbecue area and swimming pool as a value-enhancing asset of the property, it needed more than pristine white walls decorated with a scattering of souvenirs from the farm's working past. And, no matter how reluctant I may once have been to admit it, it needed more than a cosy-looking, welcoming bar in the corner. What it needed was a woman's touch, and I said so.

'Let's get into the car,' said Ellie, inspired and enthused. 'We're going to Palma!'

As with so many of the handy contacts we'd made on the island, it had been Jock Burns who'd first tipped us off about Galerías de Mueble. Situated half way up the Carrer de Oms ('Elm Street'), a busy shopping thoroughfare that runs from the top of the Passeig de la Rambla to the Plaça d'Espanya, this smart furniture store is where we'd bought some of the larger items for the house when we first moved in.

In line with a fairly common Mallorcan practice, we'd actually bought the property 'furnished' from the previous owners, the wily Francisca and Tomàs Ferrer. At any rate, that's what we *thought* we'd done. What we certainly hadn't done when signing the original contract of purchase, however, was to include an inventory of the furniture that was in the house on the day we'd agreed to buy it. We took for granted that what had been there then would still be there when we eventually arrived from Scotland to take possession of the place a few months later. Wrong assumption. Very wrong.

The Ferrers had emptied the house of everything of any worth and had left us with only the barest of essentials. Despite those things being (to put it politely) well past their use-by date, the Ferrers *had* complied with the term 'furnished', in law if not in spirit, and our gullibility had left us with no option other than to go and buy replacements. In our naivety, we had sold for a pittance, or had given away, all of the bulkier items of our own furniture before leaving Scotland. Under the circumstances, we'd decided that paying to have them transported all the way to Mallorca wouldn't have made sense. It had been an expensive mistake, but one which would have proved even more so had it not been for Jock and his introduction to Miguel, the accommodating young manager of Galerías de Mueble.

Miguel helped put an end to our furnishing nightmare. But it wasn't from the impressive array of furniture on display in his glitzy 'Elm Street' showroom that he provided what was needed. Those articles would have been both beyond our budget and much too modern for an old farmhouse. Astute man as he was, Miguel was quick to recognise our particular requirements and, thanks to our mutual friendship with Jock, he took us along the street a little way and led us into a warehouse which stored unsold stock that had become too outmoded for the floor of his trendy shop. We assumed that this was furniture destined be sold off 'to the trade', perhaps ending up in more modest retail establishments well away from the city centre. Nevertheless, Miguel told us, it was all brand new, top quality merchandise and, if we found anything there that we liked, he would happily sell it to us at a generous discount. We gratefully accepted his offer and purchased everything we needed.

At that time, we had been looking for major items, like lounge, dining room and bedroom furniture, so I hadn't paid much attention to what else was stored in Miguel's warehouse. But Ellie had.

'There are loads of things tucked away in there that'll do just fine for your games room,' she assured me as we drove into the underground car park in a nearby square.

Sure enough, an hour later, we emerged from Miguel's warehouse into the Carrer de Oms with broad grins on our faces. I also had a receipt for a long list of purchases in my pocket. The warehouse had yielded up a wonderful selection of everything from easy chairs and table lamps to wicker-seated bar stools and framed prints of pastoral Spanish scenes from yesteryear. The style of all these items had become a tad *pasado* for the owners of swanky apartments on the likes of Palma's seafront Paseo Marítimo, but would be just fine, as Ellie had predicted, for a 'tarted-up' old *almacén* away out in the sticks.

Miguel, clearly keen to grab the chance of unloading a batch of stuff that might otherwise be difficult to sell, had marked his prices down to rock bottom for us. Consequently, we'd left him in a spirit of communal self-satisfaction. We hadn't walked far, though, before I started experiencing once again those familiar old worries about the fragile state of our bank balance. I felt a bout of post-shopping depression coming on.

'Fair as Miguel's prices were,' I said, 'we've still spent quite a bit of money we hadn't bargained for. I'm not sure we can really afford it, you know.'

Ellie gave me a playful push. 'Don't be such a worry guts! We couldn't afford *not* to spend money on these bits and pieces. They'll turn the *almacén* into a really attractive room. And that, don't forget, is the object of the exercise. Adding value to the property, remember?'

'Hmm,' I droned, 'I suppose so.'

'Oh, lighten up, for goodness sake! We agreed that it's high time we started enjoying life at Ca's Mayoral a bit more, and that's another good reason for making your games room as nice as possible. Besides, we'll have great fun doing it up, you'll see!' However, no matter how convinced she was herself, Ellie could tell that I was still having qualms. She gave me another shove. 'Come on,' she laughed, 'you'd better treat me to one last lunch before we go comp*lete*ly to the wall!'

The Celler Sa Premsa restaurant is situated at the corner of the Plaça Bisbe Berenguer de Palou, the square where we'd parked the car. I couldn't tell whether Ellie had planned all along that we'd round off our purchasing trip in Sa Premsa that day, but I wouldn't have been surprised if she had. I recalled her mentioning that she'd been there a couple of times with Meg Burns after shopping sorties in this area, so she knew what to expect.

As soon as you push open Sa Premsa's heavy wooden doors, you're struck by the sheer size of the place. At first glance, you'd be forgiven for thinking you'd wandered into a German *bier keller*, but once your eyes have adjusted to the subdued lighting, you're left in no doubt about the nationality of this popular Palma eatery.

An ancient grape press, the actual *premsa* from which the establishment takes its name, enjoys pride of place in the centre of the floor, while the circular ends of huge wine butts protrude from smoke-stained walls hung with posters depicting bullfight attractions of bygone times. The place fairly oozed the very atmosphere that I'd have loved to emulate for our converted *almacén*. I had a hunch that this was why Ellie had plotted our visit, albeit that to replicate this interior (even on a decidedly smaller scale) would be an impossible task.

Here, the generous height of the beamed ceiling, together with the paved floor and rows of bare wooden tables and chairs, amplifies the noisy chatter and clatter that reverberates around every busy Spanish eating place at mealtimes. And it quickly becomes apparent why this particular eating place is one of *the* busiest in Palma. The bill of fare is more wholesome than fancy, and it's aimed primarily at local tastes. In Sa Premsa, you get a selection of the island's favourite dishes, unfussily prepared in an open kitchen, where the incessant activity of the chefs and a shuttle service of scurrying waiters reflects the popularity of what's on offer. This is typical Mallorcan country food, expertly though unpretentiously presented right in the heart of the capital city, *and* at out-of-town prices at that.

I could happily just have sat there, soaking up the ambience, without eating anything at all. Or so I thought at first. But the tempting smells wafting out of that open kitchen ensure that such undesirable self-restraint isn't likely to remain on the Sa Premsa menu for long. Accordingly, I was surprised that Ellie elected to forgo her customary rabbit or squid, or, for that matter, any other of the multitude of scrumptious meat and seafood dishes that are on the menu. Perhaps it was to pander to my sudden attack of thriftiness a few minutes earlier that she decided instead to share with me a *greixonera* of *Sopes Mallorquinas*, one of the simplest, most economical, yet surprisingly appetising of the island's peasant dishes.

This isn't, as the name might suggest, a soup at all, but (at least in its original form) rather a substantial fusion of ingredients so thick that, when 'rested' for a while after cooking, it can be cut into wedges like a pie. Nowadays, however, most restaurants, including Sa Premsa, tend to serve *Sopes Mallorquinas* in a more moist state. *Sopes* (pronounced 'so-pays') are, in fact, the thin slices of brown country bread that form the basis of the recipe, for which it's said there are as many variations as there are Mallorcan grannies. That aside, the universally accepted method of preparation involves lining the bottom of a *greixonera* (a flat-bottomed, earthenware casserole dish) with the *sopes*, which are then submerged in a savoury broth that includes an abundance of sliced cabbage. Depending on what else happens to be available, or on which particular granny's recipe is being followed, a sprinkling of easily-available vegetables, like onions, garlic, leeks and tomatoes, may also be added to the stock. But whatever else does or doesn't go in, bread and cabbage are *the* essential components of *Sopes Mallorquinas*. The only other prerequisite is that all the cooking liquid must be absorbed by the bread before the dish is served.

Mind you, it has to be said that, no matter how flattering a description is attempted, even the most fervent fan of *Sopes Mallorquinas* would be obliged to concede that it still sounds a pretty dull concoction. It isn't, though. Like that other super-simple Mallorcan delicacy, *Pa amb Oli* (in its basic form, nothing more than a slice of crusty bread drizzled with olive oil), *Sopes Mallorquinas* is, I believe, a masterpiece of the island's country cuisine.

First impressions of the interior of a restaurant can be deceptive – especially a restaurant as barn-like as the Celler Sa Premsa. Now that I had time to take it all in properly, I realised that there was a lot more to the décor than the instantly-noticeable things like big wine butts, old posters, exposed beams, bulky wooden furniture and an ancient grape press. There were some delightful little details as well.

For example, a row of miniature wooden barrels was perched in a prominent position on the bar. Their signs indicated that they contained *hierbas*, the green, herb-infused liqueur that is synonymous with Mallorca – and with thundering hangovers, if you don't treat it with great respect. It was a novelty not to see the *hierbas* displayed in the usual decorative glass bottles, in which the eponymous sprigs of herbs can be seen suspended. Like those bottles, however, each barrel was clearly marked *secas* or *dulces* – sweet or dry. As the former is considered too cloying by some afficionados, and the latter too sharp by those with a sweeter tooth, many find the best way of drinking *hierbas* is by mixing the two varieties in fifty-fifty parts, or *mig-i-mig* ('meech-ee-meech') as they say in Mallorca. It's great fun deciding which of the three choices suits your own taste buds best, but beware that dreaded *hierbas*-induced hangover at all costs. With that in mind, I had a hunch that prudence (born of bitter experience) would prompt me to display only one *mig-i-mig* bottle of the stuff among the 'clutter' in my own little bar, no matter how much I liked the look of that row of dinky barrels and the notion of bulk *hierbas* on tap.

Just as I was mulling this over, a high-pitched 'ching-ching-ching' ventured timidly through the lunchtime clamour in Sa Premsa. It sounded like the chimes of one of those dainty carriage clocks that adorn the mantleshelves above many a neat suburban fireplace. On checking my watch, I noted that it *was* three o'clock, so the chances were that the three 'chings' had actually been produced by a timepiece of some sort.

Ellie noticed me looking around for it. She gestured towards the wall behind me, where I was surprised to see a handsome grandfather clock standing semi-obscured in the shadows. It was tall, dignified and aloof. Within its plain but beautifully-proportioned mahogany case, a great pendulum, shaped like a long brass teardrop swung in languorous silence amid the surrounding babble. It seemed unbelievable that such a stalwart object as this could have chimed with so puny a voice. But that didn't diminish my admiration for it by one iota. I'd have given a marvellous clock like this centre stage in our refurbished *almacén* anytime.

Ellie was reading my thoughts. 'Forget it,' she said. 'We can't afford it.'

I was obliged to agree with her, so I could only busy my mind with thoughts of how to borrow a few of the other features of the Celler Sa Premsa for 'tarting up' that evolving games room of ours. Difficult. For a start, those huge wine butts, undeniably attractive as they were as wall embellishments here, would have looked out of place in a more modest space, even if there had been a cost-effective way of reproducing just one of them accurately – which I knew there wasn't. A gentle tap on my shoulder jolted me out of my deliberations.

It was Carmen, an amiable mainland-Spanish woman and the mother of one of Charlie's classmates. Carmen occasionally ordered fruit from us, which we'd deliver to her when picking up our respective kids from school. Through Charlie's friendship with her son, we'd got to know Carmen quite well, and the boys would spend occasional weekends at each other's homes. Despite that, we'd never found out exactly what Carmen's husband Salvador did to support the smart home and comfortable lifestyle which they enjoyed. All we knew was that he had 'business interests' in Palma.

Carmen spoke perfect English. 'You both look deep in thought,' she said after the mandatory round of hugs and air kisses had been completed.

'It's him,' said Ellie. 'He's building a games room in the house, and he's trying to work out how to make it look like a pub without spending any money on it. Typical.'

I fully expected Carmen to follow up this piece of news with a similarly dismissive anecdote about *her* other half's household efforts. Instead, she arched her eyebrows and a grin of inspiration spread over her face.

'Then this is your lucky day,' she informed me. One of Salvador's companies, she revealed, held the Mallorcan import franchise for several leading northern European beer manufacturers. Big names like Carlsberg, Kronenbourg and Löwenbräu. Salvador was forever coming home with promotional hand-outs from the various brewers, and he was like a magpie, the way he hoarded it all. Things like souvenir beer glasses, bar mirrors advertising one brand or another, ornate German *bier steins*, even repro beer-barrel bottoms. She indicated the Sa Premsa wine casks. 'Just like those ones, but a lot smaller, of course.' She went on to tell us that their garage at home was so full of these odds and ends that she'd told Salvador that very morning that he'd have to get rid of them. Why, she exclaimed, he had accumulated so much of this brewery-trade bric-a-brac that they could hardly get their cars inside because of it! I was very welcome to take as much of it as I wanted. 'But make it soon,' Carmen cautioned, 'otherwise it will all be going to the nuns for their next charity sale!'

I left the Celler Sa Premsa that afternoon a lot happier than I'd entered it, and without even the slightest twinge of guilt about overspending. From what Carmen had said, it seemed certain that the cost of a shared *greixonera* of *Sopes Mallorquinas* had turned out to be a bargain price to pay for the license I now had to plunder the contents of her garage.

– TEN –

WINNERS AND LOSERS

Unfortunately, the smile that I was still wearing as we drove back into the yard at Ca's Mayoral was not mirrored by Pablo Gomez. So pained was his expression, indeed, that Ellie poetically remarked his face looked like a smacked backside with a moustache.

'*Es un desastre*, *amigo*,' he wailed, slouching over to meet us with all the cares of the world on his shoulders. 'A disaster! It is Groucho's hole!'

Pablo led me quickly round to the front of the house. 'A disaster!' he repeated. 'Ah *sí*, *amigo*, we have *un problema grande*!' He pointed down into the void of the pool, which Abdul and two of his fellow workers had lined with shuttering timber during the previous couple of days. Abdul, for once, wasn't working, but was leaning cross-legged against the portable cement mixer that cost-conscious Pablo had provided for his men instead of having ready-mixed concrete brought in by truck. Abdul was smoking a cigarette and looking distinctly unsympathetic about whatever was troubling his distraught employer. So were the other two guys.

I was relieved to see that Abdul and his mates were all right, my first concern on hearing their boss's announcement of *un desastre* having been for their safety. 'So, what's the big problem?' I asked Pablo. 'Everything looks OK to me.'

'I told you. It is the hole. Groucho, that son of a whore – he has made it too big!'

A rumble of throaty chortles rolled over from where Abdul and company were standing.

As it happens, I had taken the precaution of measuring the length and breadth of the swimming pool plot at the end of Groucho's very first day on the job, and I told Pablo so. 'Eight metres by four,' I said. 'Just as the contract stipulates. *No problema*.'

The length and breadth weren't the problem, Pablo somewhat agitatedly informed me. *Madre de Dios*, had I not noticed that he had pegged it out himself before letting Groucho loose with his damned *aixada*? Pablo stuck his chest out and avowed that, no, there was nothing wrong with *those* measurements. Absolutely not! He pointed into the excavation again and, almost choking on his words, revealed that it was the depth that was all wrong.

'*Hombre*,' he spluttered, 'that buffoon Groucho has dug the hole almost three-quarters of a metre too deep!' Pablo then took a kick at a shovel, which went clattering down onto the concrete floor of the pool.

Out of the corner of my eye, I could see Abdul and his two comrades smirking at the sight of their boss having a temper tantrum. I was trying not to smile myself. I remembered how I'd reckoned that Groucho's work rate and enthusiasm for the job had increased after I'd started giving him a nip of *coñac* every morning, but I'd never imagined that his productivity would have been boosted to this extent. I mentioned this to Pablo in an effort to introduce a note of levity into the situation.

But Pablo was in no mood for mirth. He grumpily explained to me that Groucho had actually dug the pool to the exact depth that he'd been told to. Where the stupid *tonto* had gone wrong, however, had been in failing to take into account that the terrace round the pool would be an extension of the existing terrace in front of the house. 'And the surface of that existing terrace is, *amigo*…?' Pablo looked at me through sad eyes and awaited the obvious answer.

'Three quarters of a metre higher than ground level,' I duly replied.

Pablo was almost in tears. This was going to cost him money, and he knew it. 'Think of all the extra tiling work that will be involved,' he muttered, speaking as much to himself as to me, I suspected. 'Eight metres by four metres, multiplied by another three-quarters of a metre,' he groaned. '*Dios mío*, think of the cost of all those extra tiles!' He lowered his head and clapped a hand to his brow. '*Un desastre, amigo*,' he moaned. '*Sí, un desastre grande*.'

'Well, these things happen,' I said, in another attempt to lighten up the mood a bit. 'And don't worry – I won't sue you,' I joked. 'On the contrary, I'm more than happy to have the pool a bit deeper than expected.'

The calculating look that entered Pablo's eyes on hearing this made me instantly wish I hadn't said it. His wounded expression melted into a smile – the smile of a man-eating crocodile that's just noticed his next meal swimming unsuspectingly towards him.

'I am pleased that you are happy about that, *señor*,' he said, 'because the extra depth will cost you correspondingly more – *naturalmente*.'

I already knew Pablo Gomez well enough to realise that the sudden use of the formal '*señor*', instead of the matey '*amigo*' that he habitually employed when speaking to me, meant that we were back talking business again. I hastily purged my mind of any idea of keeping things light. 'On second thoughts,' I said, 'I'd prefer to stick to the letter of the contract. Raise the bottom of the pool by three-quarters of a metre, please.'

Another rumble of chortles from Abdul and friends.

But Pablo hadn't heard anything to be amused about. Going red in the face, he asked me if I knew how many hundreds of cubic metres of rubble he'd have to buy to part-fill the hole in the way I'd suggested. What's more, he swiftly added, the drainage sump and all the related pipe work had been incorporated into the concrete already laid in the bottom of the pool. *Sí*, and that pipe work had been connected up to the rest of the filtration system now half buried in the concrete that Abdul and his chums had started to pour between the walls of timber shuttering.

Pablo then revealed that it was only when his men asked for extra materials to be brought in that it became obvious to him that something was amiss. The quantities of cement, sand and gravel required to complete the concreting work had been calculated by Pablo himself, and, he confidently declared, there should have been *more* than enough on site.

'*Hombre*,' he said with a hurt look, 'it was on those quantities that I calculated the price for this stage of the work. So, you see why I must charge you more to cover all of this, as well as for the additional tiling that eventually will be involved – *naturalmente*.' He shot me a businesssslike look. 'A contract is a contract, no?'

'I think, Pablo, you'll find that the price in the contract can only be increased – in respect of anything relating to the "small digger" that you chose to use – *if* I default on any of the stage payments. That was the gentleman's agreement we made, no?'

Pablo raised a rather reluctant shoulder of assent.

'And I've paid everything on time so far, correct?'

Pablo nodded his head. The hurt look on his face shifted for a fleeting second into one of annoyance, before softening into a winning smile. 'Ah,' he crooned, 'but I am a fair man, *amigo*, and I am sure we can reach a compromise. Shall we, uhm, divide the extra cost, say fifty-fifty, between us?'

I had to admire Pablo's optimism. 'Horses for courses' had been the racing expression he'd used when trying to ratchet up the price of using Groucho to dig the hole in the first place. If it now turned out that he'd backed the wrong horse, then that was his problem. It was nobody's fault but his own that he hadn't bothered to check Groucho's work, and I wasn't obliged to cough up a cent for his mistake. I told him this in the nicest possible way, while reminding him that I could insist, if I chose to, that the pool be made to the exact dimensions that were stipulated in the written agreement.

'But, like you, I'm a fair man, *amigo*,' I declared to the sound of muted sniggers from Abdul and his boys. 'And don't worry about being sued,' I added, though a mite less jocularly than before. 'If you choose to make the pool three-quarters of a metre deeper than it should be, it'll be fine by me. And, better still, I won't even charge you for the extra cost of water to fill it.' I gave him a hearty pat on the shoulder. 'The choice is yours, *señor*. Go ahead with completing the pool as it is, or order those truckloads of infill and start chiselling out the pipe work.'

Pablo's laugh didn't quite reach his eyes, but the sound of it and the reciprocal pat on the shoulder he gave me were obviously intended for the benefit of his three onlooking employees. The last thing he wanted them to think was that he'd come off second best in matters of business.

'Why look so serious?' he asked me with a chuckle designed to give the impression of nonchalance, though not totally succeeding. He patted me on the other shoulder, this time a bit *too* heartily, I thought. 'Hey-y-y-y,' he beamed, 'did you not realise that I was only having a bit of fun, eh?' He shrugged again and, elbows tucked in, he half raised his hands and showed their palms in a 'what, me worry?' sort of pose. 'Three-quarters of a metre deeper for your little pool? *Hombre*, even the extra cost of a metre or two metres deeper would be nothing for the Gomez Construction Company.' He was now talking in a voice loud enough to be heard half way up the valley. '*Por favor, amigo* – accept the increased size with my compliments, and for *absolutamente* no charge.'

Despite the favourable outcome, for some reason that I couldn't quite fathom I was left without any feeling of satisfaction at the end of this little confrontation. I didn't feel that I'd come out on top, because, I suppose, I hadn't seen it as a contest in the first place. That said, I couldn't bring myself to believe that Pablo Gomez had only been having me on, as he'd ultimately claimed. If I'd been prepared to pay for his blunder, he'd have readily accepted and would have chuckled all the way to the bank. I couldn't really criticise him for that, though. Business is business after all, and Pablo hadn't made a success of his by ignoring the dog-eat-dog aspects of the game. But, by the same token, I wasn't about to become prematurely skint by being taken for a ride.

My immediate thoughts, however, were more with little Groucho. What punishment would Pablo mete out to him for his having cost the firm money by working too hard? It might even cost Groucho his job. And, for all I knew, he may well have had a large family to support.

But, perhaps not too surprisingly, I needn't have worried. I noticed him in The Gomez Construction Company's yard when I passed by a few days later, and he was looking just as miserably content as ever. He was loading his trusty *aixada* pickaxe and rubber bucket onto the back of a truck, with Pablo sitting in the cab waiting for him, a huge cigar in his mouth and a *genuine* 'what, me worry?' look on his face. Pablo knew what side his bread was buttered on. He had the best 'small digger' in the business, and he wasn't about to get rid of him for the price of a few boxes of ceramic tiles. Any builder worthy of his trade's reputation for shrewdness takes these contingencies into account when pricing every job. And if Pablo hadn't already allowed for such a mishap in his bid for our contract, it's certain that its cost would be passed on to the next 'suitable' client.

'It's a pity we couldn't fix *our* prices like that,' Ellie remarked while we were picking oranges that same evening. 'The merchant tells us what the going rate is, and we can either like it or lump it. It's not fair.'

'Yeah, well, that's the joys of farming,' I replied. 'It was the same when we were growing barley in Scotland. You have to take what you get when you sell it, and if it ends up costing you more to grow the stuff than you're paid, then tough.'

'Hmm, but at least we got government subsidies to help out a bit when we were farming barley and beef. With fruit, we have to sink or swim without any support at all.'

'True, but fruit farmers aren't unique in that respect. Most businesses have to survive without handouts from the taxpayer, don't forget.'

'It's still not fair. Why should some farmers get it while others don't? I mean, oranges are more healthy than all that smelly beer and whisky they make out of barley.'

Maybe Ellie had a valid point there, but it was unlikely to influence the EU's subsidy-shuffling decision makers. As fruit farmers, we'd have to stand on our own two feet without any financial help from officialdom, at least for the foreseeable future. I looked around the orchard at the rapidly decreasing number of oranges still on the trees.

'Another few weeks,' I said, 'and the orange season will be over.'

I didn't say any more on the subject. There was no need to. Ellie knew as well as I did that doing our sums at the end of the current harvest would give us an indicator of how viable or otherwise our little farm was going to be. The trees had now recovered well from the curative surgery that Pepe Suau had done on them the previous year. They were in fine heart at last and yielding acceptable crops of good-quality fruit. While we *might* still be able to increase production through further careful husbandry of the trees before the start of the next harvest in eight or nine months time, we accepted that it wouldn't be by much. The farm had just about reached its optimum earning level. The moment of truth, then, was only just around the corner.

I already sensed a feeling of apprehension creeping in, and although I hadn't succumbed to a serious nail-biting fit just yet, my mood wasn't exactly given a positive boost by what Jeronimo the fruit merchant told me when I was making the usual delivery to his warehouse the following morning…

There was a slump in the demand for oranges, due to a glut that was being caused, some said, because of Spain's provisional entry into the EU. The word was that the resultant increase in competition from other Mediterranean countries had flooded the market. Jeronimo wasn't sure if that was merely political propaganda, but, for whatever reason, the price of oranges *was* taking a hit. He'd even heard that thousands of tons had been bulldozed into the sea over on the mainland, some growers there preferring to destroy their oranges than sell them at a loss.

Déjà vu, I thought. Could this end up being yet another of the follies of the European Economic Community, in which there had already been grain, tomato and meat mountains, wine lakes and a mushrooming of bureaucrats employed to oversee the unholy shambles? We'd already felt the draught of this wind of change as small farmers in Britain, so we knew what to expect if a similar situation developed here in Spain. Only the strongest would survive. And in farming, the strongest usually means the biggest.

'Which is why we're building the swimming pool and doing all the other value-adding things to the property,' Ellie reminded me when I began bemoaning the situation on my arrival back in the Ca's Mayoral kitchen. 'If we do eventually have to find the means to expand, we'll need as much collateral as possible. OK, we can't do anything about the price of oranges, but we *can* do plenty about improving what this place is worth.' Ellie then tagged a physical nudge onto the verbal one she'd just given me. 'So, go on – stop worrying and get into the *almacén* and start being creative with all that pub gear you got out of Carmen's garage!'

– ELEVEN –

THE ROAD FROM ANDRATX TO SÓLLER

Keeping yourself busy is certainly a good way of banishing
worries to the back of your mind. Enjoying yourself while
keeping busy is an even better way, and Ellie's assertion
that completing the makeover of the old workroom would
give us plenty of fun proved to be absolutely correct. We'd
taken on our share of the usual DIY home-improvement
projects in the past, not least since coming to Ca's Mayoral.
But there was something a bit different, a bit less 'sensible',
about creating a room that was intended purely for
enjoyment, compared to grinding away at an essentially
functional task like stripping and re-papering the walls of a
kitchen, for example. Not that there was anything even
remotely decadent about the way we were transforming the
almacén. The idea of kitting it out with pieces of fairly
outmoded furniture, items of obsolete farm tackle and a

225

selection of beer-promotion odds and ends didn't exactly conjure up images of wanton self-indulgence, but it *was* giving us fun.

The job wasn't without its practical problems, of course. Radically changing the appearance of a down-to-earth place of work in an old farmhouse is bound to throw up certain aesthetic dilemmas. One hangover from the original use of the room that was going to be difficult to get rid of without going to a great deal of expense was what, in modern parlance, might be termed 'the utility area'. This was a corner of the *almacén* containing a fairly basic shower room with toilet. Outside it was an old stone sink that was a throwback to washboard-scrubbing days, and next to that a big, American-style fridge-freezer. This impressive-looking 'Frigidaire' had been left for us by the Ferrers, a gesture that initially struck us as being generous in the extreme, considering they'd emptied the house of just about everything else of any value. We weren't too astonished, then, when the 'Hotaire', as we subsequently dubbed it, turned out to be more impressive-looking than reliable. We lost count of how many times we had to replace an entire stock of food wasted during one of its regular breakdowns. Doubtless it would have been cheaper to have replaced the infernal machine when we moved in. Ever hopeful, though, we persevered with expensive running repairs until we ultimately got it working right by replacing *all* of its clapped-out innards in one desperate, last-ditch attempt to exorcise its devils. Then it really did become a valuable and, especially during the searingly hot months of summer, an essential addition to the smaller fridge-freezer that Ellie, in the meantime, had bought for fitting under the worktop in the kitchen.

The dilapidated and permanently-leaking washing machine that the Ferrers had more or less abandoned in the *almacén* had been chucked out by Ellie long ago. But, in the space that it had occupied, we'd been obliged to install a new electric boiler, big enough to supply the house with hot water. (You guessed it – the one that the Ferrers had endowed us with was both pitifully too small for the job and, being gas-fired and ancient, a potential bomb!) The new boiler was a fine-looking appliance, but its white-enamelled bulk was never going to harmonise with the country-pub look that I had in mind for the room. The boiler, together with what were now its equally incongruous-looking neighbours in the old utility area, would have to be moved to somewhere less conspicuous, or hidden.

It was a foregone conclusion that the first option would be rejected on the grounds of cost.

'Besides,' Ellie said to me during an on-site deliberation, 'a handy fridge, sink and toilet are essentials for any bar, and a shower would be regarded as a luxury in most, so moving them out would be daft anyway.'

'And the water boiler?'

'Well, that'll add a bit of warmth in here during the winter, which is when it's most in use.'

'OK,' I said, 'so we hide the lot. But building some sort of wall around them isn't going to be cheap either, you know.'

'Who's talking about a wall? Apart from the expense, it would only trap any heat the boiler gives off. A waste.' Ellie motioned towards the canopy I'd erected above my little homemade bar. 'Just get yourself some more of that broom-type thatchy stuff, fix it onto light wooden frames, hinge them together in twos, and you've got yourself some free-standing screens. Simple. What's more, it'll be in keeping with your rustic theme *and* it'll cost next to nothing. Problem solved.'

So the process of 'tarting up' the *almacén* continued, and as the days passed, the more satisfaction we drew from seeing our ideas take shape. Waiting in the wings to take centre stage was a snooker table I'd bought a while back from a house near the town of Sóller, the orange-growing capital of Mallorca. The boys had noticed an ad for it in the 'For Sale' columns of the *Majorca Daily Bulletin*, and although it was only a three-quarter-size model, the table would suit our purpose and the space available just fine. Despite having been tucked away in a corner with all kinds of waiting-to-be-used oddments piled on top of it since its arrival, that snooker table was already the boys' pride and joy, and I had to admit to sharing their eagerness for having it available for a game whenever it took our fancy.

Ellie's reaction to the games room idea when it was first mooted by Sandy had been predictably cool. As the lone woman in a three-male household, she'd envisaged it as an extravagant playpen for overgrown schoolboys, with me as the leader of the gang. True to my promise of keeping outlay on the project to a minimum, therefore, I'd had to ensure that I bought the snooker table for a really keen price. And closing that bargain had added an extra element of pleasure to the drive from Andratx to Sóller, always an excursion to look forward to – unless you suffer from vertigo, that is!

The last time I'd taken this most exhilarating of drives had been when Jordi accompanied me to buy tomato plants from an old crony of his who was a specialist grower in Banyalbufar, a mountain village noted for the quality of its tomatoes and for the awe-inspiring crescent of steeply-terraced land on which they're cultivated. My memories of that trip are slightly blurred by the results of Jordi's ulterior motive for making the journey, namely his determination that I should join him in sampling (liberally) his friend's moonshine liquor. Much as I'd appreciated Jordi's consideration and his friend's generosity, I was glad that today's drive was going to be in the less dissolute company of the family. There was no way the boys would have been willing to miss out on being there when the decision to buy or not to buy that snooker table was taken, and Ellie was equally determined that she'd be around if any money was likely to change hands. Indeed, as a means of insurance against my making a rash purchase, the money we'd set aside for buying the snooker table was stashed securely in her handbag.

Taking the C710 road north from the market place on the outskirts of Andratx, you climb steadily away from the town as you approach the Coll de Sa Gremola pass and continue along the wooded slopes of the Serra d'es Pinotells ridge. It's then that you catch your first glimpse of the sea, shimmering far below you on your left. And if you gulp at the sudden realisation of how high this road is, be prepared to cover your eyes a few times during the journey ahead. There are dizzying vistas to thrill (or terrify) you round almost every bend as you snake your rollercoaster way along the coastal flanks of the mighty Tramuntana Mountains. A sense of your own insignificance strikes you as you pass between sheer drops to the sea on one side and the towering, pine-cloaked spine of the mountains on the other. Here and there an overhanging cliff will suddenly loom above as you round a curve, great clefts in its rocky face exposing a wonderful range of colours from the palest dove grey through camel beige to fox red. The road continues like this, hugging the mountainsides and weaving its way through ravines and valleys all the way to Cape Formentor, some ninety kilometres away at the northernmost tip of the island. But we were going only about a third of that distance today.

For all its twists and turns and the head-spinning views it regularly surprises you with, the road is a good one, its safety having been much improved by the systematic widening of some of its tightest corners in recent years. It goes without saying that the reason for such costly upgrading is linked to tourism, and in particular to the demands of the less intrepid traveller of today. The allure of this dramatic expanse of mountain, forest and sea has attracted visitors for centuries, but it's a long time since sightseeing tourists expected nothing more comfortable in the way of transport than a mule. So, it's worth remembering that, even when driving along during the relatively quiet months of winter, it's always possible that you'll meet a huge, luxury coach bearing down on you round any one of those countless hairpin bends. And if anyone is forced to pull up and take his life in his hands by reversing out of the other's path, rest assured it won't be the coach driver!

The first of several *miradores*, or viewing places, that you encounter along the way is the *Mirador de Ricardo Roca*. This one has an adjacent clifftop restaurant, Es Grau, with a large balcony that seems to hang from invisible skyhooks high above the sea. The views are truly breathtaking, so the spot is a popular stopping-off place for car-, bicycle- and coach-borne sightseers alike. Hence the souvenir shop that adjoins the restaurant. But if you prefer to take in the scenery, and some sustenance, somewhere a bit less bustling, continue on via the short tunnel carved through the outcrop of rock on which the *mirador* sits, and make for the village of Estellencs, just a few kilometres ahead.

The Restaurante Coll d'es Pi sits on a spot where the road starts to wind steeply down towards the village. The outlook from here, although perhaps less vertigo-inducing than those from most of the recognised *miradores*, is nonetheless glorious in its own way. For it isn't the sea that first captures your attention here, but rather the landscape that surrounds Estellencs. And what a magnificent landscape it is. The ragged summit of Galatzó, the highest mountain in this part of the Tramuntana range, dominates the skyline and provides a striking backdrop to the village nestling cosily at its feet. Craggy scarps of grey-pink rock cut vertically into Galatzó's higher slopes, their natural grandeur giving way eventually to the man-made order of cultivated terraces that tumble in sweeping folds all the way to the valley floor.

The only sounds to greet your ears on this lofty vantage point are those so typical of the Tramuntanas – the drowsy chirping of sparrows in the surrounding woods, the nasal bleating of goats, the tinny tinkle of distant sheep bells and the dull clang of the village clock drifting up through the still, clear air. And everywhere, the intoxicating scents of wild herbs mixed with the resinous tang of the pines and the faint whiff of smoke from olivewood fires. This is the very breath of the Mallorcan mountains.

The restaurant is a relatively modern building, compared to those whose ochre-tiled roooftops it overlooks down in the valley. It was developed (so the locals say) on the site of a wayside tavern, where muleteers would refresh themselves and their laden animals on the tough and tortuous journey along what was then only a rutted and rocky track, and a happy hunting ground for bandits. There's no risk of being robbed these days, and you'll be served in bright, airy surroundings that pay homage to the past in a refreshingly individual way.

The front of the bar, for instance, is decorated with a series of local scenes, while the huge feature fireplace is a modern adaptation of the inglenook, or *chimenea*, the sit-in heart of many an old Mallorcan living room. It's worth a visit to the Restaurante Coll d'es Pi, if only to cast your eyes over the fireplace's amazing combination of sturdy beams, intricate filigree work, chunky masonry and finely turned wood. Love it or loathe it, this *chimenea* is truly unique, and if this kind of visual counterpoint isn't to your taste, you can always escape outside to the terrace and soothe your eyes by gazing over green waves of pine flowing gently down towards the sea.

Back on the road, the wild beauty of the landscape melds here and there into huddles of honeystone houses, as embodied in the villages of Estellencs itself and Banyalbufar with its amazing cascades of tomato-spangled terraces. The serenity of these little townships and the brilliance of the light reflected from mountain and sea are why so many artists and writers have chosen to live within their humble precincts over the years. These are priceless places of escalating, cobble-stoned alleys, of footpaths twisting between ancient olive groves to secret pebble beaches, and of magical mountain walks on which you may have only a soaring eagle for company.

Of all such villages that cling to the slopes on either side of this meandering way, the most celebrated is perhaps Deià, the home of the poet Robert Graves for much of his lifetime. Even with the inevitable summer incursion of tourists and the gradual growth of businesses created to cater for their needs, this 'unspoiled' little town of modestly-elegant buildings the colour of old straw still manages to sustain an air of almost tangible tranquility.

But the attractions of this part of the island aren't limited to the places and views you encounter around the switchbacks of the corniche road. On its seaward side, for example, there are tiny fishermen's havens like Port de Canonge, tucked into hidden coves accessible only by boat, or by steep, zig-zagging tracks that demand the utmost care when being negotiated by car. Perhaps they're best visited on foot – *if* you have the energy to trek all the way back up to the main road, that is!

Then, on the landward side, towards the sleepy village of Esporles, you can experience the rural Mallorca of yesteryear, professionally spun, woven, carved, fashioned, forged, cooked, played and danced for the visitor in and around the impressive old mansion of La Granja. The abundance of pure mountain water flowing from a spring here has made this wedge of fertile land prized agriculturally since Roman times. Today, however, La Granja's fortunes no longer depend on farming. The estate's stage-managed displays of bygone times, together with the beauty of its fountain-adorned grounds, laid out amid cool, deciduous woodland, now attract paying customers in their thousands every year.

A bit farther on, more concessions to tourism can be seen in the historic town of Valldemossa, in whose former Carthusian monastery, La Cartuja, the composer Chopin spent the winter of 1838–9 in the company of his lover, George Sand (the pen name of the French author Amandine Aurore Lucie Dupin). She wrote of Valldemossa: 'All that a poet or an artist might dream of, Nature has created here. It is the most beautiful place I have ever lived in and one of the most beautiful I have ever seen.'

These days, the spectacle of its clusters of stone houses spilling in random steps down the mountainside is as enchanting as it ever was, although I doubt if George Sand would have written so glowingly of the place if she'd had to elbow her way through the hordes of daytrippers who now mill along its narrow streets in summer. They come to see the one-time monk's 'cell' in which Chopin composed some of his most famous works, to wander round La Cartuja's museum and pretty gardens, to wonder at the painted ceilings of its church, to visit the birthplace of Santa

Catalina Tomàs, Mallorca's only saint, or just to soak up the age-old atmosphere of unhurried peace that, in spite of its status as the island's most popular coach-tour destination, this enchanting little town still retains – though, at times, only just!

Following in the pioneering footsteps of Chopin and Sand, it was the Archduke Luis Salvador of Austria, who, no matter how unwittingly, was probably more responsible than anyone for laying the foundations of modern Mallorcan tourism, following his first visit to the island as a young man back in 1867. So enthralled was he by this stretch of coastline that he bought the secluded property of Miramar, 'a dream-like vision suspended among sea, sky and land', overlooking one of the most outstanding views of all in the area. In the words of the Spanish luminary Miguel de Unamuno, 'The greatest wonder with which Majorca regales the eyes of the soul and the soul of the eyes is the superb headland of Miramar'. It's accepted, however, that the Archduke chose to buy Miramar, not just for its panoramic Mediterranean seascapes, but also for 'the natural, unspoilt charm of its surrounding woods'. From the outset, he charged his servants to 'respect the olive trees, evergreen oaks and pines, old and twisted, but magnificent in their picturesque settings'.

As such things inevitably do in country areas, news of the Archduke's deep concern for the protection of the sylvan beauty of his adopted home soon spread, and the profit-potential of this highly commendable trait wasn't slow to be exploited by the local folk. One day, according to a contemporary chronicler, the birds, which were usually chirping away happily, fell silent, and all that could be heard were the resounding blows of an axe in the distant depth of the forest. A neighbouring proprietor of Miramar was chopping down a centuries-old tree, which he was perfectly entitled to do. But *S'Arxiduc*, as His Royal Highness is referred to in *mallorquín*, regarded this as nothing short of vandalism. To put a stop to it, he promptly bought the culprit's land – at a much inflated price, of course. Shortly afterwords, the same thing occurred on the other side of Miramar, and once again the Archduke felt compelled to purchase the relevant block of land. As word spread among the fly *mallorquines* in the vicinity, it wasn't long before *S'Arxiduc* couldn't open his bedroom window in the morning without hearing the same unbearable noise of a tree being felled.

Consequently, the Archduke Luis Salvador ended up being the proud owner of a dozen conjoining estates, which he eventually presided over from the mansion of Son Marroig. Perched high above the sea, this fine house is now open to the public and, being in Mallorca, it has its own restaurant, Na Foradada, named after the spectacular 'perforated rock' peninsula it overlooks. You can see why the Archduke chose this spot in which to live for so many years of his life. It's as if you are in an eagle's eyrie, looking down along bluff after rocky bluff plunging headlong into the sea, while far below you a lone gull spirals lazily above the waves.

Although not realising it at the time, his enormous investment in saving just a few old and twisted trees was destined to result in the permanent preservation of a vast swathe of idyllic landscape that otherwise might well have fallen victim to commercial plundering of one sort or another. But the Archduke did more than just commit large chunks of his wealth to buying much of this ruggedly-beautiful coastline and its mountainous hinterland. He also dedicated himself to writing *Die Balearen*, an exhaustive study of Mallorca that is still regarded as the most complete account of the island's history, botany, geography, folklore, crafts, customs and traditional ways of working life.

It was as a result of his wish to share with others the natural treasures of his personal paradise that many dignitaries of the time, including authors, painters, scientists, aristocrats and royals from all over Europe, came to enjoy his hospitality and to fall in love themselves with this relatively undiscovered gem of the Mediterranean. His generosity towards that select group of friends was the magic bean that sprouted into the beanstalk that grew into the burgeoning Mallorcan tourism industry of today.

It isn't hard to guess what the good Luis Salvador's opinion of the worst excesses of that industry in the more easily reached parts of Mallorca would have been. Even in his wildest nightmares he could never have foreseen the concrete forests that would one day proliferate along many of the island's sandy bays and tower above some of its little coves, where once only leaning pines cast their shadows on the shore. But access to the treasures of travel is no longer the preserve of the privileged few, and even the wealth of a thousand *Arxiducs* could never have saved all the metaphorical trees that were to fall to the axe of 'progress', with the resultant 'wealth' that Mallorca now enjoys.

Nevertheless, the heritage of the area of the Tramuntana Mountains which he cherished so much is still being nurtured. And, as chance would have it, it's another prosperous and influential non-Mallorcan who has emerged as a formidable champion of the cause. Unlike the Archduke, however, he isn't a member of an ancient royal family, but one who has risen through a much less advantaged lineage. For it was on the initiative of a Hollywood film star that the Costa Nord de Valldemossa Cultural Centre has now been established in the town that bears its name.

In a fortuitous repetition of history, so bewitched was Michael Douglas by this part of the island when he first visited it, that he bought, appropriately enough, one of the estates that once belonged to the Archduke Luis Salvador of Austria himself. Subsequently, the Costa Nord project was set in place. Its declared purpose is 'to create a cultural bond between the island's inhabitants and those who visit it, and to transmit to them the fascination that this countryside has long held for writers, artists, musicians and thinkers'. An admirable commitment of which the *Arxiduc* would surely have approved.

Oh, and I should point out that, so far, there have been no reports of Michael being awakened from his early morning slumbers by the sound of even one neighbouring woodman's axe!

I could have lingered for hours at so many of the places we passed through that day, but we were on a mission, and the boys weren't likely to let me forget it. We pressed on as quickly as respect for the road would allow. Beyond Deià, it continues in a relatively unswerving way for a while, though now following contours that skirt an almost vertical drop to the sea. Then, sweeping inland, the whole world seems to fall away before you as you are suddenly confronted by a vast, basin-like valley enclosed by the brawny arms of the Tramuntanas. Imposing as they are, these encircling mountians are dwarfed by the summit of Puig Major, Mallorca's highest peak, soaring majestically on the northern skyline above the Valle de los Naranjos, the wonderful Vale of Orange Trees. And there, cradled on the valley floor at the end of yet another writhing ribbon of road, lies the old town of Sóller, its surrounding orange orchards a joy to behold and their golden fruit the basis of the town's great prosperity.

Ironically, it was Sóller's situation on the northern side of the Tramuntanas and, therefore, its relative inaccessibilty from Mallorca's capital city of Palma some thirty kilometres away to the south that was to sow the seeds of its affluence. Before the building, a hundred years ago, of the narrow-guage, 'wild west' railway that runs between the two centres, and long before the recently-completed road tunnel was even thought about, the only direct route to Sóller was by the crazily-twisting mountain road that has been described as the scariest on the island. That allegation is debatable, because there are many contenders for the most-hair-raising-road crown in the mountains of Mallorca. One thing that isn't in doubt, however, is that the severity of the gradients that have to be scaled on this particular road before reaching the Coll de Sóller pass would certainly have been a daunting prospect for even the most energetic of muleteers – not to speak of his poor pack animals. And so the businessmen of Sóller turned their backs on the mountains and the remote market places of Palma, took to the sea and established a trade exporting oranges to France, and to the Mediterranean port of Marseille in particular.

Evidence of their success can still be seen in the quality of the homes of wealthy merchants of the time, and in more recent *modernista*-style buildings that rival Palma's finest. Yet there's an unmistakable air of the south of France about Sóller as well. Handsome houses, cool under overhanging eaves and decorated with wrought-iron balconies, reach out to each other across the maze of narrow streets that radiate from the town's main square, the dominant feature of which is its magnificent old church. There can be few experiences more pleasing at any time of day than to sit under one of the huge plane trees that shade the Plaça de Sa Constitució, sipping a drink outside a pavement café and watching the townsfolk of Sóller go about their unhurried lives.

Every so often you'll hear the toot of a train whistle announcing the arrival, a couple of streets away, of one of the little 'orange blossom specials' from Palma. Then, depending on how closely the driver has been sticking to what is loosely referred to as his timetable, an ancient wooden tramcar will rattle through the *plaça* on its way from the train terminus, laden with daytrippers bound for the pretty resort of Port de Sóller, just a short ride away through orange groves and, in parts, even through people's gardens. These bell-clanging old boneshakers with their open-sided 'trailers' are said to have plied the streets of San Francisco in their youth and they do add a touch of eccentric charm to this captivating corner of Mallorca.

There was no time for us to stop and savour the special magic of Sóller on this occasion, though. We were heading for Fornalutx, a little way up the valley in the foothills of the mighty Puig Major itself.

Fornalutx has the distinction of being rated the prettiest village in Mallorca, if not in the whole of Spain. It has even been called a Mediterranean Shangri-La, and although some might judge that to be a slightly over-exalted description, it would be a callous eye indeed that failed to be entranced by such a magnificent fusion of nature's bounty and man's ingenuity. Fittingly, it is the enfolding mountains themselves that have provided the essential ingredients. They afford shelter from the cold north winds that sometimes rake this part of the island in winter, while their configuration helps create the favourable micro climates that make the Sóller valley bloom. These things, together with the abundance of water that the mountains also provide, have helped turn Fornalutx and the neighbouring hamlet of Biniaraix into rare jewels in the long, rugged line of the Tramuntana chain.

Yet, without the creative intervention of man, none of this would be.

It was during the Moorish tenure of Mallorca over a thousand years ago that the *bancales*, the cultivable terraces that are a wonder of so many Mallorcan mountainsides, were constructed. The Moors' engineering skills also made it possible to channel the waters from their high mountain sources down onto these terraces. This, in turn, was an essential contributory factor towards the mammoth task of turning an untamed wilderness into the fertile garden of delights that it is today.

Against the massive backcloth of the Puig Major, Fornalutx appears like a glorious confusion of biscuit-coloured matchboxes that have been thrown onto the landscape by a giant hand. The old stone houses cluster together amid a labyrinth of narrow lanes and stepped alleyways, winding this way and that up and around the hillsides. Terraced groves of citrus trees appear between them here and there like vibrant brush strokes applied to a canvas that even the most imaginative of Impressionists would have given his right ear to have painted.

'Aha, so *vous êtes* Scotteesh. 'ow absolutely *merveilleuse!*'

Madame Antoinette MacPherson's way of blending two languages matched the intriguing incongruity of the two halves of her name. 'Ah *oui*, Édimbourg!' she kissed the gathered tips of her fingers. 'Mmwah! What a *belle cité*! Oh yes, I know eet, because I 'ave 'ad the *plaisir* of spending a year as a student *d'échange* in your lovely capital. At the *université*, you know.' She gave a little giggle and batted her eyelashes coyly. '*Mais oui*, but that was, I theenk, a long time ago, *non*?'

Looking every bit the retired actress we'd been told she was by the elderly village woman who had directed us to her house, Madame MacPherson was reclining on a wickerwork chaise longue when we reached the top of the stone steps leading from the lane to her patio. Shaded from the afternoon sun by the fronds of a spreading palm tree, she was wearing a long sheath dress of red silk, boldly embellished with the image of a Chinese dragon. On her nose were square, bamboo-framed spectacles, and in one hand she flaunted a matching bamboo cigarette holder long enough to serve as a stake for a Banyalbufar tomato plant. Her other hand was holding a glass of buck's fizz, the orange juice for which, she proudly informed us, had been squeezed from the fruit of the trees on the *bancal* behind her house.

She invited us to sit on wickerwork chairs round a wickerwork table on which her champagne bucket and a jug of orange juice had been placed within easy reach of her wickerwork chaise longue. She was clearly a woman who favoured visual coordination. Even the varnish on her immaculately manicured fingernails matched the colour of her dress, as did the exaggerated cupid's bow of her painted lips.

'*C'est magnifique*, the perspective from 'ere, *non?*' she said with a theatrical sweep of her cigarette holder.

There was no denying that. Her house, although situated not far from the little square that is the hub of the village, was sitting in such an elevated position that all you could see of the neighbouring properties, close as they were, was their tiled roofs and rubblestone chimneys. And the predominant feature of this little balcony with uninterrupted views around the vast amphitheatre of the Sóller valley was silence. Only the tinkling of a small fountain in a shady corner of Madame MacPherson's garden interrupted the total stillness that prevailed. Geraniums, tumbling in pink profusion over the patio's drystone walls, created a touch of floral fragility to counterbalance the wild grandeur of the mountains that, no matter in which direction you looked, made their looming presence felt. No old drama queen could have chosen a more impressive set to grace her retirement stage.

'Yeah, *c'est magnifique*, right enough,' I replied, unintentionally aping Madame Macpherson's Franco-English, though inevitably making it sound decidedly less exotic than her version.

I felt an elbow nudging my side. It was Charlie, sitting next to me, looking impatient and trying to attract my attention without attracting that of our laid-back hostess.

'What about the snooker table, Dad?' he whispered. 'I mean, like when are we gonna see it?'

But Madame MacPherson's ears were obviously attuned to picking up any sound that was even slightly louder than the soft gurgle of water rising from her fountain. 'Eet ees in there, young *garçon*.' She pointed to the house door, then gave precise details of how to find the relevant room. 'Be my guest, *mon petit*. Go and 'ave a game on eet, *si tu désires*.'

Both boys immediately rose from their seats. 'I, eh, I think I'd maybe better go along with him,' Sandy said, putting on an unconvincing air of indifference. He flashed Antoinette a nervous smile. 'Just in case he gets lost... if you don't mind... ehm, Madame.'

Madame MacPherson sped them on their way with a facial shrug and some Gallic shooing movements of her hands. 'Such nice boys,' she said to Ellie. 'The, uhm-ah, the beeg one – the Sandee one...' She paused, while closely surveying Sandy's departing, denim-encased bum through the magnifying lenses of her bamboo-framed specs. 'Sandee 'as such a nice, you know, *manière*, *non*?'

Ellie didn't have much French, but she had no problem in recognising the word *manière* as being a thinly-veiled euphemism for *derrière* in this context. 'Mmm, quite so,' she replied, with the wary reaction of a mother seeing her 'wee boy' being ogled by an older woman – particularly one who looked old enough to be his granny.

The perceptive Antoinette MacPherson was swift to change the subject – temporarily, at least. 'So,' she said, 'you are *curieux* to know about my Scotteesh name, *oui*?' Without waiting for a reply, she proceeded to give us a potted history of her married life.

Richard MacPherson had been her third husband, she informed us, while skipping any reference to her first two spouses or what had become of them. Richard, or 'my beeg Deek', as she affectionately used to call him, had been a burly Scot; *une figure splendide* of a man, especially when wearing his kilt.

'*Très* sexy, the Scotchmen in the keelts, *non*?' she remarked to Ellie, a naughty twinkle glinting behind the square lenses of her specs.

Richard, she went on, had been a theatre critic for a London newspaper when they first met. He'd been on a working visit to Paris, and they were introduced at a back-stage party after the first night of a new play Antoinette was appearing in. The classic love-at-first-sight scenario took place, followed by a fairy-tale wedding in a fairy-tale *château* on the Loire and a fairy-tale life together in Montmartre, where Richard diverted his literary talents towards the writing of romantic novels.

A stoical raising of her pencilled eyebrows accompanied the revelation that she had lost her 'beeg Deek' just three years later. She neglected to reveal, however, whether 'losing' him had been the result of a deliberate act on her behalf, or had been down to more mournful causes. All she would say was that she had never remarried. But, she was quick to add, there had been no lack of young, live-in lovers in the meantime – *naturellement*.

'And thees,' she said with a sudden note of finality in her voice, 'ees why I am selling *la table de* snooker.' She studied our expressions of puzzlement for a moment, then gave us an owlish look over the top of her bamboo rims. 'You know, *bien sûr*, 'ow eet ees with these casual *affaires d'amour* with toy boys, *oui*?'

'*Non,*' we replied in unison, but our looks of nosiness-fuelled eagerness to learn were all that was needed to persuade Antoinette to enlighten us.

Roger, a twenty-something, self-styled poet from London, had been her most recent beau – a beautiful *enfant terrible*, with the body of Michelangelo's 'David', the eyes of a Raphaelesque 'Madonna', the flowing locks of Botticelli's 'Venus', and the *appétit sexuel* of three Casanovas. *Mon Dieu*, Antoinette ejaculated, it had been all she could do to keep up with him at times! But, she was quick to add, she had succeeded – *naturellement*.

For all his physical stamina, however, Roger had one fatal weakness – his mind, or rather the low boredome threshold it had been burdened with. After a few weeks of composing rhyming couplets in praise of mountains and oranges, beautiful Roger had tired of everything about the Sóller valley, except its bars. Clearly, something would have to be done to save him from becoming yet another sad immitation of a failed Dylan Thomas. Antoinette had deduced, from the amount of time Roger spent watching it on satellite television, that his other great passion in life (after sex, alcohol and, to a dwindling extent, poetry) was snooker. So, she had ordered a snooker table for him direct from the manufacturers in Britain.

'*Et voilà!*' she declared. It had done the trick.

Why then, I ventured to enquire, was she selling it?

Madame MacPherson raised those stoical eyebrows of hers again. 'Because, *mon ami*, after only a few games on eet, my beautiful paramour 'ad one beeg attack of the *ennui*.'

I shook my head in a consoling sort of way. 'You mean he grew bored with the snooker table as *well* as the scenery?'

'*Absolument!*' Antoinette was patently piqued. To emphasise the fact, she exhaled jets of Gauloises smoke through her nostrils in a convincing simulation of a fire-breathing dragon. 'But thees ees not all,' she growled. 'Because, to add *l'insulte* to the injury, he then – 'ow you say in Édimbourg? – fucked off wi' the lassie next door.'

Ellie and I struck up a coughing duet to mask our sniggers. We could see that this wasn't a laughing matter, regardless of how amusing Antoinette's unexpected announcement in earthy Scots had sounded to us.

The 'lassie' in question, she went on to clarify, was actually the Swedish au pair of her German neighbours right there in Fornalutx. This had been a truly international *ménage à trois*, but none the less hurtful to the self-confessed *cosmopolite* Madame MacPherson for that. She had already chucked out or sold everything belonging to that randy lump of *merde*, she divulged. Everything, that is, except *la table de* snooker. Spanish men didn't play snooker, she explained. Like the French, they played *le billard*, on a table not unlike its snooker equivalent, but without, as she put it, 'pockets to poke their balls into'.

I sniffed a potential bargain here. 'Not much response to your advert in the *Majorca Daily Bulletin*, then?' I suggested.

'Well,' she shrugged, 'I 'ave 'ad a few phone calls, but the *manières* of the callers offended me.' They had all been proprietors of Brit tourist pubs, of that she was sure. She swiped the air with her cigarette holder. 'Puh! I would not invite anyone into my 'ome who calls me "doll" on the *téléphone*. *Sacré bleu*,' she gasped, 'one of them even 'ad

245

l'effronterie to address me as Brigitte Bardot!' Antoinette's look of shock then melted into a lopsided smile – a little smirk of a smile that had a hint of sensuality about it. 'And thees, you see, ees why I responded *favorablement* to the phone call from your boy Sandee. *Mais oui*,' she purred, 'I do like the *manières* of your boy Sandee.'

I could sense Ellie bristling. 'Yes, well, we've always taught him to be polite,' she said, pausing deliberately for a moment before adding, '*especially* to his elders.'

If Madame MacPherson read anything even remotely catty into that remark, she certainly didn't show it. Instead, she once again steered the conversation in another direction. Adopting a confidential, girl-to-girl approach, she started to tell Ellie that, although her three marriages to men of 'comfortable means' had left her financially *bien furni*, her restless nature demanded that she keep herself active – mentally as well as physically. Physical stimulation had never been a problem, she was swift to stress, that suggestive little smirk playing at one corner of her cupid's bow again. On the other hand, keeping mentally sharp while cohabiting with a succession of pretty-boy cretins like randy Roger was another matter entirely. So, amongst other things, she had developed a little business importing ex-catwalk items of *haute couture* from the top fashion houses of Paris. Having been worn only once at their 'launch', these exclusive garments were virtually new, but, thanks to her being on first-name terms with the designers themselves, she was able to buy and, more importantly, to *sell* the dresses at a fraction of their usual cost. She gave Ellie an enticing smile. 'Would you like to see some of them, *ma chérie*?'

That was my cue to join Sandy and Charlie at the snooker table. And a fine one it turned out to be. Green baize, cushions, pockets, balls, cues and all the rest of the paraphernalia all present, correct and in good-as-new condition. We liked it – a lot. And to add to its attraction (specifically, we hoped, in Ellie's eyes) it had a removable wooden cover which, when in place, converted it into a dining table. This wouldn't be just another 'big boys' toy' for the *almacén* after all. It was a handsome piece of furniture that would add a touch of class to its rustic surroundings – provided, of course, we could afford to buy it.

As misfortune would have it, however, I was still loudly singing the snooker table's praises when Madame MacPherson entered the room with Ellie. I hadn't exactly placed myself in the most favourable of starting points for negotiating a good price. Dammit! I could have kicked myself for being so careless, especially after Antoinette's self-defeating revelation about the response to her ad in the paper. But my worries were premature. Fate was about to come to my rescue.

To reach the cue ball, Sandy was stretching over the table, his body bent forward in a jack-knife position that presented Madame MacPherson with a priveleged view of what she clearly considered to be his best feature.

'Ooh-la-la!' Antoinette squealed in pop-eyed delight. '*Formidable*!' And she wasn't expressing her appreciation of the difficult snooker shot that Sandy had just made.

Sandy stood bolt upright, like a soldier called to attention, wheeled round with a look of shocked bewilderment on his face, and stood with his backside pressed firmly against the edge of the snooker table.

'Tell me, Sandee, *mon cher*,' Antoinette pouted, 'do you 'ave a keelt?'

Sandy nodded his head, while his eyes darted from side to side in the manner of a cornered rabbit looking for an escape route from a salivating wildcat.

'*Très bien*,' his man-eating admirer purred, 'because you 'ave, I theenk, a very nice *fuselage* for the wearing of eet.'

Charlie faked a puke.

Sandy blanched.

Antoinette letched.

Ellie bristled – though slightly less so than before, I noted.

I cleared my throat, then quickly interjected, 'Ehm, just to let you know, Madame MacPherson, that we're definitely interested in buying your snooker table. It's, well, to be perfectly frank, it's really a matter of the price you –'

She cut me off with a dismissive swatting motion of her cigarette holder and asked me bluntly if I was prepared to pay for the table being uplifted and transported to Andratx. When I replied that, yes, I would be happy to, and then attempted to make the qualification that it would depend, firstly, on arriving at a mutually-agreeable purchase price, she cut me off for a second time. She turned to Sandy...

'And you, you 'andsome young Scotchman,' she simmered, 'will you come and tell me 'ow much *plaisir* the *table de* snooker 'as been giving you when next you are in Fornalutx?'

Sandy nodded his head as if in a dread-induced trance.

'And will you wear the keelt, *mon brave*?'

Sandy nodded hypnotically again.

Charlie, having taken refuge behind my back, muttered, 'Perverted old slag!'

Madame MacPherson, apparently, hadn't heard him. '*Bon!*' she said to Sandy. 'And so you will 'ave *la table de* snooker as a geeft from me! *D'accord?*'

Yet another zombie-like nod from Sandy.

She then stepped forward, held her cigarette holder dramatically aloft, kissed him on both cheeks of his face, patted him on one cheek of his bum and, with a reiterated verdict of '*Formidable*', bade us all a Thespian farewell.

Back in the privacy of our little Ford Fiesta, I fully expected Ellie to go off on one about this elderly woman's lascivious behaviour towards our nineteen-year-old son. But she didn't. I suspected that it had something to do with the large paper carrier bag in the back of the car. Curious, I drew her attention to it.

'That? Oh, it's nothing,' she pooh-poohed. 'Just a little something from Antoinette.' Ellie smiled to herself. 'Really nice lady. Quite a character, but nice.'

I caught a whiff of bullshit mixing with the citrus aromas drifting in through the car's open windows. 'You mean you bought one of those fancy Paris dresses from her. Is that it?'

'No, no, no, nothing fancy, really. Just a frock.'

I shot her a suspicious look.

'Well, OK – two frocks, actually.' Ellie headed off my next question by launching herself into a diversionary spiel about how Madame MacPherson had 'so kindly' arranged to meet her in Palma the next time she was returning from Paris with a suitcase full of exclusive designer 'frocks'. Not for Ellie to buy for herself, I would understand – more to see if there was anything she might want to sell on to some of our friends. 'Could be quite a profitable wee sideline,' Ellie enthused.

While she treated herself to another little smile, I got my question in. 'So, how much did you pay her?'

'Mm?' Ellie was still smiling.

I wasn't. 'The two frocks in the back of the car – how much did you cough up for them?'

Ellie adopted her wide-eyed, innocent look. 'For the, ehm, frocks?'

'Yeah. How much?'

'Well… nothing.'

'Nothing?'

'Yes. More or less. I mean, it amounts to nothing… in the final analysis.'

Now I got it. 'You blew the snooker table money on them, didn't you?'

As expected, Ellie went all assertive now. We were *all* better off than we had been half an hour ago, she argued. So, what the blazes was I whingeing about? The boys and I had a free snooker table, Antoinette had the money we'd been prepared to pay for it, and Ellie had a couple of new frocks. 'And just wait 'til you see me in them,' she cooed, going all coquettish now. 'Mm-hmm, you won't be complaining about how much they cost then.'

Both of the boys faked pukes, while I said 'Touché' to Ellie and drove on homeward. The ways of a woman's mind, I thought, have even more twists and turns than the road from Andratx to Sóller.

– TWELVE –

AN ISLAND HIGHLAND FLING

The Saturday that Jock had been obliged to pick for his biggest ever Burns Night was actually a couple of weeks later than the customary Saturday following the bard's birthday, which is 25 January. Firstly, the musicians and entertainers he'd booked to fly over from Scotland for the event were otherwise engaged in Burns celebrations back home on the preferred date. Secondly, Jock had had to fit in with the diary of commitments at the highly popular establishment he'd chosen to present his 'extravaganza' in. Those considerations aside, precisely when it would be held wasn't really of any great consequence. Some of the people who'd be there on the night wouldn't even be sure who Rabbie Burns was, far less his date of birth. And even those few expat Scots who were afficionados of the great man and his work weren't going to be bothered if the time-honoured date for marking his memory had been overshot by a fortnight or so. There was going to be a bumper Hispano-Caledonian fiesta in Burns' name right there in Mallorca, and that was all that really mattered to them.

Pequeño Mundo, meaning Small World, is a hacienda-style roadhouse, tucked away in a little pine grove a short way beyond the eastern outskirts of Palma. It lies just off the *autopista* highway to the airport, in a neighbourhod called Coll d'en Rabassa. Such a convenient location, together with the large capacity of its function hall, was obviously why Jock had selected this as the venue for his big occasion.

Ever alert to the possibility of getting something for nothing, Jock had pulled off a public relations masterstroke by announcing a couple of weeks earlier that 'profits' from the Burns Night bash would be donated to a Palma nunnery, where the holy sisters were particularly noted for their charitable work in the local community. The result was extensive coverage of the story in the English language and Spanish newspapers on the island, with a correspondingly large upsurge in sales of tickets for the event. It mattered little to Jock whether or not this increase in demand was due to the public-spirited nature of the customers involved. He now had a guaranteed full house, and the free press publicity he'd rustled up to achieve this happy state of affairs more than compensated for the cash he'd reluctantly forked out for that small ad in the 'Daily B' a few weeks previously. Besides, 'lobbin' a wee wedge o' moolah to the currant buns at the convent', as he poetically put it, would bathe him in a nice glow of benevolence, as well as providing him with a bit of valuable kudos 'in the right Mallorcan circles'.

Curiously, though, the self-congratulatory smile he'd been wearing since engineering this cute move was noticeably absent from his face when I called at his house on the morning of the big night. I'd volunteered to go along to Pequeño Mundo with him to help set things up for the evening. His expression was uncharacteristically glum as he got into the car.

'Hell's bells, man,' he moaned, 'ye wouldnae believe the twenty-four hours I've just had.'

'Been feeling a bit under the weather, have you, Jock?'

'Under the cosh, more like. Twice! First, the leader o' the Scottish Dance Band I booked for tonight phones up to say he cannae make it cos he's got the flu. Then, right on the back o' that, one o' the Highland dancers does the same bloody thing.'

'And you couldn't get replacements in time, eh?'

'No, no, that wasnae the problem, son. Nah, the bandleader fixed up a stand-in accordion player OK, and the teuchter hoofer managed to rope in a dep as well.'

'So, what's the problem?'

Jock looked at me as if my head buttoned up the back. 'Flights! That was the problem! Budget airline, ye see. Non-transferable tickets, right?'

'Oh, right. You've had to pay for another two Edinburgh-to-Palma return tickets. Well now, that really is a bad break, Jock. Liable to turn a potential profit into a loss, eh?'

Jock rolled his shoulders. 'We-e-ell,' he drawled, 'I maybe wouldnae go so far as to say *that*. No, but I *will* admit the chances o' the nuns gettin' a wee iron lung have been lookin' kinda bleak.'

'Iron lung?'

'Aye – the rhymin' slang. Ye know – iron lung – bung – as in slice o' the action.'

I had a quiet chuckle to myself. Good old Jock – making sure, typically, that his own arse was covered first. 'Well, it's a true saying,' I said. 'Charity begins at home, doesn't it?'

'Too fuckin' right it does,' Jock readily agreed. 'Yeah, and you better believe it, by the way.'

'Still, it's a pity you've had to fork out for two extra air fares.'

At last, the self-satisfied smile returned to Jock's chubby face. He gave me a reproving look. 'It's *me* ye're talkin' to, son! Come on – did ye honestly think I'd be daft enough to let that kinda dosh slip through ma sticky, wee fingers?' He shook his head. 'Hey, hey, no way, José!'

It had taken him every minute of the limited time available, he admitted, and he'd had to bend the ears of every contact he had in the travel business, but he'd finally managed to solve the problem of the non-tranferable tickets.

'Why the hangdog expression when I picked you up a couple of minutes ago, then?'

'For hangdog read knackered. I've been up half the bloody night, remember!'

'Anyway, all's well that ends well.' I slapped his knee. 'And congratulations. Only you could find a way round paying the airline twice.'

'Better than that,' Jock grinned, 'I've even sweet-talked *them* into payin' *me!* Well, in a manner o' speakin', like.' He slapped his own knee and let out one of the wheezy giggles that always remind me of Muttley, the conniving Dick Dastardly's dog in the *Wacky Races* TV cartoons. He then proceeded to tell me that, after immense difficulty, he'd finally managed to get through on the phone to the airline's head honcho himself. The good man, being a devout Christian, had been so moved by Jock's tear-jerking story about his intended donation of profits to the nuns now being in jeopardy that he'd not only waived the non-transferable ticket rule in this instance, but had contributed two free air tickets to the UK as a raffle prize for the Burns Night as well.

'Wow!' I said. 'Very generous. Whoever gets the lucky number's going to be well chuffed with that.'

'Aye, right,' Jock winked, 'and guess who that's gonna be.'

I looked at him askance. 'You surely don't mean –'

'Listen, son,' he cut in. 'Man mind thyself. That's the only way to get anywhere on this island. Yeah, and you better believe that as well, by the way.'

Jock's wife Meg and a few of her friends were already at work in the function room at Pequeño Mundo when we got there. Willi, the affable owner, and his staff were putting the finishing touches to setting the last of dozens of tables that had been arranged around the perimeter of the dance floor, while Meg and her little team busied themslves decorating them with nick-nacks appropriate to the occasion. Tartan-ribboned sprigs of 'lucky Scottish heather' (gathered from the slopes of the Serra de Na Burguesa mountains to the west of Palma) were being placed in little vases alongside miniature cardboard flags of Spain and Scotland. At strategic positions round the walls, they'd already pinned portraits of Rabbie himself, as well as colourful posters depicting well-known Scottish landmarks, so the desired effect was beginning to take shape.

'It's looking good, Meg,' I shouted from the doorway.

'Yeah, and it'll be lookin' even better when you two have done yer bit.' She nodded towards a suitcase standing in the middle of the floor. 'Ye'll find everything ye need in there, so get yer fingers out!' When Meg was busy, everybody was busy.

The case was packed full of tartan wallpaper; roll upon roll of it, in all sorts of clan colours.

'Fell off the back o' a van belongin' to an interior decorators' supply company in Glasgow,' Jock confided.

I didn't bother to ask how the wallpaper had found its way to Mallorca and, in particular, to Pequeño Mundo on the very day that a Scottish shindig was being held there for the first time ever. Some things are best left shrouded in mystery.

'Fix some o' that wallpaper in pleats round the front o' the stage,' Meg instructed. 'Us girls are gonna make big bows and fans and ruffles and everything out o' the rest, and you guys can hang them all over the place. Ye'll get a set o' stepladders from Willi if ye ask him nice.'

Without even having to be asked, Willi snapped his fingers and barked a command in *mallorquín* to one of his staff. A couple of minutes later, the required stepladders were there.

'I get nosebleeds up heights,' Jock informed me. 'You'll have to go up the steps.'

'But they're not much more than two metres high,' I laughed.

'For me, that's a good nostril's worth o' vital fluid, son, so up ye go.'

So, up I went.

'Seen from this angle,' Meg called to me from the bottom of the ladder, 'ye've actually got quite a tidy arse, Pedro. Got yer kilt all ready for tonight, have ye?'

Memories of Antoinette MacPherson's kilt fetish came flooding back. I told Meg and Jock all about it while taping a paper toorie to the ceiling.

'*I* know her,' Jock piped up. 'Old Auntie Annie, the kids called her. Yeah, she used to do after-hours drama classes at a couple o' the international schools. A real horny old bint. Fancies anything in trousers, her.'

'Or, better still, out o' them,' Meg chipped in. 'She used to get her hair done in my salon when she came here first. Oh aye, a real randy old raver, that one. Yeah, and she *does* like them young.'

'Hmm,' I concurred, 'Sandy was certainly glad to escape from her place before she had a chance to lock him up in a cupboard for her occasional, well, amusement – if you know what I mean.'

Meg let rip with one of her trademark cackles. 'Well, well, well, he's *really* gonna be pleased,' she declared, 'because she's comin' tonight! Honest, she phoned up a coupla weeks ago and booked a ticket. Said she wouldnae miss a kiltie do like this for *any*thing.'

'If Sandy hears about that, you won't see him anywhere near here tonight,' I cautioned. 'I'm telling you, Madame MacPherson just about scared the pants off him the first time they met.'

Meg cackled again. 'Yeah, and wi' his kilt on, he won't even be *wearin'* any pants tonight, *if* he's a true Scotsman, that is.'

Jock was taking all of this very seriously. 'Well, for Pete's sake don't tell him she's comin',' he pleaded. 'He's got an important job to do – carryin' in Master MacSporran behind the piper, so he's *gotta* be here.'

'Don't worry,' I laughed, 'mum's the word.' Little did I know then, however, that fending off possible advances from old Antoinette MacPherson would turn out to be the least of Sandy's worries.

Jock, I'd noticed, was already starting to look a bit apprehensive about the forthcoming festivities. 'Talkin' about Master MacSporran,' he muttered as I descended the ladder for the last time, 'I hope to blazes Willi's taken him out o' cold storage!'

Meg shook her head and tutted. 'Aw, stop gettin' yer breeks in a fankle about the bloody haggis!' she groaned. 'It's all taken care of. Me and Willi saw to that long before you even got here.' She folded her arms and surveyed our handy work. 'No bad,' she conceded. 'Anyway, it'll have to do.' She checked her watch. 'Hey, it's high time you two headed for the airport to meet the band and everybody off the Edinburgh plane, so get yer bahookies outta here!'

Having been a professional bandleader myself (and the leader of a jazz band to boot), I can recognise the telltale signs of a half-plastered musician a mile away. Ellie once said that's because it takes one to know one, although she was only kidding – I think. But there *is* something different about the look of a musician experienced in inebriate ways, compared to, say, the occasional tanked-up holidaymakers who stagger off aeroplanes at Spanish holiday destinations like Palma de Mallorca every summer's day. For a start, musicians dedicated to a tipple don't stagger – not, at least, on the way *to* the gig. They make sure they have someone or something to hold onto if their legs aren't responding to simple commands from what's left of their brains. That's what gave big Donald away.

I knew the accordionist he was standing in for very well. He was a bandleader who led his sidemen by example; a strict teetotaller, who expected his musicians to follow suit, certainly when working. It seemed, though, that big Donald did not subscribe to what he obviously regarded as such a spoilsport dictum as this. While the other band members and the rest of their party were bright-eyed and eagerly taking in the Mallorcan ambience and surrounding scenery as they crossed the tarmac from the plane, Donald looked straight ahead, his eyes glazed and unblinking, his face fixed in a silly grin. His arms were draped round the shoulders of two of his fellow musicians, not in a show of camaraderie, but rather as insurance against falling flat on his face.

'You better get him on a crash diet of strong, black coffee,' I said to Jock, 'otherwise he'll never make it to the do tonight.'

Jock's reply was a dejected sigh. He and Meg had put a huge amount of time and effort into planning this show, not to speak of the financial risk they'd taken. It was only natural, then, that the possibility of it all being spoiled by one drunken accordion player was hard to contemplate.

A stocky little chap, who introduced himself as Doddy the drummer, came up to us first. He'd obviously read Jock's downcast expression, and he gave him a reassuring smile. 'Don't worry about big Donald,' he said. 'He's a bit scared o' flyin', ye see. Aye, so he just had a few wee nips durin' the flight – eh, to calm his nerves, sort o' style.'

Jock was beginning to look as if he could do with a few wee nips to calm his own nerves. 'So ye say,' he grunted, 'but if the bugger's not fit to play tonight, I'll bloody well murder him with my own bare hands, no matter how big he is.'

'Nah, nah, ye won't have a problem wi' big Donald,' Doddy assured him. 'I'll make sure he sleeps it off at the hotel this afternoon. He'll be OK for the gig, never you fear.'

It was then that I noticed a familiar face among those of the other Scottish entertainers coming towards us. It was Linda, the Glasgow girl whom Sandy, not so long ago, had brought to Ca's Mayoral the day she'd missed her plane home. We'd provided her with a bed for the night, but, much to Ellie's disappointment, no sparks of romance had been kindled between Sandy and our unexpected house guest.

'Hi, Linda,' I smiled. 'This is a surprise. Nice to see you again, but what brings you back to Mallorca so soon?'

Linda did a twirl, then a few steps of an improvised Highland Fling. 'Ah'm one o' the dancers,' she said. 'Deputisin' for the lassie that's got the flu.' She fanned her face with her passport. 'Phew! What a rush it's been. Only got the call last night.' She hesitated a moment before asking, 'And, ehm – and how's Sandy, by the way?'

I got the feeling that there was a little more than just polite small talk behind her question. 'Oh, he's fine,' I replied. 'Actually, you'll see him tonight. Jock here has roped him in to carry the haggis on the parade from the kitchen to the stage.'

Linda's eyes lit up. 'So, uhm, he'll be wearin' the kilt, like, will he?'

'Yup, all the gear – kilt, Prince Charlie "bum-freezer" jacket, hairy sporran, the works.'

Linda arched her eyebrows. 'Hmm, sounds right interestin'. Oh aye, Ah'll be lookin' forward tae seein' that, but!' She then adopted a confidential mien. 'Ah maybe shouldnae be sayin' this tae you – Ah mean, you bein' his dad and that. But see your Sandy? Well, Ah think your Sandy's pure, dead sexy. Honest, Ah really fancy your Sandy somethin' rotten, so Ah do.'

I was tempted to say that she'd shown precious little sign of that during her brief stopover at Ca's Mayoral. But I decided it was all part of the mystical ways of the female mind, and best not delved into too deeply. Discretion was the safer option. 'Once he knows you're here, I'm sure he'll be looking forward to seeing you again, too,' I said, my fingers firmly crossed behind my back.

Linda skipped off into the terminal building with a cat-that-got-the-cream grin on her face.

Jock already knew all about the frosty treatment Sandy had given her at Ca's Mayoral. 'For Christ's sake, don't tell him *she's* gonna be at the do as well as old Antoinette MacPherson,' he muttered as soon as Linda was out of earshot. 'Otherwise, it's odds on I'll have to call on you to do the haggis-totin' honours instead.'

That was one honour I didn't relish having bestowed on me. I knew from past experience that, when wearing the kilt, it's best to maintain a low profile – especially at 'international' occasions like Jock's free-and-easy Burns Night. There's usually at least one tiddly woman unable to resist the temptation of finding out in public whether or not you are actually the real thing – a 'true', bare-arsed Scotsman. I told Jock he needn't worry. I'd keep word of Antoinette's and Linda's impending presence at tonight's big event well away from Sandy's ears.

I knew I should have been feeling guilty for agreeing to be so underhand with my own son, but, for some mischievous reason, I wasn't. Instead, I had a good laugh on the drive back to Andratx after dropping the musicians and dancers off at their Palma hotel. This was promising to be *quite* an evening!

Young Charlie had chosen to give the Burns Night a miss. In his opinion, such shindigs were only for weirdos who liked dressing up like the 'kilted poofs' you see depicted on Scottish shortbread tins. My assertion that all Scotsmen should be proud to wear their national dress elicited only a dismissive grunt from Charlie.

'You wore a kilt yourself when you were a sprog,' Sandy reminded him as we set off in the car for *Pequeño Mundo*.

'That's only cos Mum made me,' Charlie retorted. 'Let's face it, I didn't have much choice, did I? I was only three years old!'

'You wore your kilt until you were *seven*,' Ellie corrected, 'and you looked really cute in it.'

Sandy burst out laughing. 'Yeah, especially with the bulge in his nappies sticking out the back.'

'Very funny, big brother,' Charlie came back. 'You should try your hand at being a stand-up comedian. Yeah, just stepping on stage dressed in all that tartan drag-queen gear you've got on tonight would bring the house down before you even opened your mouth.'

And that was the type of brotherly banter the boys exchanged all the way to the O'Briens' place, where Charlie would be spending the evening.

'Remember, don't drive too fast in the Merc on your way along the *autopista* to Tito's nighclub,' Sandy shouted to Charlie as he was pressing the entryphone button by the gilded gates to the O'Brien mansion.

Charlie's response was a feigned yawn and the expected one-fingered salute.

I glanced at Ellie just as she was glancing at me. I wondered if I was looking as uneasy as she was.

Sandy noticed this visual exchange. 'It's all right, it's all right, it's all right,' he urged. 'I was only pulling his leg!'

'I hope so,' Ellie said, her tone leaving Sandy in no doubt as to how serious she was. 'Honestly, Sandy, if you know about anything dangerous that Charlie gets up to when he's with Dec O'Brien, you've got to tell us.'

All that Sandy would say in response was that we knew as much about what Charlie and Dec got up to as he did. While this left us none the wiser and did little to ease our nagging concerns, we left it at that, at least for now, and continued on our way to Coll d'en Rabassa.

If the wooded setting of Pequeño Mundo had struck me as attractive in daylight, it looked doubly so at night. Earlier in the day, I'd scarcely noticed the gnarled and ancient pine tree that dominates the courtyard in front of the main building. Now, with its contorted trunk and sagging branches cleverly floodlit, that old tree stood out as a truly stunning masterpiece of natural beauty. The Archduke Luis Salvador himself would probably have bought the whole island to protect such a magnificent specimen. Seeing the tree in that light for the first time (both literally and aesthetically), I was reminded of just how beguiling such easily-ignored details of the Mallorcan countryside can be. And this one was there for all to see in the most unlikely of locations; in a little oasis of rustic peace, tucked away between a traffic-packed highway, an industrial estate containing the local Coca Cola factory, and the fuel storage depot for one of the busiest airports in Europe. Jock had chosen his venue well, and nature had added to the charm of the setting by providing unusually balmy weather for the time of year.

When we arrived, the paved area around the old pine tree was already filled with people, all sipping bubbly, all dressed in their finery, and most of them sporting at least a glimpse of tartan in recognition of the Scottishness of the occasion. Not that anyone could fail to recognise that aspect, given that a pipe major in full ceremonial 'kiltie' uniform, complete in every detail from the black fur of his bearskin hat to the pristine white of his spats, was playing a rousing selection of Scottish tunes by the main entrance to the hall.

I was surprised, though, to see the number of male guests who'd also turned up in Highland dress. Sandy and I were far from being conspicuous in that respect, and for this I was extremely grateful. If Charlie had been there, I'd have explained that there's a difference between being proud to wear the kilt and feeling like the only technicolour guppy in a jam jar full of tuxedo-clad tadpoles. It's worth mentioning, however, that not everyone is inhibited by such Celtic self-consciousness. Jock, for instance, was positively revelling in his role of the traditionally-attired Highland laird. Standing with Meg just inside the doorway, he was cheerfully receiving everyone into the warmth of his 'castle' with hearty handshakes and hugs. These were accompanied by extravagant (and often non-sensical) words of welcome in broad Scots. 'Long may yer lum reek, hen,' he gushed to one patently confused Spanish lady, before telling her equally bewildered husband that, 'Auntie Mary had a canary up the leg o' her drawers'. Jock's earlier state of anxiety had now been ousted by a 'no business like show business' kick. He was on a high and loving every minute of being the centre of attraction at this, his very own and long-awaited 'ethnic extravaganza'.

While the interior of Pequeño Mundo may not have been an exact reproduction of the great hall of a baronial pile by yon bonny banks of Loch Lomond, it was close enough to serve the immediate purpose. Meg and her little group of helpers had done a grand job. In the soft glow of candlelight flickering from its ranks of tables, the tartan-trimmed function room had assumed a festive atmosphere that was Scottish in essence, but with due deference being paid to the host nation as well. To emphasise this, the Spanish flag and the Lion Rampant of Scotland, which share the same red-and-gold colours, had been draped on either side of a portrait of Robert Burns to form an eyecatching centrepiece on the wall behind the stage.

Nods of approval and muted words of praise were general as couples began to drift in from the courtyard to the gentle sounds of old Scots airs being relayed through the house PA system. As they were plied with more sparkling *cava* by a squad of waiters, few of these guests would have realised that their ears were merely being caressed by the lull before a musical storm. But there was much to enjoy before matters reached that state of unbridled fun.

When, at length, the gathered company had been shown to their table places, a buzz of anticipation for the forthcoming jollifications was already in the air. The hushed chitchat of the courtyard had now graduated into a laughter-sprinkled babble. Bottles of Spanish wine (included in the ticket price) graced each table in sufficient quantity to ensure that little, if any, re-ordering would have to be done by anyone. That, at least, was the theory. Jock, mindful of Burns Night convention, had also provided each table with a bottle of Scotch for toasting purposes. Given that not everyone would drink it, this meant, of course, that there was enough whisky to allow those who did partake to toast themselves silly. Again, Rabbie Burns himself would have approved, I'm sure.

His namesake Jock, now spotlit in the centre-front of the stage, brought proceedings to order. For reasons best known to himself, his accent was now switched from the broad Scots of the doorway to the usual mid-Atlantic of his public persona. His first great pleasure, he drawled through the microphone, was to thank everyone present for their support, and to welcome, in particular, several Mallorcan government dignitaries and their wives, who would be experiencing their first taste of Scottish culture. They would, he promised them, *not* forget this evening. In closing, Jock bade a special welcome to the British Consul, without whose good offices, he smiled, the evening's 'top of the bill' would not have been sprung from Sing Sing.

While the audience were pondering the meaning of that cryptic statement, they were asked be upstanding. Jock then called out, 'Now, let the festivities begin!' He gestured theatrically towards a door in the far corner of the room. 'Pipe major!' he commanded, 'let's hear it for... ANGUS MacSPORRAN!'

The hall lights dimmed, and the skirl of the bagpipes heralded the grand entrance of Jock's star attraction. To the rhythmic handclapping of the crowd, the pipe major began his slow march through the rows of tables, followed a couple of paces behind by Sandy, holding aloft Rabbie Burns' celebrated 'great chieftain o' the puddin' race'. The 'beastie' was lying in state on a silver platter, his grey skin doused in whisky, which had been set alight to add to the dramatic effect of his progress from kitchen to sacrificial slab.

I noticed a little smile of pride on Ellie's lips as she watched Sandy cross the dance floor behind the piper. Whilst not overdoing it, Sandy did include enough swagger in his step to give the kilt the required 'swing'. Wolf whistles from some of the less reserved ladies present were heard to rise over the steady beat of applause as the two-man haggis procession stepped up onto the stage, where Jock awaited their arrival. It was then that Sandy noticed Ellie and me, sitting as we were at a table directly opposite. The dirty look he gave me spoke for itself. Nevertheless, Ellie decided to put it into words for me, just in case.

'He's obviously bumped into Linda backstage,' she said out of the corner of her mouth.

'Yeah,' I muttered back, 'and she's obviously told him she bumped into me at the airport this afternoon.'

'You *will* be popular, and it serves you right for being so deceitful,' Ellie said flatly. 'You really *should* have told him, you know.'

'That's not the half of it,' I informed her. 'Just wait 'til he discovers old Antoinette MacPherson's here as well!'

The dirty look Ellie then gave me spoke even louder for itself than Sandy's had done. This time, she didn't bother to translate. She knew she didn't have to.

As the piper ended his tune, Sandy placed the flaming haggis on a small table in front of Jock.

Angus MacSporran's big moment had arrived.

And so had Jock's.

He motioned the audience to be seated. Then, after a suspense-building pause, he launched himself with gusto into Robert Burns' famous 'Address To A Haggis'…

'Fair fa' your honest, sonsie face,
Great chieftain o' the puddin' race!
Aboon them a' ye tak yer place,
Painch, tripe or thairm:
Weel are ye worthy of a grace
As lang's my airm.'

Although it was abundantly clear from the blank looks on their faces that most of his audience hadn't the faintest idea what he was talking about, Jock recited on regardless, his delivery becoming ever more animated as he approached the climax of the piece. He reached down and pulled his *skean-dhu* dagger from the top of his tartan stocking, unsheathed it with a flourish, then raised it menacingly above the hapless haggis.

'His knife see rustic labour dight…'

Jock's voice rose to a growling crescendo:

'And cut you up wi' ready slight…'

To gasps of astonishment from those in the crowd unaccustomed to this ritual 'slaughter', Jock brought his dagger down in a murderous stroke and plunged it into Master MacSporran's bulging midriff:

'Trenching your gushing entrails bright
Like ony ditch…'

Jock ripped his *skean-dhu* blade this way and that through the haggis, his voice quivering with over-the-top menace:

'And then, oh, what a glorious sight,
Warm-reekin', rich!'

His performance, blatantly hammed-up though it had been, earned Jock a standing ovation. He milked it for as long as he could, then held up a silencing hand. 'And now, ladies and gentlemen, *señoras y señores*, pray remain upstanding, charge your whisky glasses, and let us drink a toast to our honoured guest here – the haggis.'

'The haggis!' everyone chanted, glasses raised.

Then, shortcutting the lengthy proceedings that are regarded as *de rigueur* at 'serious' Burns Suppers, Jock proposed what he described as the most important toast of all, a salute to the immortal memory of Scotland's national bard, Robert 'Rabbie' Burns.

Thus, the first two drams of whisky of the night were downed by those so inclined. Many, however, opted to toast with wine. A sensible decision, considering the amount of *vino* that would soon be flowing, and the effects on human behaviour that mixing 'the barley' and 'the grape' is reputed to provoke. But Sandy, still standing on stage with Jock and the piper, wasn't afforded the same choice. Tradition dictated that he, along with his two 'performing' cohorts, had to do the honours by quaffing shots of neat whisky.

Ellie was horrified. 'He'll be sick,' she gasped. 'He's just not accustomed to strong drink.'

I said nothing. I'd have been surprised if, at nineteen years of age, he hadn't had an experimental go at most popular forms of intoxicating liquor, including his national spirit. Time, though, would tell how well he could hold it.

Jock's next master-of-ceremonies task was to invite a round of applause for the piper and the haggis-bearer as they left the stage. Antoinette MacPherson's unmistakable call of '*Bravo, mon cher! Quel beau* keelt!' warbled out from somewhere in the body of the hall. Sandy blanched visibly, threw me another dirty look and made a swift exit.

While the Scottish Dance Band was being introduced member-by-member, the ritually-slain haggis, his moment of glory gone, was unceremoniously whisked away to the kitchen, there to join his canned cousins as the mainstay of the first course of the banquet that was about to commence. An ignominious end, you might say, to the brief reign of a great chieftain of any gastronomic race. Yet it would have taken a miracle of messianic proportions to be able to feed the gathered three hundred with the 'gushing entrails' of just one haggis, no matter how ample an example. And, as I mentioned before, it's extremely unlikely that anyone in the hall would have guessed correctly whether their particular portion of haggis had come from an anonymous tin or from Angus MacSporran's fêted skin.

Jock had diplomatically arranged the menu to reflect the same Hispano-Scottish theme as the décor and the drinks. Following the mandatory Burns Supper fare of haggis with 'mashed neeps and tatties', the guests were served bowls of one of Mallorca's's most popular dishes, *Arròs a la Marinera*, a substantial rice-based stew of fish and seafood cooked in a herby saffron stock. This was followed by Scottish oatcakes and Spanish *Manchego* cheese, which, like the two previous courses, proved to be an exceptionally happy gustatory marriage.

During the hour or so that the meal lasted, the band – comprising accordion, fiddle, piano, bass and drums – had churned out medleys of deliberately subdued background music. This had been mainly Scottish in flavour, but with the occasional Spanish melody included for the sake of courtesy. Jock had left no card unplayed in his quest to impress those present who happened to be 'in the right Mallorcan circles'. Also, instead of joining in the feast, he and Meg had busied themselves going round the tables selling tickets for the 'grand raffle', which, as I overheard them repeatedly stressing, featured a star prize of two return flights to the UK. Ticket sales were understandably brisk. The Palma nuns would be eternally grateful for their generosity, the purchasers were assured.

No matter how concentrated his sales pitch, however, Jock had also been keeping a close eye and ear on the band, and on big Donald in particular. And so far so good. The recently-errant accordionist had arrived on stage looking stone-cold sober, his gormless grin of earlier replaced by a smile of such professional brightness that he wouldn't have looked out of place in a toothpaste commercial. More importantly, though, his playing had been flawless, as befits the lead instrumentalist in this type of band. Better still, Doddy the drummer's smiles and winks of reassurance to Jock suggested that all would continue to be well. The small bottle of mineral water from which Donald sipped between numbers seemed to reinforce Doddy's visually-imparted messages that the big squeeze-box player was now safely on the wagon. Jock allow himself a well-deserved sigh of relief.

No sooner had the last plates been cleared from the tables than the start of the entertainment proper commenced. Shona, a singer whom Jock introduced as coming direct from her success on 'the Scottish traditional-music charts' (as if any such list existed), got the ball rolling with a selection of tartan sing-along favourites, which the nicely-relaxed audience could 'lah-lah-lah' in tune with, *if* they didn't happen to know the words – which most of them didn't. This proved to be the shape of things to come.

After a brief intermission, which would allow everyone, in Jock's lyrical words, 'time to go and water the cactus', the pitch of the evening's revelries was ratcheted up a notch or two. The pipe major made his second appearance, the slightly jaunty angle of his bearskin hat and the pained wailing of his bagpipes as he fought to thrash them into musical submission hinting that he may have been doing a bit of clandestine bard-toasting on his own somewhere since his earlier performance. But, true to the reputation of all pipe majors worthy of the rank, he soon had his multi-limbed instrument under control.

To the stirring sound of the war pipes, Glasgow Linda and another girl in traditional dress swept in brandishing swords. These they crossed on the floor and, much to the delight of the audience, hurled themselves into a routine of tip-toed, high-speed, kilt-whirling manoeuvres around and between the razor-sharp blades.

'Half pissed,' Jock muttered, arriving crouched, unexpected and worried-looking at my side. 'Big trouble.'

I gave him a 'what the hell are you talking about?' look.

Jock continued to talk in snipped phrases. 'Your Sandy,' he said. 'In the kitchen. Her – Linda the Highland hoofer. A Spanish waitress. Half pissed. Big trouble.'

'Who's half pissed?' I asked, trying to make sense of Jock's clipped clues. 'Linda or the Spanish waitress?'

'Your Sandy,' he replied. 'Must've been the whisky.'

Ellie glared at me. 'I told you!' She then glared at Jock. 'And you should have known better – schoolteacher and everything!'

It seemed that Jock had been expecting just such a response from Ellie, and he didn't mince his words in replying. 'He's not my responsibility, darlin',' he rightly pointed out. 'He's a big boy now – old enough to make his own decisions about what he does or doesnae drink.'

Ellie acknowledged the truth of that with a tilt of her head and a rueful little smile.

In any case, it hadn't been the two nips of whisky Sandy had drunk on stage that had done the damage, Jock went on to explain. It had been the others he'd downed in the kitchen, where he'd taken refuge after hearing old Antoinette MacPherson calling out to him. 'Dutch courage, ye see,' Jock said. 'The poor laddie was in a state o' shock. Aye, and that's when the Spanish waitress zeroed in on him and did a bit o', well… comfortin', I suppose ye might say.'

'You mean they had a snogging session,' I said. 'That's what you're trying to tell us, Jock, isn't it?'

Jock pulled a 'you know how it is' shrug. 'It was the whisky,' he said. 'Mind you,' he swiftly added, 'don't get me wrong – the Spanish lassie's a real looker. Nice big, ehm – well, big brown eyes and that. Student – works here part-time.'

Ellie, for once, didn't appear at all interested in hearing details of Sandy having a romantic liason with a local *señorita*. 'Trouble,' she said to Jock, a worried frown on her brow, a hint of panic in her voice. 'You said there was trouble.' She prepared to stand up. 'I'm going to see Sandy.' She gripped Jock's arm. 'I hope the police aren't involved!'

'*Tranquilo, tranquilo, tranquilo*,' Jock implored, laying a hand on her shoulder. 'Just sit there and relax, hen. Everything's under control. And there's no police, OK?'

Reluctantly, Ellie did his bidding. She stared at Jock, her eyes urging him to get on with his story.

Jock gestured towards the dance floor, where the two featured dancers were Highland Flinging like tartan dervishes while the piper skirled them up a storm of jigs and reels. 'It was her fault,' he said. 'That Weegie bird Linda.'

'Weegie?' Ellie queried.

'Aye, ye know – Weegie – short for Glaswegian. Anyway, she's a fuckin' nut case.' Linda, Jock continued, had discovered where Sandy was holed up after his rapid departure from the hall. So, perhaps hopeful of creating some sort of love-at-second-sight reunion, she had gone breezing into the kitchen. Her entrance, Jock smirked, just happened to coincide with Sandy and the Spanish waitress 'gettin' warmed up', as he put it, at the side of the upright freezer.

Ellie rolled her eyes heavenward. 'Don't tell me there was a scene. How embarrassing!'

'Well, just a few plates,' Jock said, his deliberately casual manner clearly intended to keep Ellie's blood pressure down.

Ellie was aghast. 'You mean Linda chucked *plates* at them?'

'Yeah, one o' yer more excitable Weegies, her,' Jock said. Seeing Ellie's jaw drop, he turned up his calming tone to maximum. 'But don't worry, darlin', her aim's lousy, and anyway, the plates are covered by the insurance here.'

Ellie looked relieved. 'Phew!' she sighed. 'Thank goodness for that.'

Jock nodded towards the whirling Linda again. 'Oh aye, it was only when she lunged at the Spanish lassie wi' her sword-dance sabre there that things started to look a wee bit nasty. I'm tellin' ye, if the pipe major hadnae struck up her intro music at that very moment, ye never know what might have happened. Could've been bloody carnage in the kitchen.'

Ellie and I were both aghast, and it obviouly showed.

Jock started to laugh. 'You should see your faces!' he giggled. 'Honest, you pair would believe *any*thing!'

Right on cue, Jock stood up to leave us as the Highland Dancing display ended. 'Oh, and by the way,' he shouted over the applause, 'Sandy said to tell ye he'll see ye back at home – sometime. He's takin' the Spanish lassie out on a date.' With that, he swaggered over the dance floor and bounced up on stage to announce the next item on the programme.

'Well, Ellie,' I said, 'maybe your wish for Sandy to find Señorita Right has been granted at last.'

Ellie shook her head wearily. 'Hmm, but I won't be holding my breath.' She picked up an empty glass. 'Here, pour me some wine, please. My nerves could do with it.'

I said 'Amen' to that, and sat back to watch Jock's raffle-drawing performance, aided and abetted by Meg.

The atmosphere in the hall had reached that stage when any traces of after-dinner lethargy had given way to the uninhibited party spirit that Jock's provision of copious quantities of wine had been calculated to ensure. The more good-natured heckling he was subjected to as each prize-winning ticket was drawn, the more he enjoyed returning the accusations of 'Fix' and 'Rip-off' with slighting wisecracks of his own. He was in his element.

I was intrigued by one thing, though. Recalling his earlier hint to me that the star prize would be 'diverted' in his own direction, I could hardly wait to see how he'd pull off such an outrageous fiddle. My guess was that Meg would somehow manage to produce her own ticket out of the hat. The ensuing outburst of mock-irate objections that were guaranteed to be hurled at Jock by all and sundry would then be parried by him in the same mischievously-insulting way as had already become the norm.

But I misjudged him. His avowed sneaky intentions turned out to be nothing more than a bit of typical Jock Burns bluster. The two return air tickets to the UK were won fair and square (apparently) by a frail, old Spanish woman, whose good luck was warmly applauded by everyone present, including Jock himself. He, in turn, received a rapturous response to his announcement that sufficient had been raised by the Burns Night promotion to ensure that a 'generous donation' would be made to the nuns at the Palma convent.

Jock, therefore, was looking distinctly pleased with himself when he came off stage, after re-introducing the band and inviting everyone to 'loosen their corsets and hernia trusses and dance the rest of the night away to the best little-old ceilidh band this side of Hadrian's Wall'.

I congratulated him on doing the right thing by the free air tickets. 'You had me fooled, though, Jock,' I laughed. 'I honestly believed you were going to pocket them for yourself.'

Jock leaned in close as the amplified opening chords of 'The Dashing White Sergeant' blared out from the band. 'Aye,' he shouted in my ear, 'but like I told ye earlier, son, you'd believe anything.' Then, while dozens of revellers crowded onto the dance floor, he confided that the old dear who had 'won' the air tickets was a regular client at Meg's salon, and she just happened to have a phobia about flying. 'Ye wouldnae get her within a mile o' a plane, son.' He rubbed his forefinger and thumb together. 'So, a few coins from yours truly into her wee purse, and…'

I couldn't tell if this latest claim of skulduggery was just one of Jock's image-creating white lies, but, whether or not, his chesty giggle of delight at making it was rapidly replaced by a gasp of shock as a thunderous crash and a spine-chilling scream rang out from the direction of the stage. The music came to an abrupt halt, as did the dancing.

Big Donald had fallen off his chair. He was lying sprawled along the front of the stage, happily paralysed, his eyes glazed and unseeing, that silly smile fixed on his face again, his accordion still strapped to his chest and wheezing out its last, discordant breath.

'The bastard's blitzed!' Jock wailed. 'Imagine havin' all yer hard work and honest intentions ruined by one bloody piss artist!' He stood and watched, helpless, as the other band members dragged big Donald into the wings. Jock held his head in his hands. 'How the hell could this have happened?'

The answer was supplied by Doddy the drummer when Jock eventually clambered on stage to try and find some way of salvaging what was left of his rapidly disintegrating 'ethnic extravaganza'. It had just been sussed, Doddy told him, that the bottle of mineral water big Donald had been sipping from all evening had actually contained neat vodka. 'Must've been gettin' it refilled sneaky-like at the bar outside in the courtyard between sets,' Doddy lamented. He gave Jock an anguished look. 'Sorry about that, big man. Ah never even noticed.'

Jock wasn't even listening. Lame apologies would serve no purpose now. He glanced round at the sea of expectant faces staring up at him from the dance floor. 'What the hell are we gonna do now?' he mumbled to himself, almost sobbing.

But, as so often happens, cometh a problem to a man, cometh his wife with a slick solution to it. 'Haul the squeeze-box off that big numpty,' Meg snapped at the other band members. She turned to Jock. 'And you buckle it on. *You're* the bandleader now!'

'But –'

'Yeah, yeah, I know – ye havenae played the accordion for years. But needs must.' She gave him a slap on the back that was so encouraging he almost choked. 'Come on!' she pressed. 'You can do it. It's like drownin' or fallin' off a bike. Once learned, ye never lose the knack.'

'But –'

'No buts! Strap that box on and start squeezin' out the tunes!'

And so the evening was saved, despite Jock's understandable misgivings about stepping unprepared into the musical breach. As Meg had maintained, once he got the knack of playing the accordion again, he did surprisingly well. In fact, to paraphrase the words of the old Frank Sinatra song, mistakes, he made a few, but then again too few to mention – at least in the opinion of the majority of wine-fuelled merry-makers whose cheers of appreciation rang to the rafters at the end of each dance. Like some of Jock's notes, their improvised steps to the 'Eightsome Reel',

'Highland Schottische', 'Gay Gordons' and other Scottish Country Dance favourites may not have followed the recognised pattern to the letter, but they were having fun aplenty. And that, in the final analyisis, was all that Jock (and Rabbie Burns in his day) considered important on such occasions.

A potential disaster was turned into a belter of a Scottish knees-up, as individual musicians mucked in with impromptu solo 'turns' to help keep things going. Doddy the drummer had everyone in stitches with impersonations of legendary Scottish music hall stars, while the fiddler got toes tapping with some swinging Stephane Grappelli numbers. But, surprisingly, the star of these ad lib cabaret spots turned out to be none other than the pipe major. The ramrod bearing, which had been such a conspicuous feature of his image at the start of the evening, had gradually degenerated into a state of unkempt slovenliness as the effect of a steady intake of whisky took its toll. With military reserve finally cast off, the strict orthodoxy of his playing technique was abandoned in favour of a much more irreverent style. The essence of this involved jazzing-up well-known Scottish pipe tunes and Scotching-up jazz standards, like 'The Saints'.

The audience lapped it up, and the pipe major's accompanying footwork, which included spasms of frenzied twirling, proved to be particularly popular with a certain ageing French actress. So fascinated was Antoinette MacPherson by all this flying tartan that she was moved to station herself in poll position at the edge of the dance floor for the duration of the pipe major's act. She grinned, squealed and applauded in delight as the piper's abandoned kilt-whirling proved that he was, without a shadow of doubt, the truest of true Scotsmen.

'I am *très* disappointed not to 'ave seen more of your son, the Sandee one,' Antoinette told us with a saucy smile when we chanced to meet on the way outside after the mandatory community singing of 'Auld Lang Syne' at the end of the night.

'Yes, well, he had to rush off to another engagement,' Ellie politely lied.

Antoinette ignored that and winked at me. 'And you are poking your balls into your pockets, *oui*?'

'Oh, the snooker table,' I replied with a circumspect cough. 'No, haven't quite got things in place to set the balls running yet, I'm afraid. But, ehm, soon, I hope.'

'*Merveilleux*.' She winked again. 'And I 'ope you will enjoy the poking of them.'

Just then, the pipe major appeared by her side, his bearskin hat now being worn so jauntily that it completely covered one eye. 'Your place or mine, beautiful?' he slurred, while his free eye attempted to focus on Antoinette's heavily made-up face.

'I theenk your 'otel will be the place most *approprié*, my beeg, 'andsome keeltie,' she cooed, pecking his cheek before taking his arm and spiriting him away.

'How's he going to feel when he wakes up next to *her* in the morning?' Ellie somewhat scathingly remarked as the odd couple disappeared into the night.

'Probably about as bad as *he* feels good,' I said. I gestured to where Jock was glorying in a scrummage of handshakes and backslaps with some guests whom I took to be from 'the right Mallorcan circles'. All of the dignitaries looked unashamedly mellow and much the better for their first taste of Scottish 'culture'. Yes, despite a few heart-stopping moments along the way, Jock's big gamble had paid off, and no-one could have begrudged him the obvious pleasure (and sense of relief!) he was now basking in.

★★★

'You look a bit rough,' I said to Sandy when he arrived late and dishevelled in the Ca's Mayoral kitchen for breakfast the following morning.

'Your date with the Spanish girl go all right?' Ellie probed, unable to contain her pent-up nosiness.

'Never happened,' he grunted

Ellie and I were all ears as he poured himself a black coffee, but Sandy said no more. Instead, he slumped down at the table and cradled his head in one hand.

'Don't tell me she stood you up,' Ellie eventually ventured, her curiosity getting the better of her again.

Realising that he'd get no peace until he spilled the beans, Sandy took a deep and laboured breath. 'Right, mother,' he sighed, 'here's the full, unabridged account…'

What had happened, he glumly recounted, was that Magdalena the waitress had gone home to change after the last of the dinner plates had been cleared from the tables. The arrangement was that they'd meet up again at the bar in the Pequeño Mundo courtyard half an hour later, and from there they'd go on to a Palma nightclub that Magdalena had suggested. What Sandy hadn't realised until it was too late, however, was that when Magdalena had casually mentioned that she hailed originally from a small village in the mountains of southern Spain, she had actually been indicating that certain 'old fashioned' Spanish formalities were still adhered to by her family. And the custom that was observed on this occasion was the one they call *la acompañata*, the chaperoning of unmarried girls on rendezvous with members of the opposite sex.

'When I crept out of the kitchens at the appointed time,' Sandy disclosed, 'she was sitting at the courtyard bar with what she said were her three older brothers and what looked like her parents and a few aunties and uncles as well. Half the population of Andalusia!'

'Maybe they were just interested in seeing a bloke in a kilt,' I glibly suggested, trying not to laugh.

Sandy hadn't been amused at the time, however, and he still wasn't. He dryly informed us that he'd assessed the proposed 'date' situation in the blink of an eye, and had decided to make his second swift exit of the night.

Ellie was following all of this as intently as she would one of her favourite soaps on telly. 'I don't blame you,' she said, 'but if you left the Burns Night early, how come it took you so long to get home? I heard you coming in, and it was *long* after we got back.' In sudden anguish, she clapped a hand to her cheek. 'I hope the brothers didn't take offence at you snubbing their sister and ganged up on –'

'No, no, no, mother,' Sandy butted in, 'nothing like that.'

'Well, I *am* relieved,' Ellie gasped.

'You won't be,' Sandy countered, 'because what actually happened was a lot worse than being duffed up by three ex-gypsies from the Sierra Nevada or wherever.'

What *actually* happened, he went on, was that, after fleeing the Pequeño Mundo, he hailed a taxi and went to a Palma bar that he knew was frequented by his Mallorcan chums in the La Real football team. Just what had possessed him to do that dressed in a kilt he couldn't now imagine. Maybe he hadn't been thinking too clearly because of the whisky he'd drunk earlier. Anyway, sure enough, he'd found three of his teammates there and, after a few more drinks, had been persuaded to go on to a nightclub with them. They'd promised him it was a fun place, where he'd soon forget his traumatic Pequeño Mundo experiences. In the mood he was in, that had suited Sandy just fine. Even when the 'fun place' turned out to be a sleazy strip joint in the armpit of Palma city, he'd only laughed at what he regarded as his chums' roguish sense of humour in trying to cheer him up. They'd meant well – or so he'd thought at first.

Sandy stroked his brow and shook his head slowly, a look of utter abjection on his face. 'Why oh why,' he moaned, 'did I take the boys' dare to go up on stage and ask that erotic dancer to join us?'

'The whisky again?' I suggested, hoping that Sandy wouldn't notice the snigger-stifling yodle in my voice.

'I'll never drink that stuff again,' he muttered, 'and I should never have drunk the two large ones the lads bought me in there.' He was almost whimpering now. 'Carla the Human Python, she was billed as.' He massaged his temples. 'Oh-h-h-h, my poor head.'

If we hadn't known him for the honest lad he is, what Sandy told us next would have seemed like pure fiction...

Carla the Human Python had joined them, as invited, at their table at the end of her act. She sat down next to Sandy and wasted no time in making it abundantly clear that she'd taken quite a fancy to him, and, he admitted, the feeling was mutual. In addition to all the stunning physical attributes that she had flaunted so graphically on stage, there was something about her sultry, dark-eyed features, her long, raven hair, her smooth, dusky skin and, most of all, her husky, sensual voice that made him go weak at the knees. And it was those knees, or rather one of them, that would lead to his undoing.

First one of Carla's fingers stroked Sandy's knee under the table, then it was joined by its neighbours as they worked their way with practiced skill slowly and seductively up his bare leg. '*Madre mía*,' the Spanish siren rasped in his ear, 'for me, the keelt of the Scotchman ees a beeg turn-on, eh!'

'The brazen trollop!' Ellie gasped in motherly indignation. 'I hope you slapped her face!'

No, that was hardly the sort of thing a bloke would do in front of his mates, Sandy wearily informed her, even if the bloke didn't find the female attractive – which, in this case, he did. But that was beside the point, because what happened next wasn't something he could have controlled, anyway. The combination of too much whisky, the stuffy atmosphere in the club, the fevered rhythms of electric flamenco music and the effect of Carla's wandering hand on his pulse rate suddenly made him come over all woozy and wobbly. Slurring his apologies in faltering Spanish, he'd disentangled himself from the clinging *señorita* and staggered off towards the gents' to freshen up.

'I hope he knows what he's let himself in for!' he heard one of his friends guffaw as the toilet door swung shut behind him.

'That went in one ear and right out the other,' Sandy confessed. 'I was so befuddled by then that I didn't even realise that the "he" he was referring to was me. Hmm, and after that I was too busy splashing cold water on my face to even notice the other person coming into the toilets just after me.'

Ellie tensed over her toast, patently dreading what her son might come out with next.

Sandy continued with his tale…

'*Hombre*, I have never had a Highland Fleeng before!' he'd heard a gravelly voice say in a disturbingly familiar Spanish accent. He'd then looked in the mirror to see someone having a pee in the urinal behind him, lecherous eyes giving him the once over. Sandy spun round, unable to take his eyes off his admirer's hitched-up mini skirt and what was pointing at porcelain from beneath it.

'Carla?' I said.

Ellie was flabbergasted. 'Sandy! You *don't* mean to tell me that Carla was…'

'Yes, Mother, this particular Car*la* was actually a Car*los*! Yeah, and he'd obviously been told I was some kind of kinky kiltie, a tartan transvestite touting for a one-night stand with a female-impersonating snake-dancer! No wonder the boys were in hysterics when I flew out of that toilet, bolted past them and shot straight out into the street! Honestly, I didn't stop running until I reached the taxi rank in the Born – half way across the city!'

Even Ellie now joined me in a good laugh about Sandy's latest Burns Night misadventure. Sandy didn't see the funny side of it, though, so I thought an attempt to draw an apt and jocular line under events was now called for.

'Well, Sandy,' I said, 'it just goes to show, doesn't it?'

'Show what?'

'That, no matter how *attractively* disguised, in the immortal words of Rabbie Burns himself – a man's a man for a' that!'

– THIRTEEN –

SPRINGTIME IN A BASKET

Our arrival at Ca's Mayoral fifteen months earlier had been greeted by a freak flurry of snow, the first in the valley that any of our elderly neighbours could remember. Having just left the Scottish winter behind us, we'd been more than a little dismayed to think that the same weather had followed us all of fifteeen hundred miles south to a Mediterranean island where, according to a popular eulogy by Santiago Rusiñol, 'the sun shines all day long'. And so it does, for most of the time, as we would discover to our even greater dismay during our first summer there. For there's a world of difference between relaxing under a parasol with an ice-cool drink (as, sensibly, most choose to do while holidaying in Mallorca) and having to work in the blistering heat of the fields, week in, week out. But we had survived our introduction to the latter by gradually adapting to the pace

285

and rhythm of life in the Mallorcan countryside. You ultimately have to accept that the climate dictates such things. Take, for instance, the Spanish custom of having an after-lunch siesta, especially in summer. That isn't laziness, but simply common sense.

Now that we were nearing the end of our second winter, memories had all but faded of that first November day, when the freaky little whiteout turned our unpicked oranges into exotic snowballs and transformed every palm tree in the valley into a grenade burst of cottonwool. Imagine my surprise, then, when I now heard Ellie shout:

'Peter! It's snowing!'

'Would you *ever* credit it?' I muttered through clenched teeth, 'Only two falls of snow in living memory, and both since we arrived on the scene. We must have brought a jinx to this valley!'

I was busy putting up some shelves on the wall behind the little bar in the *almacén*, and I'd been so engrossed in what I was doing that I hadn't even bothered to look outside for an hour or so.

'That'll put paid to the work on the swimming pool for a while,' I called in full defeatist mode to Ellie when I heard her coming along the corridor. 'Snow today, slush and muck tomorrow. Everything out there will be an absolute quagmire.'

As deflated as I was by her piece of bad news, Ellie was cheerfulness personified when she came into the old workroom. Looking as happy-go-lucky as Dorothy skipping down the 'Yellow Brick Road', she was swinging one of the little wicker baskets we used for orange-picking. But, significantly, it didn't contain any oranges.

'See,' she breezed, 'I've brought you a basketful of snowflakes!'

My spirits rose the moment I realised what she meant – a natural occurrence that transforms the island's landscape into a living 'snowscape' every February. But this wonder of nature has nothing in common with the white blanket depicted on those Christmas cards that feature dead-of-winter scenes in Olde-Worlde England. This version is the very antithesis of that. It heralds, in one sudden blizzard, not death, but the arrival of new life. It's the glorious birth of spring in Mallorca. It's almond blossom time.

'You should see it,' Ellie enthused. 'As soon as the sun came out from behind those clouds that have been hanging about this morning, the valley was smothered in this lovely, pinky-white stuff.' She showed me the contents of her basket. 'It was just as if someone had thrown confetti everywhere.' She thrust the basket at me. 'Look how beautiful it is. And the blossom comes out even before there are any leaves on the trees. Isn't that wonderful?'

'I hope old Pep didn't see you taking it off our trees,' I said, only half jokingly. 'He'd convert that little bunch of blossom into so many potential almonds that I'd be on the receiving end of another tongue-lashing for throwing away money again.'

'Well, we only have half a dozen almond trees to Pep's hundreds, and half a dozen almond trees are about as profitable to us as six of our hundreds of orange trees would be to him. So, a few blossoms more or less are neither here nor there.' Ellie went over to the sink, poured some water into a jug and deposited the flowering almond twigs in it. 'Anyway,' she said as she placed the jug on the bar top and fussed with the blossoms until they were arranged to her liking, 'they'll brighten the house up for a couple of days, so who cares what Pep thinks!'

She took the electric drill I'd been using from my hand. 'The shelves can wait 'til later,' she said, leading me by the elbow out of the *almacén*. 'Let's go and have an angels' eyeview of the blizzard. It happens, as they say in the tourist brochures, but once a year.'

We'd been caught up in such a whirlwind of work the previous February that we'd hardly even noticed the coming of the almond blossom, a spectacle for which Mallorca is rightly famous. There had been so many things to do about the farm after it became apparent just how run down the orchards were, and we were in such a flap to put everything right as quickly as possible, that taking time out to admire pretty flowers on almond trees had been the last thing on our minds. But now, Ellie was invoking our recently-adopted principle of 'work to live, not the reverse', and she wasn't about to let my programme of urgent tasks to be done in the emergent games room get in the way of it.

There are *santuaris*, literally religious 'sanctuaries' in the form of old monasteries, on the highest hilltops all over Mallorca. Among the most famous of these is the Santuari de Nostra Senyora de Cura, built on a mountain called the Puig de Randa, a flat-topped prominence rising more than five hundred metres above the rolling countryside of the southern heartland of the island. The Puig de Randa is considered to be one of Mallorca's holiest places, and, due to its historical association with Ramón Llull, the island's legendary thirteenth-century theologian, the Cura Monastery is one of its most revered. These days, though, the number of pious pilgrims and sanctuary-seekers visiting the place is likely to be far outstripped by sightseeing tourists, young hostellers taking advantage of the simple lodgings available, and even flocks of local folk out for celebratory meals. Yes, this *santuari*, like many of its counterparts around the island, has its own restaurant and bar, originally established to take commercial advantage of the public's appetite for religious refreshment, and prudently developed to cater for its alimentary hunger as well. And who would criticise such a pragmatic principle? After all, they say the way to a man's heart is through his stomach, so why not the way to his soul as well?

Ellie's reason for making the sixty kilometers journey from Andratx to the Puig de Randa today was neither gastronomic nor spiritual, however. Well, not entirely, anyway...

After bypassing Palma on the Via de Cintura *autopista*, we took the eastbound C715 highway to the little town of Algaida, where we branched off south towards the massive, table-top outline of the Puig de Randa. I noticed a little smile cross Ellie's lips as we left the main road, and I suspected that this might have been a hint that she was harbouring an ulterior motive for making this trip. Although I had a gut feeling about what that might be, I reckoned it would be more fun to keep it to myself for the present

We had left Es Pla, the great, windmill-bristling central plain of Mallorca, far behind, and we were now in an undulating landscape flecked with little farmsteads that nestle amid pine groves and a random patchwork of stone-walled fields. Although we had passed this way a few times previously, the scenery had never appeared like this before – simply because we had never realised just how many almond trees were dotted about those fields, especially when the land was blanketed in the summer colours of poppies and wild marigolds. But every tree, like every dog, has its day. Although not the most eye-catching of nature's creations during the rest of the year, in late February the scrawny-limbed and sparsely-foliaged almond tree becomes the Cinderella of the arboreal ball.

Suddenly, we were passing through a wonderland of white, tinged here and there with splashes of the palest pink.

For the 'snowfall' of blossom hadn't turned just one plain-Jane tree into a fairy-tale princess. As though by the waft of a magic wand, it had also dressed her hundreds of ladies-in-waiting in matching gowns of finest lace. At any rate, that was Ellie's impression of what we were seeing, and, however unromantic in such matters I may be, I have to admit that she'd probably come up with as good an analogy as any.

Before starting the long climb up the Puig itself, you have to pass through the hamlet of Randa, snuggling on the mountain's lower slopes. There's a little church here, and just up from the church there's a little restaurant called the Celler Bar Randa, which serves up typical Mallorcan country fare in a homely, round-the-fire atmosphere. A bit farther up the winding street there's yet another restaurant, this one called Es Recó de Randa. While also specialising in Mallorcan country cuisine, Manolo Salamanca, the proud proprietor of Es Recó, presents his version in a more sophisticated (and correspondingly more expensive) way than his near neighbour. It's horses for courses again, and going by our own experience, both eateries are justifiably well patronised. So, I believe, is the church. It strikes me as unlikely, then, that the inhabitants of this tiny village risk going under-fed or under-blessed. But it strikes me even more strongly that merely having the privilege of living in such an idyllic place as Randa is blessing enough in itself. If I were to be marooned there for ever, I'd make no complaint at all.

There's an air of true timelessness about Randa. In that respect, it's by no means unique among Mallorcan villages, of course, but there *is* something subtly different about the age-old tranquility that pervades this one. Perhaps it has something to do with the fact that many of the houses here are built, not with the honey-hued stone that predominates throughout the island, but with a rock that is veering more towards a pale grey. It gives the elegant old homes that border the steep main street a soothingly cool appearance, even in the heat of summer. Complementing this is the tinkling sound of water, flowing freely down a little, stone-lined *canaleta* from its source farther up the mountain. This is collected in an ancient communal wash trough, also made of stone, before continuing on it way to irrigate the gardens of the village houses lower down the slope. The lush vegetation that consequently abounds here, together with cascades of flowers tumbling in profusion over every wall, helps make Randa a little corner of heaven on earth. Yes, the monks who, all those centuries ago, chose this place in which to devote their lives to their maker were wise men indeed.

The sinuous road out of the village soon enters a very different landscape. The higher you climb, the more sparse the greenery becomes, as the track twists round bends where the cut-away rock of the mountain lies in broken tiers so even that they could have been the work of a fastidious bricklayer. The *monte bajo*, which is the scrubby, evergreen maquis of Mallorca, eventually surrenders to rocky slopes, where only an occasional mastic bush stands out against the meagre ground cover of asphodels and thorns. But the poorer the vegetation, the richer the outlook. Each corner turned presents a different and wider aspect of what you have left behind. Yet, although these views down the mountainside are spectacular, they're but a teasing taste of what's to come at the summit.

Imposing as the gateway to the Cura Monastery is, and impressive as its arcaded cloisters and chapel façade are, Ellie and I paid them only a nodding homage on this visit. No disrepect was intended. We were about to pay our respects in a more informal though no less profound way.

We strode straight over to the vast courtyard's perimeter wall, took a deep breath, and looked over.

'Feast your eyes on that!' said Ellie.

On a perfectly clear day like this, it really is possible to see almost the entire island of Mallorca from here – all the way to the sweeping Bay of Alcudia in the north, southwards to the Salines Cape, as far as the ragged spine of the Tramuntana Mountains occupying the entire western skyline, and to the Serra de Llevant uplands in the east. This was the angels' eyeview of the island that Ellie had alluded to back in the *almacén*.

Your first glimpse of such a glorious panorama really can leave you speechless. There are reputedly eight million almond trees in Mallorca, though some say there are *only* six million, while others would have you believe that there are as many as twice that number. I don't suppose anyone every actually got round to counting them, but however many almond trees there are on the island, those that you can see from the Puig de Randa at blossom time do add up to an unforgettable sight.

Looking out over the fertile plain of Es Pla, where neat, rectangular, windmill-irrigated fields are given over to the intense production of vegetable, soft fruit and cereal crops, the presence of the drought-resistant almond tree is understandably limited. Yet, even here, the delicate bloom of almond blossom, when seen from above, appears like a dusting of snowflakes blown across a quilt of many muted colours. At the other extreme, there are waterless *bancales*, the wedding-cake hillside terraces built by the Moors for the prime purpose of planting almond groves, where the blossom now materialises as distant drifts of deep snow.

Ellie's decision to down tools and go to witness this Mallorcan phenomenon from one of the best vantage points on the island had been inspired. I complimented her on this as I drove back down the mountain.

'Well,' she modestly conceded, 'you have to grab these chances when you can.'

'Very true,' I readily agreed.

Ellie gazed out of the car window, a dreamy look in her eyes. 'Yes,' she mused, 'as Jock's poetic namesake Rabbie Burns once wrote, "But pleasures are like poppies spread – You seize the flow'r, its bloom is shed; Or like the snow falls in the river – A moment white, then melts forever".'

Astonished, I pulled up at the T-junction beyond Randa village. 'I never knew you were a Burns scholar,' I said, staring incredulously at her.

'I'm not,' she chirpily replied. 'I memorised that quote from the back of the Burns Supper menu the other night.' She gave me a 'gotcha' wink and nudged me in the ribs. 'Now let's grab a bite to eat. All that holy-mountain air's made me really peckish.'

I looked at my watch. 'A bit early for lunch, isn't it? Not even midday yet.'

'Yes, but I only meant a titbit. You know – just a nibble to keep us going.'

'OK. There are loads of eating places between Algaida and Palma – all those huge country restaurants that families from the city head out to on Sundays. But, ehm, why don't we go home a different way for a change? Try somewhere different.'

'Go home a *different* way?' There was a definite note of dismay in Ellie's voice.

Now I knew that my hunch about her having a hidden agenda for making this trip had been correct. 'Yes,' I said, 'Llucmajor's a big town, so we're bound to find a snack bar there.' I selected first gear and indicated to turn left. 'It's only a few kilometres down the road here.'

Ellie grabbed the steering wheel with one hand and jerked the thumb of her other to the right. 'But Algaida's *that* way,' she protested.

I started to laugh. 'You've had this planned all along, haven't you?'

Ellie's expression was as innocent as a saint's in one of the Randa church's stained glass windows. 'Planned?' she piped, her eyebrows rising with the pitch of her voice. 'Planned?' she repeated, batting her lashes. '*Moi*?'

'OK, OK,' I chuckled, 'you win.' I signalled to turn right. 'We'll go home via Algaida. Anything to keep you happy.'

Cuina Casolana, meaning Home Cooking, is what the sign outside the Es Hostal d'Algaida announces in *mallorquín*, and I admit I looked forward to sampling some of it again as much as Ellie clearly did. Situated on the busy C715 road just outside Algaida village, the Hostal, as its name suggests, was originally a wayside inn, in which those making the long journey by coach and horses from Palma to the manufacturing town of Manacor in the east of the island could find lodgings for the night. Nowadays, when the same journey can be completed by car in well under an hour, there's no need for a half-way sleep-over, so the Hostal d'Algaida concentrates instead on just feeding its customers. To say 'just' feeding, however, creates a woefully ungenerous impression of the fare on offer inside this interesting old establishment.

The four stocky pillars supporting the open *porche* which extends along the front of the building look as though they've been there long enough to have overheard many a traveller's tale, right back to the days when the fastest vehicle passing by would have been a donkey-drawn cart. And once you're within the Hostal's thick, stone walls today, the diesel roar of buses and trucks speeding past is so faint that you can't even notice it above the buzz of conversation rising from the marble-topped tables that line one side of the long snack bar area. Again, to use the word 'snack' does scant justice to the wonderful food on offer, and tasteful mahogany furnishings give the place more the atmosphere of an old-fashioned coffee house or tea room than the fast-food-joint image that the term 'snack bar' suggests. We'd dropped by here a couple of times before, and we'd have done so a lot more frequently if it hadn't been such a long drive far from Andratx.

Ellie paused at the glass-fronted display counter opposite the entrance. 'Mm-mm-mm,' she hummed, her eyes popping, her tongue moving expectantly over her lips, 'just *look* at those homebaked cakes!'

'Don't yield to temptation,' I warned.

'Why not?' Ellie's eyes were still fixed hypnotically on the goodies in the glass case. 'I yielded to temptation the moment I hit on the idea of taking you to see the almond blossom from the top of that mountain back there.'

'Yeah, I'd already twigged that. But what about all the moderation-in-all-things stuff you preached at me after my kidney problem?'

'That was different.'

'How come?'

'Because cakes aren't bad for your kidneys.' Before I could come back with the obvious response, Ellie cut me off with a statement that clearly wasn't up for debate: 'Anyway, the cakes here are so good I don't even care if eating them kills me.' She tore her eyes away from the contents of the display cabinet for just long enough to throw me the briefest of glances. 'Can *you* suggest a nicer way to go to heaven?'

There was no answer to that, so I toddled off to the gents' toilet and left Ellie to drool in peace. I wasn't just visiting the loo to perform the necessary, though. The men's room in Es Hostal d'Algaida is unique, and the reason for its individuality never fails to fascinate me. On the assumption that most, if not all, of the ladies reading this have never been inside a males' piddling parlour in Spain, let me explain the basics...

The usual urinal is a long ceramic or stainless steel gutter, along which the needing stand in line abreast and do what comes naturally. This trough is either fixed half a meter or so up the wall or laid into its base. The Hostal d'Algaida version corresponds with the latter floor-channel design, so there's nothing unusual there. No, it's the method of flushing involved that sets this one apart from the mundane.

In a bog-standard gents' loo of the type described, the 'waste liquids' (and the occasional fag end) are washed away at regular intervals by a downwards spray of water squirting from a perforated pipe that runs the length of the gutter and is fixed horizontally at a suitable height above it. Very often you can even see the water cistern mounted at a suitable height above that. All fairly dull stuff when the only other thing you have to look at is a featureless, tiled wall right there in front of your face while you do what has to be done. And don't expect any inspired conversational input from your fellow piddlers. While they await the conclusion of their individual calls of nature, they, like you, are doing nothing but stare straight ahead at that same boring, blank wall. Well, you *hope* that's what they're staring at! Praise be, then, to the genius responsible for dreaming up Es Hostal d'Algaida's answer to the monotony (and possible embarrassment) of going for a pee.

The inevitable wee-wee wall is there, of course, but in this case the tiles are an attractive dark green, as opposed to the ubiquitous 'public lavatory' white. All well and good, but hardly a stroke of genius, you might say. Just wait, though. Set against that green is the rich terracotta red of

Spanish roof tiles – the type that look like elongated flower pots that have been halved length-ways. These have been fixed to the wall, one fitting into the next, to form a Tom Thumb's water chute that zig-zags downwards the full height and width of the room, so that the open end of the lowest tile sits just above the sunken piddle tray. The tilted letter 'Z' thus formed looks for all the world like the slash of Zorro, if you'll pardon the pun. To complete this work of deceptively simple-looking ingenuity, a ceramic fish has been attached to the wall just above the the top, left-hand extremity of the 'Z', and it's from the fish's gaping mouth that the water to purge the system gushes. Fantastic! Something interesting to look at, a talking point and a functional sanitary contrivance all in one.

On this occasion, there was no-one else present, so, totally mesmerised, I just stood waiting for the fish to flush a few of times, then left, having forgotten what I'd gone in there to do in the first place. Sad, but true.

Back out at the display cabinet, Ellie had made her selection. To her credit and my surprise, she had avoided all of the cream-laden confections in favour of a plain *ensaimada*, Mallorca's incomparable, sweet, spiral pastry. Basic though the ingredients of an *ensaimada* are (essentially flour, yeast, egg yolks, sugar and lard), to make a perfect one is an art, and there are no greater exponents of that art than the three middle-aged sisters, Titi, Tika and Esperanza Piza Cañelas, who own Es Hostal d'Algaida and, between them, work its culinary magic.

When Ellie looked at the golden, fluffy Catherine wheel of pastry now on her plate, she declared that this, and only this – no matter how tempting the other cakes looked – had been the cause of the craving that had triggered our trip today. It was just one of those inexplicable things, she admitted – one of those wild urges that *must* be obeyed. She *had* to have an Algaida Hostal *ensaimada*. But today!

'Hey,' I gulped, 'you're not pregnant are you!'

Ellie fired me one of her you-must-be-joking looks, then sighed, 'Just order what you want to eat.'

Not having much of a sweet tooth, I was more interested in the three sisters' array of savoury creations, and there were plenty of those. Little vegetable-, fish- or meat-filled pies called *empanadas* and *cocarrois* – some round, some half-moon-shaped like a pasty, others like miniature swag bags with the pastry casing gathered at the top as if by a draw string.

'Oh, and while you're at it,' Ellie appended, 'I'll have a cup of hot chocolate, please. Mm-mm-mm, *ensaimadas* and hot chocolate… buh-liss!'

A *coca* is what Mallorcans call their version of a pizza, but unlike its better-known Italian cousin, the typical *coca* doesn't have cheese as a basis for its topping. Also, it's square instead of round, and its thin, bread-dough base is usually topped with a succulent selection of chopped peppers, onions, tomatoes and a few cloves of garlic, sometimes scattered on a bed of baby spinnach or Swiss chard. Like an *ensaimada*, a well made *coca* is as delicious as it sounds ordinary, and that's the wonder of so many Mallorcan country recipies. The rectangular slice of *coca* I had at Es Hostal d'Algaida that day was sufficiently scrumptious to set me thinking about ordering another, and I could see from Ellie's finger-licking, lip-smacking, eye-rolling reaction to the last bite of her *ensaimada* that it would have taken little to persuade her to do likewise. But there was pressing work to do back in the *almacén* at Ca's Mayoral.

I stood up. 'Time to go, Ellie,' I said. 'Your choice of a pit-stop place was a good one, but we'll have to get back on the road now.'

Ellie stole a glance at the entrance to the adjoining dining room, then looked appealingly at me. 'Maybe, just to try it, we could –'

'No! Doubtless their lunches will be as fabulous as their snacks, but we won't get anything productive done by sitting about in there stuffing our faces for the next couple of hours.' The old Scots work ethic was having a tug of war with my hard-won attitude of *mañana*ness and, much to my regret, it was winning. '*Vámonos*!' I said. 'Let's go, Ellie!'

However reluctantly, she complied, but not without first playing a compromise card. She walked back over to the display counter and ran her eyes over its contents one last time. 'We can't *possibly* leave without taking some of these jars of homemade jams and pickles and chutneys and things with us,' she informed me. 'Just look at the little gingham tops they've tied on them. Isn't that pretty?'

'Yeah, yeah,' I mumbled, showing about as much interest as I would in being told I had ingrowing toenails. 'I'll go and fetch the car. See you outside.'

When Ellie did finally emerge, she was toting not just two plastic bags bulging with jars, but a couple of cake boxes as well. I lifted the lid of one of them and stared at the nine evenly-spaced, yellow domes protruding from a square base of sugar-dusted sponge.

'A fried egg cake?' I queried. 'What the blazes sort of weird idea is that?'

'They're not fried eggs, silly. They're apricot halves. This is a *tarta de albaricoques* – an apricot tart – another Mallorcan masterpiece.' Ellie licked her lips again. 'Hmm-mm, a nice, big slice of that with a dollop of whipped cream... *fabuloso*!'

I gave her a reproachful look. 'And I thought you were showing such restraint in there, too – limiting yourself to just one plain *ensaimada*.' I shook my head in despair. 'Well, well, I suppose I should've known better.'

'No, no, it's all right,' Ellie objected in a guilt-inflected treble. With great urgency, she raised the lid of the other box. 'See! I've bought you a treat as well!'

'But I don't like cakes, Ellie.'

'Aha, but you *will* like this one.' She lifted it out carefully. 'Look, it's a sponge, with thick layers of egg custard and ice cream, and all topped with caramel and nuts and things. Honestly, you'll *love* it!'

'Don't think so. Too rich by far for me.'

Ellie gave me a playful wink. 'But it's called *tarta al whisky* – whisky cake.'

I lowered my head and sniffed it. 'You've been ripped off. There's not even the slightest whiff of whisky in that.'

Ellie allowed herself a triumphant little smirk. 'That's because there's no whisky in it, and therein lies the secret.'

'You're talking in riddles again, Ellie.'

'Not at all. The thing is that it's up to you to add as much or as little whisky as you want.'

I pricked up my ears.

'Yes,' Ellie continued, 'one of the sisters in there told me. You just pour your whisky over it and that counteracts all the sweetness and richness and everything. *Estupendo* is how she described it. Stupendous!'

I indulged myself in an intrigued little smile. 'Yeah, maybe joining you in a cake-eating session a bit later isn't such a bad idea at that.'

As it turned out, the sister at Es Hostal d'Algaida was right. The *tarta al whisky* really was *estupendo*, and it got me wondering just why it had taken a Spanish cook to dream up such a wonderful way of 'tarting up' Scotch whisky. Sweet tooth or no sweet tooth, I had to concede that the result was a helluva lot nicer than the old Scots habit of pouring whisky on your porridge. I was still mulling over the thought when Ellie and I stepped out onto the Ca's Mayoral balcony after our evening meal that night.

It was dark, but a full moon was just peeping above the Serra Garrafa ridge away to the east. Tinny bells tinkling farther down the valley shook me gently out of my *tarta al whisky* reverie, pulling my thoughts back to a similarly still and silent night on the eve of our first Christmas at Ca's Mayoral. We had been standing on the same spot, and hearing old Pep speaking softly to his sheep as he watched over their nocturnal grazing had had a profound effect on us both. It had brought home to us just how fortunate we were to be living in such a privileged place and to be experiencing the sounds of a shepherd tending his flock by night in a way that hadn't changed here for thousands of years.

The same feeling returned now, yet Mallorca was seducing our senses in a way that it hadn't done then. That had been in the depths of winter, while all the wonderful sights that nature had presented us with today were heralding the arrival of spring.

'Look,' Ellie murmured.

I followed her gaze as she slowly cast her eyes round the valley. The rising moon was bathing the ancient almond groves that occupy the mountain terraces in its pale light, and turning the newborn blossom into a gossamer haze of silvery-blue. It gave all of the world that we could see from there a strange, dream-like quality – almost like looking at the stars of the Milky Way reflected on the ripples of a lake on a summer's night.

Neither of us spoke. There was no need to. We both knew that, whatever difficult decisions we'd soon have to make about our future at Ca's Mayoral, and no matter where those decisions might eventually lead us, memories such as the one that was being made at that moment would remain with us forever. Sometimes, just sometimes, the best things in life really do turn out to be free.

QUE SERÁ, SERÁ

We picked the last of the season's orange crop in the middle of March. Our next harvest wouldn't start until November, so our income in the intervening months would be limited to the comparatively small amounts that could be earned from the smattering of non-citrus trees on the *finca*. We had summer-ripening and autumn-maturing things like plums, cherries, little dessert pears, apricots, persimmons, pomegranates, loquats, figs, quinces, almonds and carobs. The snag was that there wasn't sufficient of any one variety to make our output of it attractive to the wholesale merchants, except on the odd occasion when they might want a crate or two to top up a larger order from one of their clients.

Obviously, those trees had been planted in the days when earning a few pesetas from farmgate sales or a stall at Andratx market on Wednesday mornings had made a worthwhile contribution to the farm's income. But those had been the days of subsistence farming, when the only 'vehicle' to be fuelled and maintained was a donkey, and when growing some vegetables between the trees, rearing a family pig and keeping a few hens and sheep would supply the farmer's family with most of its food throughout the year. Those had been the days that our elderly neighbours Maria and Pep still tried gamely to hold onto in the face of unstoppable change. Those had been their halcyon 'old days' – simple times, when generation automatically followed generation into the little family farm, when everyone in the locality knew everyone else, when one farmer's son married another's daughter from only a few fields away, when a visit to Palma might be an annual or even a once-in-a-lifetime event, when tourists were as few and far between as old Maria's top teeth, and when anyone predicting a farmer's conversion from the undemanding donkey to the clunk, clatter, fumes and expensive appetite of a diesel tractor would have been dismissed as a lunatic.

No matter how sad for the old folk of the Mallorcan countryside, however, those days were largely over, and what few traces of their cherished lifestyle still remained would all too soon disappear in the name of 'progress' as well. For ourselves, having come to the island, not to escape the drudgery of an urban rat race, but to seek a livelihood from a farm even smaller than the Scottish one from which modern agricultural economics had squeezed us, the situation was very different. Whilst having the deepest respect for the traditional ways of old stalwarts such as Pep and Maria, we had to look forward, not back. Farm-gate sales of a few kilos of fruit here and there wouldn't even cover the price of petrol to take Charlie to school and back every day, never mind pay his school fees.

From our experiences as farmers 'back home', Ellie and I had known from the start that, if we were to carve a viable future for ourselves and our two sons at Ca's Mayoral, then any notions of enjoying an idealistic 'good life' in the sun would be anathema to the likelihood of succeeding. Ca's Mayoral wasn't just our home, it was also our business and our sole means of earning a living. It was, moreover, by far our greatest asset, as virtually all of our capital was tied up in it. Protecting and developing that asset, therefore, was the only way that we could hope to safeguard our long-term solvency.

Hence the reason for undertaking the building of a swimming pool, the creating of a picturesque barbecue area and the conversion of the *almacén* into a games room. As Bernat, the young Mallorcan water-tanker driver had assured me at the Sant Antoni's Eve bonfire celebrations, it was a form of insurance – nothing more, nothing less, and we shouldn't be concerned about the opinion of any 'old-timers' who couldn't appreciate the sense of that. I'd become resigned to this pragmatic way of thinking now, although the farm muck that was mixed inexorably with the blood in my veins still delivered occasional pangs of remorse to my concience. Pep's mischievous question as to how much more orchard land I could buy with the money being poured into the swimming pool project also still rankled a bit. But the decision had been made, there was no turning back, and I knew deep down that the right thing had been done.

I was putting the finishing touches to the reformed *almacén* one evening, wiring up the last of some lantern-style wall lights we'd bought from a second-hand store called Victoriana in Génova village, when Ellie came clip-clopping on high heels along the corridor. She'd been to see Victor, our *gestor* (tax advisor), in Palma for his assessment of the farm's profit-and-loss accounts for the preceding twelve months. My back was to Ellie as she came in, but I heard her stop by the door.

'Oh, these lanterns *will* look nice,' she said. 'Oh yes, *very* effective!'

I heard a click, then lightning struck. Or I thought it had. There was a loud 'BANG!' and a simultaneous blue flash exploded in my face. I was blinded for a few moments, but the stench of burnt plastic and melted wire left me in no doubt as to what had happened.

'Hell's teeth, woman,' I spluttered, once I'd coughed the fumes from my lungs and blinked the stars from my eyes, 'what the blazes possessed you to switch the damned lights on?'

'Oh, sorry, I thought it'd help you to see better.' Ellie was doing her Little Miss Innocence turn again. 'It *is* a bit dark in here, you know.'

'Yes! I know it's a bit dark in here, you raving dingbat! That's because I had the lights switched OFF! And the reason I had the lights switched OFF is because I'm working with bare electric wires here, for God's sake!'

I looked at the welded metal strands smoking in my fingers, then glared over at Ellie. Although she had one hand covering her mouth as if in shock, I could see in her eyes that she was actually sniggering.

'Sorry,' she twittered. 'I was only trying to help.'

'HELP? You say you were only trying to HELP? Jesus wept, Ellie, you could have killed me, you bloody maniac!'

For some reason, Ellie thought this highly amusing. Unable to conceal this perverse reaction, she stood cross-legged against the door jamb and started to giggle. 'Are you all right?' she whimpered, tears of glee trickling down her cheeks. She attempted to say something else, but gave up. Her bizarre sense of humour had gone into overdrive, and all that came out of her mouth was the sound of high-pitched, hysterical laughter as she slithered down the door post and hunkered down on the floor, her knees clutched firmly to her chest. 'Oh, too much,' she warbled after she'd pulled herself sufficiently together to utter a few gasped words. 'No more, *please*. I think (titter) – I think I'm going to wet my knickers!'

'I think I already have!' I panted. I clasped my heart. 'No kidding, I've never had such a fright in my entire life!'

'Just look at you,' Ellie wheezed, 'standing there on that little stool with your face all sooty.' She wiped the tears from her eyes with the back of her hand. 'Honestly, you're just like that Wally Coyote after he's had another go at blowing up that bird thingy in the *Roadrunner* cartoons!'

Uplifted by the realisation that I'd just survived a near-death experience, I was beginning to see the funny side of it myself now. 'Yeah, well,' I sighed, 'as I regularly say, anything to keep you happy, Ellie.'

'Much appreciated,' she laughed, almost crying. She pointed a shaking finger at me. 'Honest – just like the *Roadrunner* cartoons.'

'Meep! Meep!' I replied, deadpan.

'Meep! Meep!' Ellie echoed, then burst into another fit of the giggles.

'And, eh, I think you've missed the point about the Coyote's name,' I casually remarked.

'Really?'

'Yes, it's Wily, not Wally, see?'

Ellie gave that but the shortest moment of thought, then shrugged, 'Well, he always seems like a Wally to me.'

As so often happens in such conversations with Ellie, there was no answer to that. So, well aware that I was looking like a singed cartoon loser, I stepped down from my little stool and made as dignified an exit as possible under the circumstances. To the sound of Ellie's continued tee-heeing, I went and re-set the blown fuse box through in the back hall. Getting Ellie's news of Victor the *gestor*'s appraisal of our state of financial fettle would have to wait a bit.

Sandy had been picking up Charlie at school for us, and by the time they came back I had completed the rudely-interrupted electrical work in the *almacén*. I was stocking the shelves behind the bar with a selection of bottles, intermingled with some of the beer-company nick-nacks I'd salvaged from Carmen's garage. Ellie, meanwhile, was busy arranging the various items we'd bought from Señor Miguel's 'old stock' furniture warehouse in the Carrer de Oms, Palma's 'Elm Street'. Now that everything else was in place and the desired *rustica* look achieved, even those slightly old-fashioned couches and easy chairs looked perfectly at home, just as Ellie had said they would. The *almacén* was no longer a scruffy, old work room, but rather a comfy lounge in a Spanish country pub. Admittedly, this meant that it was something of a hybrid, since there are no country pubs of that essentially English type in rural Spain. But the cross-breeding had worked, and we couldn't have been happier with the progeny.

'Hey, looks all right!' Charlie declared when he came through the door.

'Yeah,' Sandy agreed. He nodded his head approvingly. 'Hmm, not bad at all!'

'Wait 'til you see this, though,' I said. I'd deliberately turned off the newly-wired wall lights when I heard the boys coming. I reached for the switch again now.

'Wow!' beamed Charlie. 'Cool!'

Sandy gave me a pat on the back. 'Your very own private pub at last, Dad! Paradise, eh?'

I stepped back behind the bar again. 'Drink, sir?' I said to Sandy, grinning like a kid on Christmas morning as I produced a bottle of Spanish *Cruz Campo* lager and a German *Dortmunder Pils* beer stein from under the counter. 'We pride ourselves on the, uhm, cosmopolitan nature of our humble establishment.'

'Hold it! Hold it!' Ellie called out. 'Before you start celebrating...' She gestured towards the spot-lit centre of the room. 'I think you've overlooked one very important item, haven't you?' She then motioned towards a dark corner concealed by one of the 'thatch' screens I'd made.

'Yeah, the snooker table!' Charlie exclaimed. 'How could we have forgotten about that!'

Half an hour later, Antoinette MacPherson's generous gift was in place, its woodwork dusted and polished, green baize carefully brushed, balls being poked into its pockets at last. And it certainly did add the final touch to the transformation of the old *almacén*. Even Ellie's previous disinterest in pubs, and her take-it-or-leave it attitude towards what they plied, appeared to have been ousted, at least temporarily, as she and Bonny the boxer sat side-by-side on two high stools at the bar. Ellie had a glass of wine in her hand and a contented smile on her face, while she and Bonny watched the boys and me enjoying our long-awaited first game of snooker in our very own big boys' playpen.

With the completion of the games room and work on the barbecue area now also finished, our two do-it-ourselves improvement projects had been realised in good time, and for a surprisingly modest outlay as well. If we indulged in a bit of quiet self-congratulation when we sat down to eat in the kitchen a bit later, perhaps it was justified. Achieving what we'd set out to do had involved a lot of hard work, but the satisfaction we could now draw from seeing the results was reward aplenty.

All that remained now was for Pablo Gomez to make his contribution to this welcome feelgood mood by promptly completing the building of the swimming pool. He'd promised that he would, and, judging by the good progress made to date, there was no reason to suspect that he wouldn't be as good as his word.

In the meantime, however, there was the little matter of our accountant's assessment of the health of our business to consider before we allowed ourselves to get too euphoric about the achievement of *any* 'leisure-activity' improvement to the property. Ellie and I decided it would be only fair to lay the facts before the boys at the dinner table that night. They had a right to know. Sandy's decision about his own course in life would be influenced by them, and young Charlie, though only just thirteen, needed to be reminded of the facts of our family finances, if for no other reason than to keep his feet on the ground.

'Well, boys,' Ellie said, 'there's good news and there's not-so-good news.'

'Just give us the good news, lady,' Charlie flippantly chipped in. 'I've had a tough day at the office.'

'Ignore him, Mum,' Sandy said. 'He spends half of his life in a different world from the rest of us. Millionaires' yachts and all that stuff. Just tell it how it is – good or bad.'

'Well, Victor the *gestor* hasn't really told me anything we didn't already know. Just confirmed it, I suppose. So, the good news is that we're making ends meet, and we should continue to do so this year, provided orange prices don't go further down and overheads don't go further up, that is.'

'One of the basics of life,' I said, principally for Charlie's benefit. 'You have to live within your means.'

'And what's the not-so-good news?' Sandy asked his mother.

'Simply that, in the longer term, we'll have to produce more to cover the cost of unavoidable things like having to replace the tractor or even the car. Wear and tear will take their toll, and just making ends meet won't leave any leeway to cover the cost of whatever major repairs may have to be done, never mind pay for replacements.'

'And, boys,' I said, 'the cold truth is that we've more or less reached the limit of how much fruit we can produce on a farm the size of Ca's Mayoral.'

'Aw gee,' Charlie moaned, 'don't tell me we're gonna be skint. What a drag.'

'Well,' I told him, 'the trick is not to let things go that far, so we'll have to do something about it before they do.'

'Which means getting more land,' Sandy immediately concluded.

'That's it in a nutshell,' I concurred. 'We'll be financially OK for the immediate future, but, in the longer term, we'll have to expand to stay viable.'

'Not a problem,' Charlie declared. 'Just buy out old Pep. Yeah, he's past his sell-by date, anyway.'

It was clear from the look on Sandy's face that he knew the solution to our impending problems wouldn't be as simple as that. Mallorca was a holiday island, and even ostensibly-unsophisticated old *campesinos* like Pep were well aware that their farms were worth a great deal more than just their agricultural value to potential foreign buyers who wanted to develop them in non-agricultural ways. Bernat, the young truck driver, had marked my card about that on Sant Antoni's Eve as well, and Sandy was bright enough to have worked out the reality of the situation for himself. Consequently, what he said next came as no great surprise…

'Well, that pretty well decides it for me.' He hunched his shoulders and gave a weak little smile that was part regret and, I guessed, part relief. 'I'll go back to college in Scotland at the end of the summer. It'll mean one mouth less for you to feed here, and I can get weekend work on the farms over there to keep me in student grub 'til I qualify.' Then, glancing at Ellie, he added as if to reassure her, 'It'll be for the best at the end of the day, you'll see.'

For once, Charlie was stuck for a cute quip. Insulting brotherly banter aside, he was extremely fond of Sandy, and although he didn't make it very apparent most of the time, he really did look up to and admire him. If truth be known, Sandy was, in many ways, Charlie's role model, his hero, who, despite outward appearances, did always manage to put up with being put down by his junior sibling. In Charlie's eyes, Sandy was… well, Sandy was quite simply his big brother. He would miss him.

We all would.

The day that Pablo Gomez declared the new swimming pool ready to be filled with water dawned bright and clear, although clouds gathering over Ses Penyes Mountain in the north of the valley were a reminder of the approaching storms that local folk regard as the final roar of their mild-mannered lion of winter. Apart from the pool being a bit deeper than originally intended, its construction had been completed without a glitch and in admirably quick time by Pablo's team of hard-working, mainland Spaniards. I congratulated him on this as the outflow of a hose from our field well topped up the five tanker loads of water that Bernat had predicted would be *almost* adequate. He hadn't known about the extra three quarters of a metre deep that Groucho had eventually dug the pool, so I had to use much more well water than originally anticipated.

'It stinks, *amigo*,' Pablo said of the water surging from the hose. 'Dead animals, for sure. Mice, birds, everything.'

'But Bernat told me the chlorine would fix that,' I said, suddenly worried that I might have contaminated so many thousand cubic metres of bought-in water that had to be translated into the value of so many thousand kilos of hand-picked oranges.

Pablo pulled one of his one-shoulder shrugs. '*Sí*,' he said. '*No problema*. Compared to what all those *tourista* kids do when swimming in their hotel pools, the *polución* caused by a couple of dead rats in your well is nothing.' He slapped me on the back. 'Hey, *no problema*, *amigo*. Bernat was *correcto*. The *cloro* will fix everything.'

Well, I thought, at least mainland Spain and Mallorca were agreed on one point.

When the water finally reached the required level, I turned off the hose. Immediately, Pablo produced a small plastic bottle from his breast pocket, unscrewed the top and poured the contents into the pool.

It was only a few drops of mineral water left over from his lunch, he informed me. 'But,' he added, raising a point-making finger, 'every little counts, as the mouse said when he pissed into the sea.'

'Amen to that, Pablo,' I acknowledged, and handed him his final cheque.

Ellie and the boys spent so much time in the new pool that first evening that I fully expected to see their skin wrinkled and prune-like when they finally climbed out to join me in the barbecue area for our first alfresco meal of the year. On the contrary, though, they were looking the picture of health, their faces glowing with the exhilaration of swimming, and already showing the first traces of the light golden tan that the rapidly warming spring sunshine was bestowing on them.

We would have five months, a full summer, to enjoy our new 'leisure facilities' as a family before Sandy finally left us to go his chosen way, as I think Ellie and I had always known in our hearts that he ultimately would. But, for little more than pocket money in return, he had done his full share of work to help us get established in our new life in Mallorca, and then to make all the improvements to the property that we were now looking forward to enjoying together. He had fulfilled what he felt was his obligation to the family, while, we were sure, also enjoying the experience of living and working in a foreign land. That he didn't eventually see his own immediate future in that land was a decision that we could only respect, while wishing him every success in following his own path and promising whatever support we could give. A page in Sandy's life was about to turn, but many more exciting chapters were there for him to open up and to write in his own way.

For young Charlie, no less excitement beckoned, except that, in his case, it beckoned from a diametrically opposite direction. Whilst the 'exotic' attractions and distractions of Mallorca had quickly palled for Sandy, Charlie had positively lapped them up and had taken to the high life as if born to it. The memory was still fresh of him coming into the house-warming party at the O'Briens' mansion a few months earlier, dressed in a borrowed tuxedo and looking every bit the young blade about town – although he'd only been twelve years old at the time. His casual claim of having been driven in one of the O'Briens' many luxury cars to the bright lights of Tito's nightclub in Palma that same evening still had Elle and me unconvinced about how to take the 'jocularity' of how he'd said it. His assertion that Dec O'Brien, only a year or so his senior, had driven the car that night still troubled us, despite our having been assured by the likes of Jock and Meg that we had only been having our legs pulled by Charlie. Sean and Colleen O'Brien, they'd stated categorically, would never have condoned such behaviour from any of their offspring. I decided to find out the truth once and for all, however, and what better time and place than now?

We were sitting round the chunky wooden table under an almond tree by the old wall, enjoying a celebratory feast of barbecued pork sausages and chicken legs, our mood made all the more mellow by the soft lighting illuminating the aged stonework of the wall and the gnarled branches of the nearby pines.

'OK, Charlie,' I said right out of the blue, 'Sandy has been open about what he wants to do with his life, so how about you being equally honest about what you've been doing with yours?'

Taken aback as he obviously was and veiled as my question had been, it was clear by the way he lowered his eyes that Charlie knew what I was getting at. 'It was only the once,' he muttered, 'and Dec got such a fright when he scraped the wing of the Merc on the gate pillar coming back in that he vowed he'd never do it again, if he got away with it that time.'

'And how did he get away with it?' I asked bluntly.

'He told his dad that his mum pranged the car when she was tipsy, and he told her his dad did it when he was in the same state. It wouldn't have been the first time that something like that had happened with them, so they both believed him.'

Ellie was visibly shocked, and the lecture she then gave Charlie was prompted as much by concern for his wellbeing as by anger at what he'd done. What dampened the powder of her reprimand slightly, of course, was the underlying fact that Charlie had actually been honest with us about the incident all along. It was just that we hadn't allowed ourselves to believe him. The gravity of the situation wasn't diminished by that, however, and I made it plain to Charlie that if he was ever tempted to get involved in such an irresponsible caper again, his association with the super-rich set of Mallorca would be terminated – forever.

'But remember, Dad, it isn't just rich kids who get up to these tricks,' Sandy quietly interjected, in a sort of back-handed way of defending his younger brother, whilst also chastising him. 'You get more boy racers who nick cars and and go on motorway burn-ups in poverty-stricken ghettos than you do in Millionaire Rows anywhere. So, clipping Charlie's wings won't make a blind bit of difference, *if* he decides to behave like an idiot in any case.'

Charlie gave me a sheepish smile. 'Yeah, Sandy's dead right in what he says.' His smile then changed into the disarming grin that he knew only too well how to use to his own advantage. 'Well, he *nearly* right in what he says. But I still reckon you're safer hanging out with the rich kids.'

'Uh-huh?'

'Yeah. I mean, Dec O'Brien's got no need to do anything as nuts as borrowing the Merc for *autopista* thrills and trips to Tito's Palace any more.'

'And how's that, then?'

'Just because his dad's bought him a natty, little speedboat.'

Ellie, Sandy and I looked at each other, dumbstruck.'

'Oh yeah,' Charlie breezed, 'if we ever get fed up on weekends now, we just jump into the boat and roar round the coast to McDonald's at Palma Nova for a burger and fries. *Defi*nitely the sensible option – *and* you can tie up right alongside, so no need to go anywhere near a road!'

While Charlie and Sandy shared a brotherly chuckle, Ellie and I exchanged confused smiles.

Charlie still worried us.

Leaving the boys to go indoors for a game of snooker, we took a stroll through the orchards with Bonny. It was a balmy, moonlit night, totally still except for the merest whisper of a breeze sighing through the trees, and the distant, sleepy, nocturnal chirruping of the first crickets to herald the coming summer. We stopped by the old well in the farthest field and looked back over the same view of the farm that had charmed us into buying it when being taken on that fateful guided tour by Francisca Ferrer just twenty months earlier. The leafy domes of the ranks of trees filling the orange groves were still as beguiling as they'd appeared then, the surrounding mountains still as secure, solid and serene, the air still as perfumed by wild herbs. Only the house had changed.

Then, in daylight, its white walls, faded wooden shutters and terracotta-tiled roof had smiled back at us in a bewitchingly drowsy way. Now, with its outline silhouetted against the moonlit mountains, the place had taken on a new, almost sprightly air. The welcoming glow shining from its open windows indicated that it was very much awake, the flickering reflection of the swimming pool lights wandering over its face added a flirtatious touch to that bewitching smile, and the subtle lighting of the old wall in the background wrapped a golden cape around its shoulders. The old house of Ca's Mayoral seemed as happy with her little face-lift as we were.

A peal of thunder rumbled far away in the north. Ellie gripped my arm. Bonny growled bravely and slunk in behind my legs.

'That's just Mother Nature telling us that tomorrow's going to be, not just another day, but another season as well,' I told them as we headed back towards the house. 'Nothing to be scared of.'

'Do you really think so?' Ellie said, sounding uncharacteristically unassured. 'Oh my,' she sighed, 'if only we knew what all our tomorrows will bring.'

'Well, as I've said many times before, when in Rome…'

'Meaning?'

'Meaning, you're in Spain, so adopt the Spanish philosophy about all our tomorrows.'

'Which is?'

'*Que será, será*. Whatever will be, will be.'

We both said 'Amen' to that.

Bonny barked at the moon.

THE END

www.peter-kerr.co.uk

Oasis-WERP

Printed in Great Britain
by Amazon